770.03
E56p
V.12

The Encyclopedia of
    photography

770.03
E56p
V.12

The Encyclopedia of
    photography

DATE DUE	BORROWER'S NAME	NUMBER

CHRISTIAN HERITAGE COLLEGE

2100 Greenfield Dr.
El Cajon, CA 92021

Volume Twelve

The Encyclopedia of

Photography

THE COMPLETE PHOTOGRAPHER:
The Comprehensive Guide and Reference for All Photographers

WILLARD D. MORGAN
General Editor

GREYSTONE PRESS/NEW YORK

Title Page Picture Credits:

Copal Company Limited

HANS BURST/*Zeiss Ikon Photo*

LOU BERNSTEIN

GEORGE L. HONEYCUTT/*Charlotte Observer and News*

The editors wish to express their appreciation to The Ridge Press, publishers of "Creative America," and Magnum for their permission to use the color photographs in this volume.

Cover and Book Designed by Harold Franklin

MANUFACTURED IN THE UNITED STATES OF AMERICA

Table of Contents   Volume Twelve

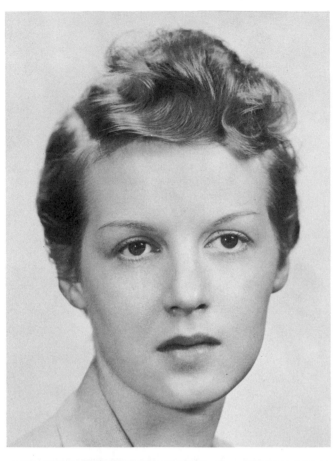

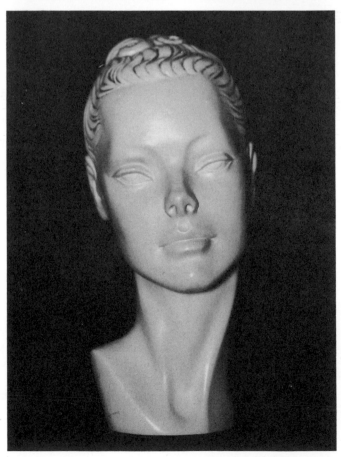

LIGHTING IN PORTRAITURE

LEWIS TULCHIN
Instructor, New York Institute of Photography
[A thorough understanding of the basic techniques in the portrait field will help to improve your work. The author's ability as photographer and teacher has provided the background for this presentation, which includes illustrations to point up the text.] All photographs by Lewis Tulchin.
• *Also see: Lighting section; Portraiture section; Psychological Portraiture.*

THE TECHNIQUES OF PORTRAIT lighting are not complicated if we condition our minds to the fundamentals of the natural light around us. If we can artificially duplicate the phenomenon of light as it exists in nature, and if we can simulate what have come to be known as "available light" conditions, we can produce a wide range of lighting styles which are esthetically appealing.

In applying these artificial methods, we will consider the light of the sun as a directional and high-lighting source—one which varies its light pattern upon the subject in relation to its position in the sky and to the subject. Call this bold, strong source the "modeling light." The sky is another light source. It produces a soft, even, over-all illumination which fills the entire picture area with light. Think of the light of the sky as "fill-in light" and "hairlight."

To develop your skill in the use of portrait lighting, it is helpful to practice light placement with a plaster manikin—the type used for display purposes in women's hat shops. Follow, step by step, the text and its accompanying illustrations. Through trial and experiment you can perfect your techniques in the various lighting styles.

Varying the position of the modeling light produces interesting light patterns, but this does not mean that the angle and elevation of the light can be varied at random. Photographers and artists have developed three major lighting styles which are generally suitable for portraiture: 1) glamour lighting; 2) 45-degree lighting; 3) split lighting.

GLAMOUR LIGHTING

Glamour lighting is also referred to as "butterfly" or "Hollywood" lighting. In this lighting style, the shadow beneath the nose is shaped like a butterfly. Glamour lighting reveals the eyes to their best advantage, minimizes skin-pore shadows, blemishes, and facial lines. It also emphasizes and flatters good facial structure.

Using glamour lighting does not in itself produce an enchanting and glorifying portrait. In one way or another, we must "gild the lily" still further. The ingredients of glamour in a photograph also encompass costume elements, make-up, hair styling, pose, and expression.

Figure 1 is an example of a very unglamourous portrait. Although the girl's face appears symmetrical in most of its parts, it lacks accent. Lighting is flat, pose is uninteresting, and in general the photograph is unappealing. Figure 2 shows the same girl. The portrait speaks for itself.

Study Figure 3. Notice that the modeling light (spot or flood) is centrally located on the face and elevated to a point where the nose shadow is approximately halfway between the nose and upper lip. If the face were turned to a 45-degree angle off the camera axis (three-quarter view), or 90-degree angle (profile view), the light would also have to be rotated to these angles to retain the same light pattern.

Fill-in Light
The fill-in light, Figure 4, is primarily a frontal illumination, to lighten shadow areas. Used by itself it does not record a good representation of roundness and structure. There is little relief or depth. It lacks visual interest.

To obtain a proper balance or ratio of light between the shadows and highlights on the face use the following procedure: 1) place fill-in light close to the camera; 2) study the shadow and highlight areas of the face; 3) move the fill light back, forward, or "feather" it to the side; 4) when the shadow areas appear to be about the right density, brighten them just a little more.

This method will insure proper fill-in illumination, because black-and-white or color film records shadows a little darker than the eye sees them.

The fill-in light is placed as close to the camera as possible, at a height about level with the subject's eyes. It should be positioned on the side of the camera opposite the modeling light. Once you have placed the fill-in light correctly, forget it. You will return to it only to vary the intensity, either by moving it closer to the subject, farther away, or to "feather" it to the side.

When using a short focal-length lens, the subsequent short distance between camera and subject requires placement of the fill-in closer to the subject, if you are to keep the light unit close to the camera. This shorter distance concentrates the light rays into a narrow area, creating shadow pockets. The closer the fill light is to the subject, the greater the tendency toward shadow pockets.

Shadow pockets may occur with the subject posed at a 45- or 90-degree angle. If this difficulty arises, place the fill-in light on the same side as the modeling light—again as close to the camera as possible. Two fill-in lights may also be used, one on each side of the camera.

Most of these shadow problems can be eliminated by using a longer focal length lens. The shortest practical focal-length lens for head and shoulder portraits is found by adding the measurement of the shortest side of the film used to that of the longest side. If your film size is 4×5 inches, $4 + 5 = 9$-inch focal length.

Top, left: *Figure 1. Before make-up.*

Top, right: *Figure 2. After make-up.*

Bottom, left: *Figure 3. Glamour (butterfly) light.*

Bottom, right: *Figure 4. Fill-in light.*

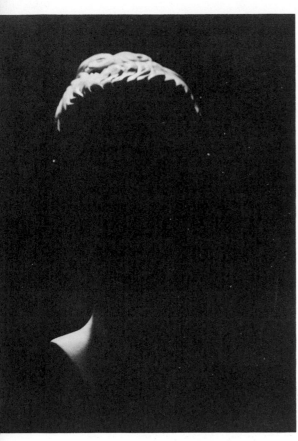

Hairlight

The hairlight, Figure 5, reveals texture and detail in the hair and adds highlights to it. The light unit is directed from above and slightly toward the back of the head and is aimed at the greatest area of hair facing the camera. Rays from the hairlight must not fall on the face.

Dark hair requires more light to record its detail and highlights. On the other hand, blond hair will appear burned-out or chalky if too much light is used.

BACKGROUNDS

Backgrounds are basically a matter of personal taste and interpretative judgment. In portraiture, interest must be concentrated on the subject, not on the background. Therefore avoid strong background designs and drapes producing highlight and shadow patterns which call attention to themselves.

Background materials are a matter of personal choice. Plain painted walls of light or medium tone and

Above: *Figure 5. Hairlight.*

Below: *Figure 6. Background light.*

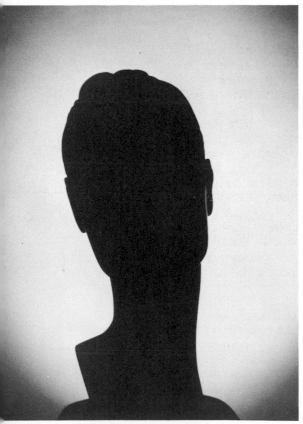

Figure 7. *Glamour (butterfly) lighting.*

muslin or similar materials used on stretcher frames form excellent backgrounds in flat white, flat gray, or flat black colors. Light, airy, youthful interpretations are best produced with light-colored backgrounds; character, dramatic, and somber studies are more suitable with dark backgrounds.

Separate the subject from the background by at least four to five feet. This will give you greater freedom of background light placement to avoid or control background shadows.

The background light can create atmosphere and a feeling of dimensional depth between the background and the subject. By lighting a broad or controlled area of the background, the head will be set off from it, guiding the viewer's eyes to the focal point of interest, the face. Figure 6 illustrates the use of one type of background lighting. The light may be placed on a short tripod directly behind the subject or to one side.

Figure 7 shows the glamour lighting style using only a modeling and fill-in light. Figure 8 illustrates the same lighting style for a profile view.

BASIC LIGHTING

In 45-degree lighting there are two separate styles: 1) basic lighting; and 2) Rembrandt lighting. Each produces a distinct and different lighting effect, but common to both is a triangular-shaped patch of light beneath one eye.

Used correctly, the light-and-shadow pattern of basic lighting is suitable for all facial structures. Unlike other techniques described and illustrated, it will not radically alter the appearance of any area of the face. If you are unsure about which lighting style to use, you will find basic lighting safest and easiest to handle.

In a full-face view, the modeling light is rotated approximately 45 degrees off the camera axis to the side of the subject, and then raised or lowered to a point where a triangle or V-shaped patch of light is formed on the cheek, as in Figure 9. Notice the following: 1) both eyes are illuminated; 2) the

Above: *Figure 8. Glamour lighting (profile view).*

Right: *Figure 9. Basic light.*

point or apex of the triangle is aligned with the tip of the nose; 3) the highlight area between the nose and the upper lip points to the outer edge of the mouth.

The easiest way to produce the triangle is: 1) with the light unit at arm's distance, position yourself directly in front of the subject's face; 2) move the light unit on a parallel plane toward the side of the subject's face until the triangle is seen; 3) elevate or lower the light until the highlight between the nose and the upper lip points to the outer edge of the mouth.

Figure 10 illustrates full-face basic lighting using modeling light, fill-in, hairlight, and background light.

If the face is turned a 45-degree angle off the camera axis (three-quarter view), the light unit will have to be rotated to this angle to retain the same light pattern (Figure 11). Notice that the triangle is now on the side of the face farthest from the camera.

REMBRANDT LIGHTING

In three-quarter and profile views of the face, the light-and-shadow pattern of Rembrandt lighting produces a feeling of roundness quite unlike any other lighting style. It is admirably suited for character and dramatic studies. Rembrandt lighting's greater shadow area facing the camera lends itself as a slenderizing medium. To understand this statement fully, keep in mind that shadow areas appear to recede or look smaller.

In a three-quarter view of the face, the modeling light is rotated approximately 135 degrees off the axis of the camera to the far side of the subject's face and pointed toward the camera, but not into the lens.

Now proceed as described for basic lighting: place yourself in front of the subject's face with the light unit at arm's distance. Move the light on a parallel plane to the far side of the subject's face, until you see the triangular patch of light on the side of the face closest to the camera. Now elevate or lower the light until you see the highlight area between the nose and the upper lip pointing to the outer edge of the mouth.

Figure 12 illustrates Rembrandt lighting using modeling light, fill-in, hairlight, and background light. Figure 13 represents a Rembrandt profile.

Top, left: *Figure 10. Complete basic lighting (full-face view).*

Bottom, left: *Figure 11. Complete basic lighting (three-quarter view).*

Right: *Figure 12. Rembrandt lighting (three-quarter view).*

Above: *Figure 14. Split (side) light.*

Above: *Figure 17. One backlight.*

Below: *Figure 18. Two backlights.*

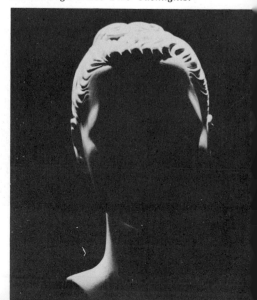

Above: *Figure 13. Rembrandt lighting (profile view).*

SPLIT (SIDE) LIGHTING

In a full-face view, the modeling light is rotated 90 degrees off the camera axis to the side of the subject's head and elevated to approximately the eye level of the subject or slightly above (Figure 14). With this lighting pattern, just half the face is illuminated; no light should spill over the shadow side of the face.

If the face is turned 45 degrees off the camera axis (three-quarter

Figure 15. *Complete split lighting.*

Figure 16. *Split (line) lighting in profile.*

Figure 19. *Complete backlighting.*

Figure 20. *A full-scale print.*

Figure 21. *Low key.*

Figure 22. *Semi-high key.*

view), the light unit should be rotated to 135 degrees off the camera axis to retain the same light pattern.

A modeling spotlight is not recommended for this lighting style, because it is likely to cause a deep shadow around the subject's eye socket on the highlighted side of the face. Use a floodlight instead.

Figure 15 illustrates split lighting, with a modeling light, fill-in, hairlight, and background light. Figure 16 illustrates the use of the same lighting style; in a profile view, split lighting is also called "line lighting."

BACKLIGHTING

Backlighting is used as a supplementary light to add highlights and accents to the contour edges of the face. It also adds depth and brilliancy to the photograph as a whole. While it can be used with any lighting style, it is especially effective in low-key photography.

A spotlight is placed behind and to the side of the subject and elevated 45 degrees to the subject's face. It is then directed at an angle toward the camera (Figure 17). The light must not spill onto the

side of the nose or cheek; the beam should be so controlled that its rays do not strike the camera lens and cause light flare.

Figure 18 illustrates two backlights modeling both sides of the contour edges of the face. Figure 19 is a good example of the use of two backlights, a modeling light, and a fill-in.

LOW KEY

If we study a scale of the tones most commonly used in an esthetically appealing photograph, we would probably find a range from deep black to pure white, together with a full range of intermediate half-tones. This is called "a full-scale print" (Figure 20).

A low-key photograph contains a predominance of dark tones, ranging from deepest black to approximately the middle of the gray scale. There will be a few accenting highlights to add brilliancy and a feeling of depth. Low-key photography is ideally suited for character, dramatic, somber, and so-called interpretive mood studies (Figure 21).

Low key is achieved by proper selection of subject matter, background, lighting, and film develop-

ment. The negative should possess delicate gradation of skin tone as well as a certain degree of contrast to lend a strong and forceful presentation of the subject. The negative should appear a little thinner than normal. In most instances, the shadow areas are registered in perceptible detail, and in other cases they may disappear into total inky blackness.

The author's method of producing a low-key negative is: 1) illuminate and balance the shadows and highlights correctly; 2) expose the film slightly less than the film manufacturer's recommended ASA rating; 3) process the film longer than normal with a diluted developer.

To add brilliance and contrast to a thin negative, longer-than-normal development of the film can be tried. An inherent characteristic of black-and-white film is that the longer it is developed, the more the contrast is built up. If the film is slightly underexposed, there still will be plenty of gradation in the skin tones of our subject through longer development. You can also gain more contrast and brilliance by using a higher-contrast paper. The

Left: *Figure 24. Glamour lighting as a corrective.*

Center: *Figure 25. Forty-five degree lighting as a corrective.*

Right: *Figure 26. Split lighting as a corrective.*

personal taste and judgment of each photographer, based on experience, preferences, and experimentation will be the deciding factor.

You may think that experimenting by trial and error to determine the best film exposure under your par-

Figure 23. *High key.*

ticular working conditions is a time-consuming procedure. Actually, a few trial-and-error experiments will take relatively little time and, if you

keep an accurate record, will provide all the information you need for future reference.

HIGH KEY

While low-key photography contains a predominance of tones from black to the middle range of the gray scale, with a few highlights to add brilliance, the tonal make-up of a high-key interpretation is exactly the opposite. There is a predominance of light tones, ranging from almost white to the middle tones of the gray scale (or even a complete absence of middle tones), but containing a few dark tones.

Essentially a good semi-high-key or high-key photograph contains either a very light and delicate gradation of skin tones (Figure 22) or an almost complete omission of skin texture and middle tones. Such a photo will have a two-dimensional line-drawing effect along the outer edge formation of the subject (Figure 23).

As you can see in both interpretations, the mood is in a lighter vein; high-key work does not lend itself to so-called character or dramatic studies.

Lighting techniques for the high-key approach are comparatively

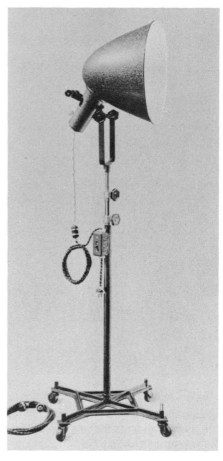

Above: *Figure 27. Photogenic Mazda floodlight.*

Left: *Figure 28. Baby Keg spotlight.*

Right: *Figure 29. Photogenic Sunspot hairlight.*

simple: any lighting style may be employed, providing the shadow areas are made very light. This is accomplished by using a fill-in light which will record shadow areas almost as bright as the areas lighted by the modeling light. Two fill-in lights may be used—one on each side of the camera.

CORRECTIVE LIGHTING

The art of correcting structural facial faults rests upon a fundamental principle of the phenomenon of light: shadows recede, highlights advance. Areas of the face which are dark in tone will appear to recede or look smaller; areas of the face which are lighter in tone will appear to stand out or look larger.

Figure 24 illustrates glamour (butterfly) lighting. Notice that this lighting style produces a wide band of illumination which would tend to call attention to discordant features. Therefore this lighting pattern is not suitable for use as a corrective. It should be used only with symmetrical features.

A few of the undesirable effects produced by this lighting pattern are: 1) dimensions of a heavy-structured or round face will appear magnified; 2) a wide jaw will appear wider; 3) a wide nose will appear wider and flat; 4) high cheek bones will be accented; 5) a wide forehead will appear wider.

Figure 25 illustrates 45-degree lighting. Its band of illumination is narrower than in butterfly lighting, and it has greater shadow area. Structural faults will appear to recede or become less noticeable, so we have an effective means to "correct" structural faults of the face. Using the Rembrandt lighting (triangle on the far side of the face in a three-quarter view) will make a heavy-structured or round face appear slimmer. A wide jaw or wide nose will appear narrower.

Figure 26 illustrates split (side) lighting. Here a further narrowing of the light band produces an even greater shadow area, offering a wide range of use as a corrective.

The fill-in light also plays an important part as a corrective, since a bright fill-in light will make a face appear wider, and a weak fill-in will make it appear narrower.

LIGHTING EQUIPMENT

A properly designed floodlight projects a broad field of illumination. This is accomplished by the design of its reflector, which deflects the light rays in many directions, reaches the subject from several angles, and thus produces a soft, even field of illumination. A floodlight can be used as a fill-in as well as a modeling light.

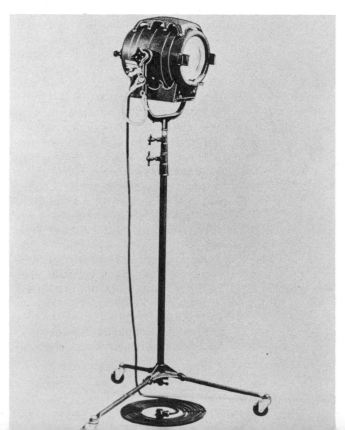

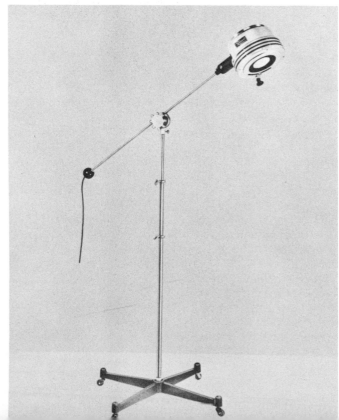

Figure 27 shows an efficient floodlight. The parabolic reflector projects a broad and even field of illumination. It is equipped with a 500- or 750-watt pear-shaped mogul base lamp and a diffusion screen to create a shoft, shadowless light. The stand extends the reflector to more than nine feet high.

A spotlight is a light source which concentrates the light rays into a narrow beam of illumination. One type of spotlight is equipped with a Fresnel lens, consisting of a small central plano-convex lens surrounded by a series of prismatic rings. This produces a strong light, but with a soft indistinct edge. Since the light rays from a spotlight travel in near straight-line directions, the shadows cast have more sharply defined edges than those produced by a floodlight. A spotlight is suitable for a modeling light, background illumination, and for backlighting.

Figure 28 shows a properly designed spotlight. The construction of the lamp house provides a clean field of illumination throughout its focusing range, from a spot to a large flood. It accommodates either 500- or 750-watt clear lamps. "Barndoors" are available as an accessory. Because backlighting is usually directed towards the camera lens, the light can be controlled by adjusting the barndoors so that light rays do not directly strike the lens and cause flare.

A hairlight is most useful when a light is required close to a picture area, such as a hair illuminant, or with a full-face view employing the butterfly lighting style. By design, this unit has a wide range of positions, making it practical for a variety of uses.

Figure 29 shows an efficiently designed unit for highlighting the hair. Its "boom arm" can be tilted, turned, or swiveled to any angle. The light is controlled in graduated volume with an iris diaphragm, permitting any size opening from ¾ of an inch to 4½ inches. It accommodates a No. 1 or No. 2 Photoflood, 500-watt 3200 K or T20 Mazda Lamps; a simple adjustment centers any of the lamps with the reflector; raises to a height of over nine feet to direct the light downward.

COLOR-WAVELENGTH RELATION

COLOR	WAVE LENGTH IN ÅNGSTRÖM UNITS
ULTRAVIOLET	SHORTER THAN 4000
VIOLET	4000 TO 4300
BLUE	4300 TO 4600
BLUE-GREEN	4600 TO 4900
GREEN	4900 TO 5500
YELLOW	5500 TO 5900
ORANGE	5900 TO 6300
RED	6300 TO 7600
INFRARED	LONGER THAN 7600

Figure 1. *Color of visible light correlated with the approximate wavelength region generating the light.*

LIGHTING SOURCES FOR COLOR

Ralph R. Winn and Gilbert H. Reiling
Photo Lamp Department, General Electric Co., Cleveland, Ohio

[Color photography with artificial light requires that the lighting sources be correctly balanced to color sensitivities. Here experts in the field discuss the color of light sources, color temperature, and luminous intensity. All types of lights—flood, flash, fluorescent, mercury vapor, xenon flash-tubes, battery-powered lamps—are covered. The article includes information on light reduction, exposure, reflectors, and diffusers.]
• *Also see: Color Fundamentals; Color Temperature; Flashlamp Characteristics; Lighting.*

For best results in color photography, the color quality of the light used for exposure should match, or balance with, the color response of the film. Color film is sensitive to all colors, but its degree of response varies. Also each type of color film has a specific color response of its own, i.e., it is more sensitive to some colors than others. Therefore any light source used with a color film should radiate the proper amount of energy in each of the color response areas of that film.

Since light travels through space as a vibration of various wavelengths, with each wavelength exciting a specific color response, it is possible to designate the exact areas in which a light source should radiate its energy. The wavelength for each color has been measured and specified in Ångström units. Each Ångström unit (A) is equal to one hundred millionth of a centimeter. Figure 1 shows the relationship between the wavelength of light and various colors.

Light is the visible portion of the radiant-energy spectrum. It extends from the short wavelengths of 4000 A (violet) to the long 7600 A area (red). Arranged in their progressive order of length (from 4000 to 7600 A), they form the "visible spectrum." When the spectrum also includes the intensity per wavelength, it is called the spectral distribution of the source emitting the light.

A light source is said to balance with a color film when the spectral distribution of the source matches the color response of the film.

COLOR OF LIGHT

In black-and-white photography the color of light has a greater effect on film "speed"—that is, more effect on film response to equal intensities of light than on the quality of the negative. Since most black-and-white photographic materials are more sensitive to blue light than to light of a longer wavelength, sources rich in blue are more efficient photographically. The relative amount of energy radiated in the blue increases as the color temperature of an incandescent body is increased. However, in the case of color photography, a definite color temperature must be used to insure proper color reproduction—the reproduced color should correspond to the impression the eye would have seen had the subject been in daylight.

Since the color process, in general, involves the exposure of more than one emulsion layer, it is necessary to have the correct exposure for each emulsion layer at the same time. The opacity produced on the emulsion varies with the intensity of light and the exposure time. It will be sufficient here to refer to the "characteristic film curve" which relates the density of an emulsion to exposure.

Figure 2 shows such a curve. The region which yields satisfactory

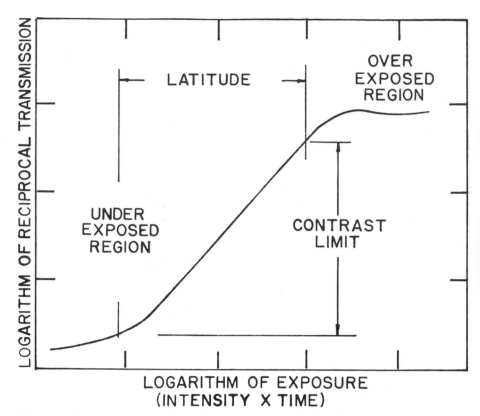

Figure 2. *Characteristic curve for an emulsion to show exposure range.*

contrast and quality is the sloping straight-line portion. Too low an exposure at the "toe" and too much light in the vicinity of the "knee" are unsatisfactory. A curve of this type is generally expressed as the logarithm of the quantities, which is a mathematical expression more closely related to the tone values of the subject than a simple linear relation.

Actual physical reproduction of the visible radiation is not presently possible in color photography. Rather, the film manufacturer resorts to the principle that, in general, it is possible to mix three primary colors and secure a given color. Usually a red, green, and blue color band are used in the emulsion.

Once the primary radiation components are chosen, it is still necessary for the film manufacturer to combine the components into the three light characteristics which make up the broad term "color":

1) brightness or intensity of light; 2) dominant wavelength or radiation component of maximum intensity; and 3) saturation or spectral purity of the radiation. The process is further complicated by the aim to reproduce not the actual color of the subject as seen under artificial photographic lighting, but rather as it would be seen if placed in average daylight.

Ordinarily observers make an unconscious adjustment in the color sensation gained from objects under different illumination, due to their knowledge of its daylight color. Film will not perform this action. The reason a subject has different apparent color is that it reflects light dependent both on its color and on the composition of the light received. That is, subjects found most often in photography are opaque and nonluminous and, therefore are seen by the light reflected from them.

If a subject whose source is composed of white light reflects all the colors or wavelengths equally, it appears white. However, if it absorbs part of the color (light spectrum)

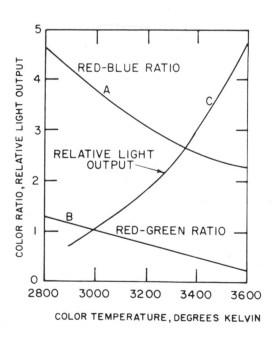

Figure 3. *Curve* A, *the red-blue ratio; curve* B, *the red-green ratio; curve* C, *the relative light output. Ratios vary with the color temperature of a photographic lamp.*

and reflects other parts, it appears the color of the reflected light. Since the amount of reflected light is dependent directly on the amount received, the object has its true color only when observed by light which contains equal portions of all wavelengths of the spectrum. For instance, a mercury-vapor lamp is somewhat lacking in red radiation; hence a red object appears black under such a lamp.

The film exposure latitude mainly determines the subject brightness and contrast (Figure 2) on film. It is also necessary to have proper color temperature of the light source and the desired amount of illumination on the subject in order to produce the subject's image on the film correctly. That is, color of the external light determines to a large extent the hue and color saturation of the subject.

COLOR RATIO

For color photography not only should the exposure fall properly on the characteristic curve of the emulsions used, but also the red to blue to green color ratios must be correct. More than any other factor, this latter requirement is controlled by the color temperature of the lamp. The relative amounts of energy radiated in various parts of the spectrum can be described by giving the intensity ratio for three primary colors.

Figure 3 shows an example of the ratio variation for the color temperature of a photographic lamp. A change of 100 K can have a noticeable effect on film—that is, the color rendition can be discerned as different. Film manufacturers balance their film for 3200-3400 K or have one film for 3200 K and another for 3400 K sources.

Aside from the color balance, a 100 K (180 F) change in source temperature changes the over-all photographic effectiveness (response) of the light by approximately two percent. Not all light sources are incandescent radiators this adds another element to the analysis.

Figure 4 shows the spectral-energy distribution of a number of sources. In the figure, curves are plotted to show the relative spectral distribution within the visible spectrum for A, and ordinary 120-volt, 500-watt incandescent lamp; B, a photoflood used by amateurs (3400 K); C, an ideal photoflash lamp; D, the relative energy radiated by the average noonday sun; and for comparison, E, the sky directly overhead on a clear day (zenith sky). These curves are plotted on the basis of equal light intensity from each source. They were adjusted so that the intensity of radiation was approximately equal at 5500 A wavelength.

COLOR TEMPERATURE

Noting the color temperature of a light source is a short-cut method of describing the integral color of the light emitted by a particular source or the relative amount of energy in different wavelength bands of its spectrum. The color temperature of a source is defined as the temperature at which it is necessary to operate a blackbody (perfect radiator) so that the emitted light is color-matched approximately with that of the source considered. (The term "blackbody" is rather unfortunate, because such a body does radiate and can be very luminous. However, the term is used to denote that the blackbody absorbs all the radiation incident upon it.)

Generally color temperature is applied to the matching of visible radiation. Color temperature can be used most exactly when describing sources emitting continuous radiation, but it has been found that

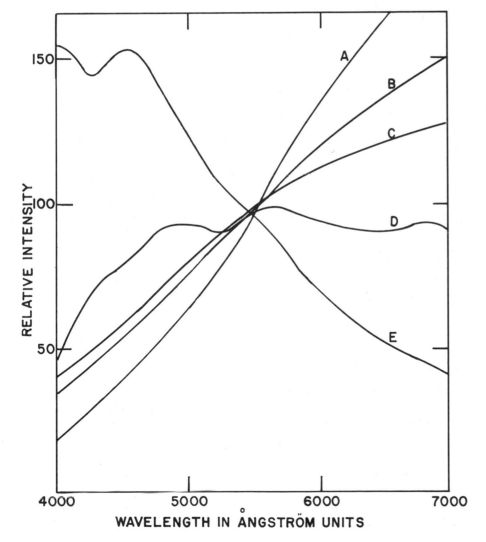

WAVELENGTH IN ÅNGSTRÖM UNITS

Figure 4. *Spectral energy distribution of a number of sources. Curve A, 120-volt, 500-watt regular incandescent lamp (2960 K); B, photoflood lamp (3400 K); C, photoflash lamp (3800 K); D, direct sunlight; E, zenith sky (13,700 K).*

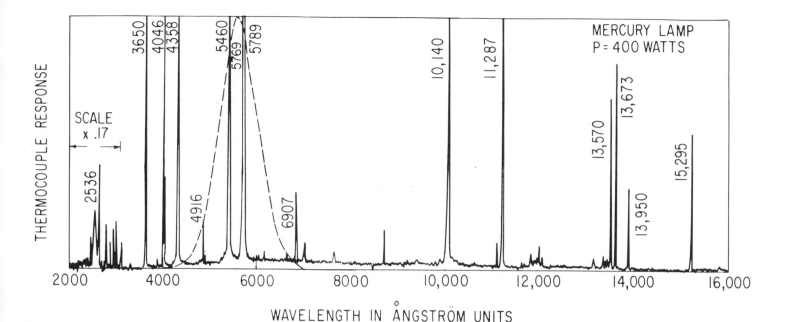

Figure 5. *A curve of a 400-watt four-atmosphere mercury-vapor lamp commonly used for road illumination.*

color of practically all sources emitting radiation can be matched with that of a blackbody—that is, such sources have a color temperature.

The curves in Figure 4 show the change in the relative amount of energy radiated in the various parts of the spectrum as the color temperature of the source is changed. For example increasing the color temperature by 1000 K decreases the intensity of the radiation in the red portion of the spectrum about 30 percent and increases the intensity of the radiation in the blue portion about 60 percent, if the radiation in the green is held approximately constant.

A source is said to emit continuous radiation if there is no sharp break in the spectrum of the radiation for any color or wavelength. This type of radiation is emitted by most sources that are luminous because they are composed of dense, incandescent particles.

However, there are other sources which emit a spectrum more characteristic of the material because they have low density or are otherwise capable of independent molecular radiation—for example, a discharge of electricity through a gas or vapor yielding a spectrum in which the energy is concentrated

in definite narrow wavelength or color bands. Such a source is obviously discontinuous with respect to color or wavelength.

The most common examples of this type of radiation are medium-pressure mercury-vapor arcs, and neon and sodium lamps. Figure 5 shows a mercury-vapor lamp of medium pressure. Occasionally photographers have to use this lighting for photographic illumination.

It has been found by experiment that most sources giving continuous radiation show the same relative spectral distribution when set for the same color temperature. While these sources vary in intensity, they all radiate energy having the same

Figure 6. *Color temperatures of various natural and artificial light sources. Note that color temperature for fluorescent lamps is based on eye response rather than on photographic response.*

COLOR TEMPERATURES	
SOURCE	COLOR TEMPERATURE K
ELECTRIC RADIANT HEATER	1000
CANDLE FLAME	1850
SUNRISE (APPROX.)	1900
500 WATT INCANDESCENT LAMP	2960
PHOTOFLOOD LAMPS	3200–3400
FLASH LAMPS – CLEAR	3800
WHITE FLUORESCENT LAMP	4500
AVERAGE NOON SUNLIGHT	5350
BLUE COATED PHOTO FLASH LAMP	6000
DAYLIGHT FLUORESCENT	6500
BLUE SKY	11,000–25,000

relative spectral distribution. Therefore it is sufficient to give color temperature and energy intensity to describe different sources.

Hence, the use of the term "color temperature" is satisfactory photographic shorthand for a set of scientific data. When a source is said to have a color temperature of 2960 K, it has an energy distribution in the visible part of the spectrum that is the same as that shown by curve *A*, Figure 4. This source's radiation has a red-blue ratio and a red-green ratio shown in Figure 3 for this temperature, which is that of a 500-watt tungsten-filament lamp. It is as easy and nearly as definite to say a photoflood lamp is designed to have a color temperature of 3400 K as to show curve *B*, Figure 4, and the curves in Figure 3. The color temperature of some well-known sources are given in Figure 6.

It is necessary to caution the photographer about fluorescent lamps which have a color temperature largely based on the chromatic response of the eye. In most cases, this is different from the response of photographic emulsion because of the more extensive range of the eye. Also, the fluorescent lamp gleans its radiation from nonthermal radiators and therefore is a more selective radiator than a photoflood lamp.

Figure 7 shows curves of orthochromatic and panchromatic film sensitivity and the relative light output of a daylight fluorescent lamp compared with a photoflood. The curves show that the film will respond differently, since the lamps are totally different in the blue-light output which is the region of maximum sensitivity of the film.

Today's color films are usually available in four types. These are balanced for either daylight, clear photoflash lamps, 3200 K studio lamps, or 3400 K photoflood lamps. In each case, the relative amount of blue, green, and red radiation emitted by the source is properly balanced for the color sensitivity of the film when the recommended source is used. If the source is not operated at the correct color tem-

perature, the red-green and red-blue ratios will not be correct for the film and the transparency or print will show too much of one color for correct rendition. As a result, the dominant wavelength, one of the light characteristics, will not be the same in the film image as on the subject.

PHOTOFLOODS

Photoflood lamps are special incandescent sources designed specifically for color photography. They provide a tremendous amount of light of a specific color temperature for short exposure and correct balance with certain types of color film.

G. F. Prideaux, a General Electric engineer, discovered the principle of photofloods many years ago. During experimental work, he found that a 60-volt, 100-watt tungsten-filament lamp operated at 120 volts (double-design voltage), consumed 250 watts (instead of 100), while providing light intensity equal to

Figure 7. *Data comparing two common film sensitivities (curve* A, *orthochromatic; curve* B, *panchromatic) with two light sources, daylight fluorescent lamp,* C, *and a photoflood lamp,* D, *near 3400 K.*

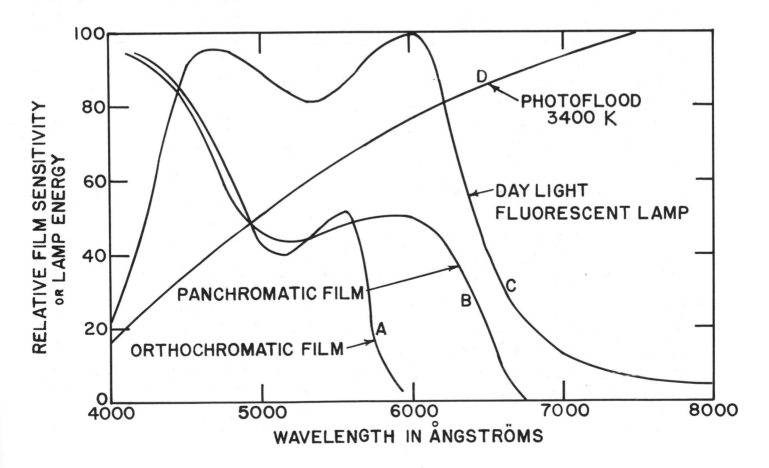

Characteristics of Photoflood Lamps

3400 K PHOTOFLOOD LAMPS (115-120 volts)

Lamp No. & Code	Appr. watts	Amps at 118 volts	Rated life at 118 volts	Rated lumens at 118 volts	Beam spread	Bulb	Bulb diam. in inches	Max. over-all length in inches	Base
BBA No. 1	250	2.2	3 hrs.	8500	....	A21	$2^5/_8$	$4^{15}/_{16}$	med.
EBV No. 2	500	4.4	6 hrs.	17000	....	PS25	$3^1/_8$	$6^{15}/_{16}$	med.
DXR No. 4	1000	8.7	10 hrs.	31000	....	PS35	$4^5/_8$	$9^3/_8$	mog.
DAN	200	1.7	4 hrs.	10500*	med.	R20	$2^1/_2$	$3^{15}/_{16}$	med.
BEP	300	2.6	4 hrs.	11000*	med.	R30	$3^3/_4$	$5^1/_4$	med.
EBR	375	3.3	4 hrs.	14000*	med.	R30	$3^3/_4$	$5^1/_4$	med.
BFA	375	3.3	4 hrs.	16000*	med.	R40	5	$6^1/_2$	med.
DWA	650	5.5	8 hrs.[1]	25500*	med.	PAR36	$4^1/_2$	$2^7/_{16}$	special 2-pin
DKX Uniflood	650	5.5	16 hrs.[1]	30000*	med.	PAR36	$4^1/_2$	$2^7/_{16}$	special 2-pin
DXC RFL 2	500	4.4	6 hrs.	6500*	flood	R40	5	$6^1/_2$	med.
DXB RSP 2	500	4.4	6 hrs.	50000*	spot	R40	5	$6^1/_2$	med.

*Reflector-type lamp. Approximate initial mean candlepower in 10° cone.
[1] at 120 volts.

3200 K STUDIO TYPE LAMPS (115, 120, 125 volts)

Lamp Number & Code	Appr. watts	Amps at 120 volts	Rated life at 120 volts	Rated lumens at 120 volts	Bulb	Bulb diam. in inches	Max. over-all length in inches	Base
ECA PH/250A23	250	2.2	20 hrs.	6500	A23	4	$6^1/_{16}$	med.
ECT PH/500PS25/5	500	4.4	60 hrs.	13650	PS25	$3^1/_8$	$6^{15}/_{16}$	med.
EAL PH/500/32R7	500	4.4	15 hrs.	8200*	R40	5	$6^1/_2$	med.
DMS PH/500T20	500	4.4	50 hrs.	13200	T20	$2^1/_2$	$5^1/_2$	med.
DMX PH/500T20P	500	4.4	50 hrs.	13200	T20	$2^1/_2$	$5^3/_4$	med. pf.
ECV PH/1M/PS40/1	1000	8.7	60 hrs.	26500	PS40	5	$9^3/_4$	mog.
DPT PH/1M/T20	1000	8.7	50 hrs.	28000	T20	$2^1/_2$	$9^1/_{16}$	mog.
DPW PH/1M/T20P	1000	8.7	50 hrs.	28000	T20	$2^1/_2$	$9^1/_2$	mog. pf.

*Initial candlepower in 10° cone; beam spread to half intensity 60°. Reflector-type lamp.

4800 K BLUE BULB LAMPS* (115-120 volts)

Lamp Number & Code	Appr. watts	Amps at 118 volts	Rated life at 118 volts	Rated lumens at 118 volts	Bulb	Bulb diam. in inches	Max. over-all length in inches	Base
BCA No. B1	250	2.2	3 hrs.	5000	A21	$2^5/_8$	$4^{15}/_{16}$	med.
EBW No. B2	500	4.4	6 hrs.	10500	PS25	$3^1/_8$	$6^{15}/_{16}$	med.
DXT No. B4	1000	8.7	10 hrs.	19200	PS35	$4^3/_8$	$9^3/_8$	mog.

*To supplement daylight for color photography.

an ordinary 500-watt lamp. At double voltage the 100-watt lamp provided about five times its normal light output and operated at about 3400 K.

Since photofloods are essentially filament-type lamps operating in a controlled over-voltage state, their life span is somewhat shorter than normal lamps of the same wattage. This is because lamp life depends on the rate of evaporation of the tungsten filament, and photoflood filament temperatures range from 200 to 500 C hotter than those of ordinary lamps of the same wattage.

There are three main types of photoflood lamps. Those designed to operate at 3400 K, others at 3200 K, and blue floods which are filter-corrected to an effective 4800 K. Lamp characteristics for all three types will be found in Figure 8.

The best known photofloods are those which operate at 3400 K to match the color sensitivity of Type A color films. They range from 200 to 1000 watts and are available in three different types, BBA, EBV, and DXR (American Standards Association lamp code), and look like regular household bulbs. They are normally used in separate reflectors for controlled lighting in still photography.

The second 3400 K group of lamps has its own highly efficient, built-in reflector. The DXB and DXC types are generally used by amateur and professional photographers for still pictures. DAN, BEP, EBR, and BFA are called "movie lights," since they are primarily used on portable light bars attached to movie cameras.

The remaining 3400 K lamps are the DXK and DWA, each of which looks like an automotive "sealed-beam" lamp. DXK is radically different from all the other photofloods because it is actually a lamp within a lamp. The thick glass, sealed-beam type outer bulb (PAR lamp) is hermetically sealed to enclose a shiny reflector and a quartz-iodine lamp. The quartz lamp contains iodine gas and a special tungsten filament. This high-

Figure 8. *Characteristics of photoflood lamps.*

output lamp, which changes negligibly in intensity and color temperature during its life, features a rectangular beam pattern matching the shape of the 8 mm movie frame for which it was designed. It is a one-lamp movie light.

DWA is also a one-lamp movie light, similar to the DXK in all physical respects except one. The DWA has a tungsten filament and collector grid instead of the quartz-iodine source. Its performance characteristics are similar to those of a rectangular photoflood, except that it features the rectangular beam pattern and an eight-hour life, about half as long as the DXK rated life.

Figure 8 also shows representative 3200 K lamps. These sources are called "studio lamps" and are designed for still and movie uses by professional photographers. They balance with Type B or tungsten-type color films. Generally speaking, they have a much longer life and somewhat lower light output than the 3400 K lamps. Both of these effects are the result of the lower color temperature.

The third type of photoflood (Figure 8) is rated at 4800 K. These lamps are the blue-bulb versions of the BBA, EBV, and DXR floods. They are designed to provide supplemental or fill-in lighting, when daylight is used to expose color film. Blue photofloods are not ordinarily used as the sole source of illumination because their color temperature is about 700 K lower than the color response of daylight-type color film. This significant difference in color balance produces warm or reddish results.

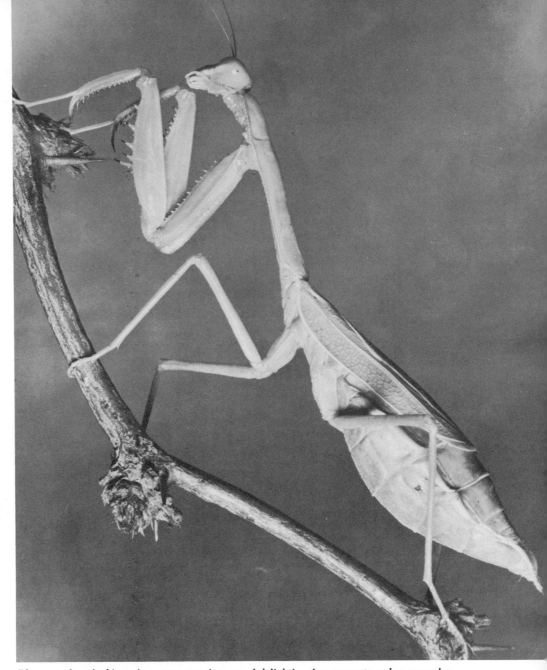

Photography of objects in nature requires careful lighting for accurate color reproduction. (Photo: George Bradt)

CAUSES OF LIGHT REDUCTION

The light output of incandescent lamps is reduced during their life as a result of several factors, all the consequence of the evaporation of the filament resulting from the high temperature of operation. This evaporation reduces the diameter of the filament, and a filament of the same length but of smaller diameter operates at a lower temperature for the same applied voltage than a filament of larger diameter, which means less light output.

The material evaporated from the tungsten filament is deposited on the walls of the bulbs and blackens them, thus reducing their transmission and preventing some of the light from getting through the bulb. As a result, in the conventional lamp the light output is reduced to about 70 percent of its original value at the end of life of the lamp. These same factors also reduce the color temperature of the lamp at the end of its life.

In 1959 the General Electric Company developed the quartz-iodine line of tungsten incandescent lamps. In these lamps iodine vapor, by a regenerative chemical cycle, redeposits evaporated tungsten evenly on the filament. The lamps not only burn longer, but they also retain their original color and brightness to the end of their life. Presently the filament is enclosed in a special quartz envelope which maintains the temperature to operate the iodine cycle properly. A variety of photographic lamps is available using this principle.

Ordinarily a photoflood lamp is operated at high temperature to obtain the maximum actinic quality (photographic effectiveness) and at the same time the maximum efficiency. For incandescent lamps, this

Food advertising is at its most persuasive when photos are reproduced in color. The rendition of the natural colors of food greatly enhances its appeal.

automatically means relatively short life. However, the efficiency goes from 17 lumens per watt of a general lighting lamp to 35 lumens per watt for a photoflood. More important, the blue output has increased greatly. Photoflood lamps have life ratings from three to approximately twenty hours. Since the melting point of tungsten is 3650 K, lamps generally cannot be operated even for short periods above 3400 K due to excessive evaporation.

LIGHT AND VOLTAGE

Since one of the important factors in making acceptable color reproductions is the color of the light used, care should be exercised by the photographer to select the proper light source for the particular type of film and to see that the source, if an incandescent lamp, is operated at the suggested voltage.

If the voltage that is applied to a gas-filled incandescent lamp is varied, changes are produced in the lamp characteristics. These changes may be transient due to the periodic nature of the variation, or they may be constant due to operating the lamp at other than the designated voltage. The changes produced in the operating characteristics of a tungsten lamp by a change in operating voltage depend upon the lamp size. But for a small change from the design voltage for 120-volt lamps, the following rules show approximately the correct effect on some lamp characteristics.

1. A one-volt change in lamp voltage raises or lowers the temperature 10 K.
2. A five-volt change in lamp voltage changes the lamp life by a factor of two.
3. A one-volt increase in lamp voltage raises the light output two and one half percent.
4. The inrush current to the lamp when turned on is ten to fifteen times the normal operating current, and the lamp requires about a quarter of a second to stabilize to the normal value.

The curves in Figure 9 show how color temperature changes with the life of the lamp. Figure 10 shows the color-temperature variation with line voltage. Thus, if a particular film for taking color pictures is balanced by the manufacturers for a color temperature of 3400 K, and if this film is best exposed within a latitude of ± 50 K, the voltage at which the lamp is operated must be kept within plus or minus five volts of that for which the lamp was designed. Due to the heavy flow in wiring, it is necessary to determine if the service lines will maintain a voltage that is accurate enough. It may be necessary to provide a constant voltage transformer or other device to insure that the lamps are operated within the correct limits.

To conserve power and reduce heat on the subject, lamps are frequently operated at half voltage until the photographer is ready to take the picture, then they are turned up to full voltage. This action does not limit the lamp life but it must be remembered that it requires about a quarter of a second for the unit to reach full brightness.

BATTERY-POWERED LAMPS

In 1962 General Electric introduced a 3400 K movie lamp operated from a rechargeable battery, which allows greater portability. The lamps, while operating at 3400 K, are designed for lower wattage. They

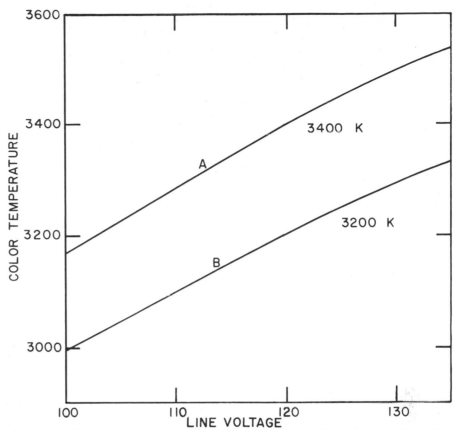

Figure 10. *The variation of the color temperature of photoflood lamps with applied voltage. Curve A, 3400 K photoflood; curve B; 3200 K lamp.*

are intended for use with higher-speed films. These lamps have the same sensitivity to voltage as the 120-volt lamps, and they have a short life if the battery operates at above normal voltage. Certain lamps

for this use have a sealed-beam construction resulting in increased reflector efficiency and increased light-collecting ability from the lamp. This construction is necessary to reduce the size of the power pack.

Perhaps the best known battery-operated lighting sources are flash-lamps, commonly called flashbulbs. More than 500 million of these lamps are used yearly in the United States in all types of cameras.

The small flashlamp with its intense, short-duration burst of light offers many advantages over other photographic light sources. Its flash is so bright that pictures may be taken with it over a wide range of distances, even with the slowest color film. The quick flash minimizes camera and subject movement. Flashlamps are now so small that some manufacturers build a flash unit into the camera body.

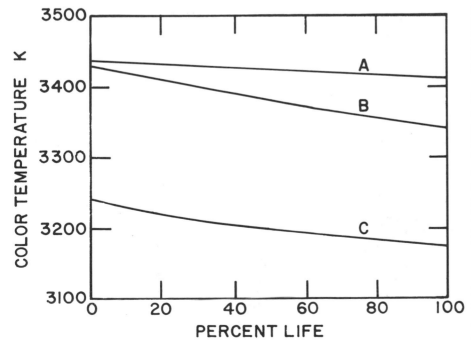

Figure 9. *The variation of color temperature of three photographic lamps with lamp life. Curve A, quartz-iodine 3400 K lamp; curve B, nominal 3400 K photoflood; curve C, 3200 K lamp.*

With flash the photographer can use fast shutter speeds to stop action and small *f*-stops for greater depth of field. In addition, the photographer is assured of the same color quality and light intensity for every picture, with the correct camera setting.

XENON FLASHTUBES

If the photographer wishes to stop action on film, a flashtube is the answer. The flashtube produces a bright flash which can last from $1/_{200}$ of a second to as short as $1/_{1,000,000}$ of a second. An average xenon flash in photographic equipment lasts approximately $1/_{2000}$ of a second, the length of time depending both on the lamp design and on the power supply.

The singular advantage of the xenon arc is that its peak energy and temperature can be increased beyond that found in incandescent sources. It produces a brilliant white light of relatively high efficiency (40 lumen seconds per watt second). Since the color temperature of the xenon flash is near 6000 K, the light can be used for black-and-white film and also for daylight color materials. In critical work, a warming filter is occasionally used, particularly with high-voltage flashtube lamps.

Usually the flashtube consists of a small-diameter helical quartz coil with metal electrodes at the end. The tube is filled to a partial atmosphere of xenon gas through which the electrical discharge is excited. Figure 11 shows several electronic flashtubes used for photographic

Figure 11. *Common electronic flashtubes.*

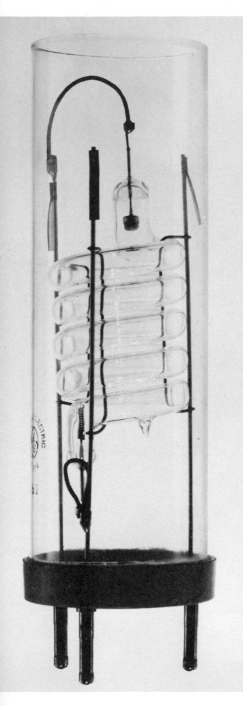
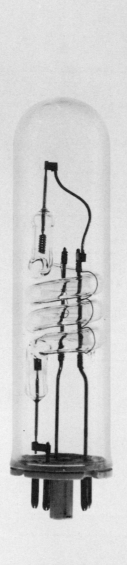
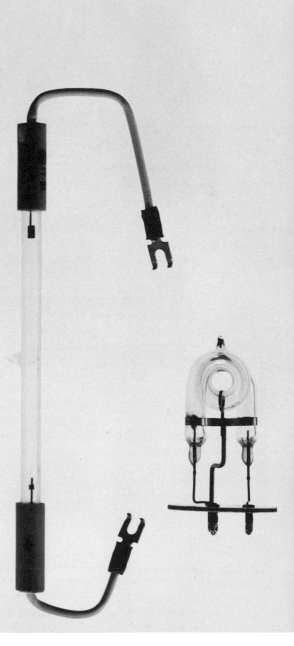

purposes. The energy burst needed to operate a flashtube is generally obtained from a storage capacitor charged to high voltage. A high-voltage ignition pulse ignites a weak arc in the flashtube enabling the capacitor to release its energy.

The spectrum of a standard flash-tube is continuous except for a few isolated atomic-radiation lines. A typical spectrum is shown in Figure 12. The higher-voltage flashtubes produce a bluer color (higher color temperature) than do the lower-voltage tubes.

Cameras with X synchronization fire the lamp when the shutter is wide open and, therefore, have no delay. Other synchronizations require a delay mechanism to fire the lamp at a time when the shutter is open. Often photographers resort to the open-flash technique where the shutter is opened and the action itself triggers the flashtube. While many elaborate triggering devices can be used, such simple mechanisms as a thread attached to the moving object or two wires which touch when the action passes are often employed. A guide number can be found from the following formula:

Guide number $= \sqrt{0.18 \times M \times S \times J}$
M is the reflector factor; S, the exposure index of the film; J, joules or watt-seconds input to the lamp. A reflector factor of 6 to 8 is representative of the average 50-degree beam-spread reflectors. Figure 13 lists various types of lamps and their input and output.

Occasionally fluorescent lamps and mercury-vapor arcs are used for color photography since such lighting may be readily available for photographic work in a store, in a factory, or on a road. Used properly,

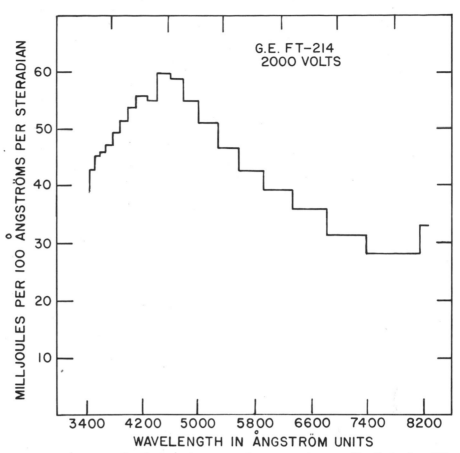

Figure 12. *Energy distribution of a general-purpose photographic flashtube. This is a helical, five-turn, 200-watt-second flashtube.*

the color reproduction by the film can be very good. However, since the intensity of the light emitted by these lamps is generally low, compared to a photographic lamp, the exposure times are long. Because of their high efficiency, these lamps have a cooler light than incandescent lamps, and they are occasionally used in studios.

Figure 14 shows the filters recommended for use with fluorescent and mercury lamps. Since there are many variables in color photog-

raphy, these filter types are only a guide and may need some variation for critical work. Although filters for clear mercury lamps are shown, these lamps are always deficient in the red. In Figure 14, directly below the filter recommendation is a fraction. This number is the suggested increase in the f-number due to light absorbed by the filter, that is, "$1/_3$" means to open the camera lens one third more than that already indicated by the exposure-meter reading.

Figure 13. *Typical flashtubes and their photographic applications.*

PHOTOGRAPHIC APPLICATIONS OF FLASHTUBES AND APPROXIMATE RANGE OF ENERGY INPUTS AND OUTPUTS

	TYPICAL ENERGY INPUT WATT–SECONDS	OUTPUT LUMEN–SECONDS	TYPICAL LAMPS
AMATEUR UNITS	25 TO 125	750 TO 5,000	FT–106,118,218
PROFESSIONAL PORTABLES	50 TO 200	1700 TO 10,000	FT–118,120,217,218
SMALL STUDIO UNITS	50 TO 500 (PER LAMP)	1700 TO 20,000	FT–217,221,220,403 FT–506,306
LARGE STUDIO UNITS	1000 TO 24,000 (PER LAMP)	50,000 1,200,000	FT–503,623

Suggested Filters for Various Light Sources

Type of Film	FLUORESCENT								MERCURY		
	WWX	CWX	WW	CW	PG	W	SW	D	Color Imp.	White Coated	Clear
Ansco Sheet Daylight	20C 20M 1/2	20M 20Y 1/2	10M 10Y 1/3	10M 20Y 1/3	20M 30Y 2/3	10M 10Y 1/3	10C 10M 1/3	30M 50Y 1	20M 1/3	50M 30Y 1 1/3	50M 50Y 1 2/3
Ansco Sheet Tungsten	10M 10Y 1/3	20M 30Y 2/3	40M 20Y 2/3	40M 50Y 1 1/3	50M 60Y 1 2/3	40M 40Y 1 1/3	30M 40Y 1	85B 20R 1 1/2	30M 1/2	Not Rec.	Not Rec.
Super Anscochrome Roll Daylight	30C 20M 1/2	No Fil.	20C 20M 1/2	10M 10Y 1/3	No Fil.	10C 10M 1/3	20C 10M 1/2	40M 60Y 1 1/2	30C 10M 1/2	20M 40Y 2/3	50M 50Y 1 2/3
Super Anscochrome Roll Tungsten	10M 20Y 1/3	20M 40Y 2/3	10M 10Y 1/3	40M 60Y 1 1/3	40M 70Y 1 1/2	20M 40Y 3/4	10M 40Y 2/3	85B 20Y 1 1/2	10M 10Y 1/3	50M 50Y 1 2/3	Not Rec.
Ektachrome Sheet E3 Daylight	80C 50M 2	50C 20M 1	80C 70M 2 1/2	40C 40M 1	40C 50M 1 1/3	50C 50M 1 1/2	50C 40M 1 1/3	20M 40Y 2/3	Not Rec.	40C 20M 1	Not Rec.
Ektachrome Sheet E3 Tungsten	10M 20Y 1/3	10M 30Y 2/3	10M 30Y 2/3	20M 30Y 1	30M 30Y 1 1/3	20M 20Y 1/2	20M 20Y 1/2	85B 30M 1 2/3	No Fil.	60M 60Y 1 1/2	Not Rec.
Ektachrome Roll E2 EF Flash	20C 20Y 1/2	20Y 1/3	No Fil.	10M 20Y 1/3	10M 30Y 1/2	10Y	10C 10Y 1/3	50M 50Y 1 2/3	20C 1/3	30M 50Y 1	20M 50Y 1
Ektachrome Roll EH Daylight	20C 1/3	20C 1/3	20C 30M 1/2	20M 20Y 1/2	20M 30Y 2/3	10M 10Y 1/3	10C	30M 30Y 2/3	20C 1/3	40M 20Y 1	50M 50Y 1 2/3
Kodachrome Roll K Daylight	30C 1/3	No Fil.	20C 20M 1/2	20M 10Y 1/3	20M 20Y 1/2	20M 1/3	20C 1/3	30M 30Y 2/3	30C 1/3	20M 40Y 2/3	50M 50Y 1 2/3
Kodachrome Roll KF Flash	No Fil.	10M 20Y 1/3	20M 10Y 1/3	30M 30Y 2/3	30M 40Y 1	20M 10Y 1/3	10Y	30M 50Y 1 1/3	20C 20M 1/2	30M 50Y 1	50M 50Y 1 2/3
Kodachrome Improved K II Daylight	30C 1/2	10C	20C 20M 1/2	10M 10Y 1/3	10M 20Y 1/2	20M 1/3	10C 10Y 1/3	40M 40Y 1 1/3	30C 10M 1/2	30M 40Y 1	50M 50Y 1 2/3

WWX — Warm white deluxe
CWX — Cool white deluxe
WW — Warm white
CW — Cool white
PG — Power groove
W — White
D — Daylight
SW — Soft white
Imp. — Improved

Figure 14. *A table showing the suggested filters for various films in combination with fluorescent and mercury light sources. Directly below the filter number is the suggested increase in* f-*number above that read on an exposure meter.* (T. Knowles / General Electric Lamp Division)

REFLECTORS

The discussion so far has been concerned with the characteristics of the light source only, but the choice of the reflector is also important. While an open lamp radiates light in all directions, a reflector directs the light and, if properly designed, concentrates the light on the area of interest so that the output is efficiently used. The amount of light falling on a given area may be increased several times by using proper reflectors.

A reflector for general photographic use should uniformly illuminate the area covered by the camera lens so the negative does not appear spotty and, for greatest efficiency, it should concentrate the energy on this area alone. Ordinarily a reflector should illuminate an area of 50 degrees with a maximum variation of not more than 2:1 from the edge to the center of the beam.

It is important to have a reflector surface which possesses the same reflectivity for all colors and, of course, it must reflect a large percentage of the light falling on it. Magnesium oxide as a diffuse reflector does this most efficiently, but photographers are usually interested in polished or semipolished reflectors to obtain directivity. Aluminum is excellent for the purpose, and chromium can be used. Often reflector surfaces are coated to prevent tarnishing. Other materials, such as white paper, nickel, or gold reflect less blue light and thus lower the color temperature of the light.

Reflector shape and size are important. Reflectors can be plane,

A good photograph of this night scene in color might be hard to produce—lights may not be correctly balanced for color film and voltages may vary. A longer-than-normal exposure also may throw off the color. (Photo: Robert Yarnall Richie)

conical, spherical, parabolic, or elliptical in shape. A flat or conical reflector, for example, will usually double the intensity of illumination coming from a bare lamp. More efficient reflectors can increase the light on the subject up to 20 times.

The use of directional light from polished reflectors frequently causes excessive contrast with color materials. The addition of a diffusing screen in front of the reflector will usually lower the lighting contrast while smoothing out uneven levels of intensity throughout the picture area.

Care must be taken in the selection of a screen, since even a trace of coloration within the material will influence the rendition of the final color picture. Spun-glass screens are designed to transmit all colors with the same degree of fidelity. Other substances such as oiled silk, tracing paper, or tissue paper are usually unsuitable because they are somewhat warm in tone and may lower the color temperature of the light by as much as 200 K. Any material that shows the slightest color when viewed by transmitted light is unsatisfactory as a diffusing material for color photography.

EXPOSURE

Correct exposure, with the limited latitude of color materials, is of great importance. Too little exposure darkens colors with a tendency to shift color balance; too much exposure gives a washed-out effect.

Interesting color pictures with daylight color film or with indoor film and the proper filter can be obtained on a clear moonlit night. The color temperature of the moon is about 4100 K and that of the sky at night is high. The exposure has

Top, right: *Correct color rendition is vital for scientific purposes. This photo of a sun eclipse, if in color, would be an even more valuable tool for studying stellar phenomena.*

Bottom, right: *The use of color in the advertising of cosmetics helps the prospective customers to judge the product's effect.* (Photo: Revlon)

Left: *Candid color photos with ordinary artificial light may result in a yellowish cast to the subject. Film should be balanced for the specific light source for best results.*

Lighting for photos of people must be carefully controlled so that skin tones will appear lifelike. (Photo: Silvester / Leitz)

to be about 2500 times greater in moonlight than in sunlight.

A good exposure meter provides the best method of determining exposure when incandescent sources, such as photofloods, are used for illumination. Exposure meters offer the best method of exposure measurement with continuous light sources, but they are useless with flashlamps. For flashing sources, the guide-number system of exposure is used. Many photographers also prefer this system with photofloods and movie lights because it eliminates the need for an exposure meter.

In this system, each lamp is assigned a table of numerical values known as exposure guide numbers, which vary according to the ASA rating of the film and shutter speed used. Simple division of the proper guide number by the distance (in feet) between the light source and subject determines the correct lens setting or f-stop to use. When a particular f-stop and shutter speed is used with a given film, division of the guide number by the f-stop used will indicate the correct distance (in feet)the light source must be placed from the subject for best exposure.

LIGHTING WITH MULTIFLASH

[Flash photography, particularly in the field of photojournalism, has been vastly improved by the multiflash technique. The author describes simple experiments showing the effects of multiflash and single-flash illumination, special multiple-flash equipment and techniques of light arrangement and exposure. The uses of multiflash at home, for portraiture, and in newspaper work are covered.]
• *Also see: Banquet Photography; Flash Photography; Lighting.*

MULTIPLE-FLASH PHOTOGRAPHY WAS born of the numerous attempts of press and commercial photographers to mitigate the undesirable effects of single-flash techniques which produce the flat, chalky faces so characteristic of news photography. The simultaneous use of several flash-bulbs was suggested by observing the modulation and depth produced by two- and three-source lighting in regular portraiture and commercial photography, and was used first without synchronization—that is, with the open-flash method.

The rapid development of multiple-flash photography gives adequate testimony to its effectiveness. Amateur and professional alike discovered the brilliance and increased lighting quality made possible by the use of one or more bulbs placed at a distance from the camera. They likewise discovered that more than one bulb could be synchronized to the shutter without the purchase of new equipment. The old synchronizer could do the job well.

When electronic-flash or "strobe" lighting was introduced in the 40's, it was found that its naturally softer light avoided the washed-out effects resulting from the flash-on-camera technique. At the same time, it was also discovered that multiflash was even easier with "strobe" light—several flash heads could be connected to a single power pack, with all firing simultaneously. In the more elaborate units, a "modeling lamp" of low wattage was provided in each head, and the units could be set up by observing the light pattern produced by each.

In electronic units, when several heads are connected to one power source, the available power is evenly divided among them. If three heads are used, each will be one third as bright as if it were the only one connected. Many photographers, though, wanted to use a number of heads for increased illumination, and means were devised to interconnect a group of power packs,

The illumination for this familiar scene came from two light sources. The flash unit attached to the camera was held above and to one side, while a Kodak Slave Unit was placed to the left. The synchronized flash at the camera triggered the electric eye on the slave unit, which then flashed.

An example of open flash exposure with one flashbulb on the flash gun without reflector, second flash to the left. 4×5 Graphic View camera, 8½-inch lens, f/16, two No. 5 flashlamps. (Photo: Interstate Photographers)

each with only one flash head connected to it.

At the same time, electronic specialists found that an electronic-flash unit could be triggered by a photoelectric cell. Each flash unit was equipped with a photocell, except for the one connected to the camera; when the unit on the camera was flashed, the others all went off at just about the same time. (Actually, there is a delay of a few millionths of a second, but with the camera shutter synchronized at $1/200$ of a second, all flashes will reach the film before the shutter closes.) Electronic specialists soon adapted the photocell tripper

to ordinary flashlamps, and small "slave units" weighing less than a pound were successfully marketed.

Those who are familiar with the time-lag characteristics of ordinary flashlamps (essentially, it takes about $1/50$ of a second for the lamp to reach peak brilliancy) were dubious of the action of photocell slave units—it seemed certain that the slaves would fire much too late to be useful. Actually, the photocell on the "slave" is extremely sensitive, and makes contact with the extension lamp at practically the first sign of light from the main lamp, long before it has reached its peak. The delay is on-

ly a few milliseconds, and with the camera shutter set at $1/100$ of a second, both main flash and "slave" units will register fully on the film.

MULTIFLASH AND SINGLE FLASH

All you need to try the multiflash technique is a camera with a flash unit having an outlet at the side for an extension; practically every flash gun, except those for box cameras, is made in this way. About 15 or 20 feet of lamp extension wire is used on the extension unit, which need be nothing more than a regular clip-on socket with reflectors.

Set up your subject in a chair, a short distance from the background, and put the clip on something fairly tall (not a chair back) like a hatrack, etc. Set this so it is about halfway between the camera and the subject and just about as far to the side. The actual distance from the extension light to the subject should be about the same as from the camera light to the subject. To calculate exposure for this lighting arrangement, use the regular guide number divided by distance, but close down an additional half stop.

EQUIPMENT

We have already discussed general principles, and for the sake of simplicity we have assumed that your camera has built-in provisions for synchronization. Actually, most modern cameras do have this, and there is little reason, at this late date, to discuss mechanical or magnetic shutter trippers.

Nevertheless, the magnetic tripper has one advantage—it can be used as a remote release for the shutter, so that you can make your multiflash picture with all lights, including the main one, off the camera. With this arrangement, you can hold the camera light in your hand, and move enough to one side, while holding the lamp up high, to eliminate the disturbing shadows on the background wall; meanwhile the extension light is placed at the usual 45-degree angle to the subject and provides the modeling.

If you are going to do much multiflash work, you might as well invest in two or three "slave" units with photocell tripping. They are easier to handle, require no interconnecting cords, and as currently made, cost about the same as simple extension flash heads. This arrangement is particularly useful with the 35 mm camera, which usually has a tiny flash gun sitting right on stop, and a short cord to the shutter. By using photocell "slaves" you can move around freely with your camera, unhampered by trailing wires, and still be sure that all lamps will fire when you trip the camera button.

Of course the same applies if you are using one of the midget strobe lights designed for 35 mm cameras; they will also operate "slave" units of either type. It is perfectly possible to make a picture using a "strobe" light as a main light source, and flashlamps in the extensions. It is only necessary, in this case, to be sure the shutter is set to "X" synchronization and a relatively slow speed. The reason here is that the "strobe" fires at the instant the shutter is fully open, with the flashlamps taking about $1/50$ of a second to reach their peak. Thus we have to keep the shutter open for about $1/25$ of a second to catch both the strobe and the flashlamps.

This technique is excellent for black-and-white. In color, there is a problem since "strobe" is of approximate daylight quality, while flashlamps emit light at about 3800 K. The easiest way to balance this matter for indoor flash is to use daylight-type film without a filter, and *blue* flashlamps in the extensions. (Caution: if you are shooting Kodacolor, the finisher will balance for tungsten and the pictures will be too blue.) Or, alternatively, you can use *clear* flashlamps in the extension, and cover the strobe with a piece of Wratten No. 85 filter gelatin. This is really

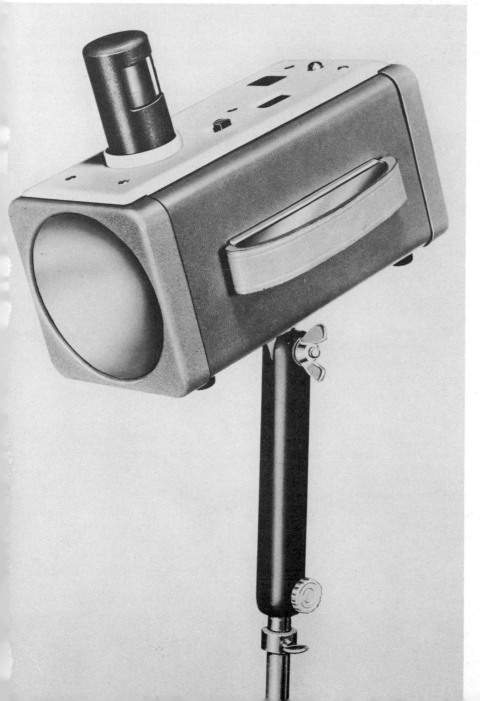

The Hi-Pro Sun-Lite is shown with a phototube for triggering the flash in this slave unit.

practical only with the very small units used on 35 mm cameras, but it does permit the use of tungsten-type films, or Kodacolor films with commercial processing.

LIGHT PLACEMENT

The most important phase of multiple-flash photography is the arrangement of the auxiliary flash-lamps. Not only does the placement of tandem lights determine the quality, balance, and effect of multi-flash, but it also governs the amount of exposure required for each set-up.

Essentials of proper light placement may be learned by first using photofloods, and, when the correct effect is obtained, substituting flashbulbs of corresponding light intensity. "Pilot lighting," as this flash-for-flood substitution method is called, can be accomplished

The two-light flash for this school year-book picture gives good detail and modeling. Note that the flash was kept to the side to avoid overlighting the foreground. (Photo: Irving Lloyd)

simply and easily. After the photographer has arranged the photofloods and noted the effect and balance contribution of each, all connections are transferred from the house current to the synchronizer. The photoflood bulbs are then removed and the photoflash substituted.

From this method of substituting flashbulbs for photofloods a number of general multiple-flash rules can be learned:

1. Usually any lighting possible with photofloods is feasible with flash.

2. Either the flashbulb on the camera or any one of the auxiliary flashes may be employed as the main or key light. If the tandem light is the principal source of illumination, a flashbulb is usually placed at the camera to provide a balance of light to fill in and cut shadows, making them "transparent."

3. General auxiliary flashlights

should be placed only where light might be expected to originate. For natural effects, tandem flash reflectors should be placed where windows, house lamps, and ceiling lights, are located.

4. The final "must" of multi-flash is that in ordinary use all flash-bulbs should normally be above the level of the lens. If bulbs are placed below the lens, an unnatural, unflattering result is certain.

As progress is made in the use of multiple flash, the substitution method of flash-for-flood can be eliminated and experience will tell the photographer where to place the flashbulbs and what size to use for the effect he wants. The photographer can be aided in arranging flashbulbs without the use of photofloods by sighting from behind each reflector and making a mental note of where each will illuminate the subject.

Extreme care must be taken to avoid shadows where they are not

desired in the final print. This is the function of the fill-in bulb. On the other hand, the fill-in flash should not be so intense as to eradicate the highlight details. This can be controlled by varying the distance of the fill-in bulb from the subject, or by changing the size of the bulb. For example, a large photoflash may be used in the auxiliary and a small flashbulb in the synchronizer reflector.

EXPOSURE IN MULTIFLASH

Most people know that to calculate exposure for a flashbulb you look up the guide number for the film and shutter speed you are using, divide it by the distance from the lamp to subject, and get the f-stop. Thus, if your film requires a guide number of 110 when used at $1/100$ of a second, and your subject is 10 feet from the lamp, the exposure setting is $110 \div 10 = 11$. So at $1/100$ of a second, you use $f/11$.

What frightens most amateurs away from multiflash is the calculation of exposure when more than one bulb is used. Starting with the simplest case, suppose we put two bulbs on the camera. Obviously we will now have double the light. To allow for the increase we will have to stop our lens down one stop, permitting one half the amount of light to reach the film.

Note that this is not the same as doubling the guide number: If we had decided upon $f/11$ for one bulb, then we'd use the next smaller stop for two bulbs, and that would be $f/16$. This, though, is equivalent to raising the guide number from 110 to 160. And if we look into the arithmetic here, we find that this is what we get if we multiply the guide number by 1.4, which happens to be the square root of 2.

But most people don't like doing mathematical problems when taking a picture, and the simple rule about closing down one stop is easier. From this, we can derive a whole system, which will work for any reasonable number of lamps, all based on calculating the exposure for the main frontlight and then closing the lens down a certain amount for each additional lamp. To do this for front lamps is

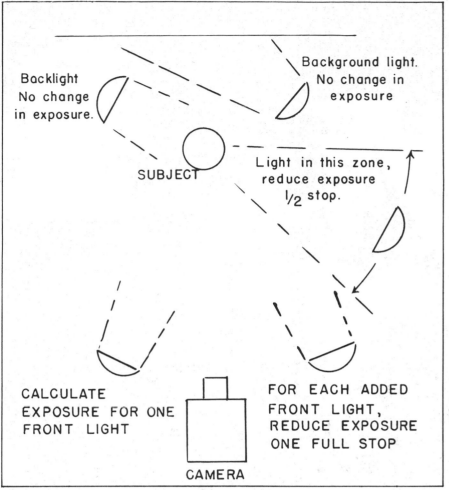

Figure 1. *This diagram is a graphic guide for calculating exposure when using various lights in different positions.*

easy enough. If we assume that all front lamps are equidistant from the subject, we have only to stop down the lens one full stop for each extra lamp. But when the extra lamps are not right in front of the subject—then what? The following three-part rule covers the situation adequately:

1. For each additional light falling full front on the subject, stop down one lens stop.
2. For each additional light falling from the side, stop down one half stop.
3. For backlight, rim light, background light, make no allowance at all. (Figure 1.)

These rules assume that all lights are about the same distance from the subject. They apply just as well to strobe lights or any other kind of light, as you can easily verify for yourself by setting up a few floods and taking meter readings.

Exposure in multiflash photography is affected by a number of other factors in addition to lens aperture, film speed, shutter setting, bulb size, and the distance from the main light to the subject. Pictures taken inside with light-colored walls and a low ceiling require considerably less exposure than photographs taken in dark-colored rooms with high ceilings, or outdoor photos at night. As much as three and four times more exposure must be given in night-clubs, auditoriums, and other places where smoke is excessive. Exposure allowance must also be made when photographing hockey and skating in interior ice rinks.

Occasionally, to produce a beautiful diffused lighting, the photographer may cover one or more flashbulbs with a handkerchief or cheesecloth. The cloth cuts down light from 30 to 60 percent, depending on its density, and exposures

Plenty of floor action was caught in this basketball scene. The use of two flashlamps directed from the sides helped to preserve detail and depth. (Photo: G. A. Smallsteed, Jr. / Columbus Dispatch)

must be increased accordingly. All these allowances, for background color, smoke, etc., should be made after the exposure has been calculated for all bulbs in use.

MULTIFLASH AT HOME

Merely by substituting flashbulbs in regular house lamps and plugging the lamp cord into a synchronizer, the novice photographer can secure a natural reproduction of the home setting. In addition, he may employ tandem flash reflectors to improve close-ups of family members, to illuminate several rooms at one time, and to control backgrounds accurately.

Emphasizing the principal subject is a general rule of composition easily applied in home photography by the use of multiple flash. Concentrate the light on the subject by means of a tandem reflector, and leave the synchronizer light source to fill in the shadows. For example, if the face of the subject is to be featured, direct the tandem reflector upon the head and shoulders. If the principal interest is centered on two or more persons in a room, the interest can be directed to the group by concentrating the tandem flash on it. The camera light source will provide sufficient detail to tell the rest of the story.

The rule, then, for multiflash photography at home is to place auxiliary flash reflectors where they will emphasize the center of interest, and where light can be expected to originate naturally. In short, place lights where they will be most beneficial and most natural.

Texture and depth, two requisites of a good picture, are made possible by the use of top- and sidelighting, placing auxiliary lights above or to one side of the subject. This arrangement produces modulation of surfaces and roundness, while backlighting is frequently employed to make the subject stand out from the background, giving a feeling of three dimensions to the print. Backlighting is obtained by directing the tandem flash toward the subject from behind. Care must be taken to prevent any backlighting from striking the camera lens.

Light, shaded, or completely black backgrounds can be obtained by varying the placement of auxiliary flashbulbs. If the background is to be well lighted, one or two lights should be placed behind the subject and directed toward the background. If a partially lighted background is desired, a strong frontlighting must be employed near the camera, and only a small bulb used for the background. However, if the background is to be dark, tandem flash reflectors are used to concentrate light only on the subject, and no on-the-camera illumination is employed. By this arrangement, light reaches only the subject, and the background, receiving no illumination, appears black.

Multiple-flash picture ideas for home use are practically inexhaustible. For the family youngster in his bath, try an extra bulb to one side and slightly above and see how "wet" the water drops appear and how many glimmering highlights are reflected from his moist features. For Dad reading the newspaper at his desk with the study lamp casting long, interesting shadows, substitute a flashbulb in the desk lamp and record those shadows and his expressions as he reads.

To simulate firelight place a tandem flash in the fireplace—a large bulb between the andirons and a small bulb in the camera reflector will do the trick. To give real depth to an interior view place the camera with a small flash in one room and shoot through the doorway into another; light the second room with a tandem flash above the doorway. To make living-room silhouettes place the tandem bulbs behind the subjects and directed toward the wallpaper. Try shooting into the house through the windows, lighting the interior by flash.

MULTIFLASH AND PORTRAITURE

In flash portraiture the photographer must first decide whether the main source of light is to be the bulb on the camera or one of the auxiliary flashes. Excellent results are possible with the camera

Lighting this storage room scene called for good placement of three No. 5 flashlamps —single flash on foreground without reflector, and two flashlamps directed on background. Note that the ceiling light behind the foreground figure gives a silhouette effect. (Photo: Interstate Photographers)

bulb as the key light and one of the auxiliary lamps as a side-, back-, or toplight.

Another interesting variation, giving life and interest to the portrait, employs one auxiliary lamp as the main or key light and the camera bulb to fill in the shadows and provide balance. When the auxiliary lamp is placed almost anywhere above and in front of the subject, character-revealing detail will result. However, in the more formal science of portraiture, several definite light positions have been found to be most advantageous and pleasing.

Practically all of the regulation lighting arrangements—the 45-degree, the Rembrandt, profile lighting, "glamour" lighting—can be produced with multiflash equipment without establishing electrical connection with the house current. As portraiture is a highly specialized field of photography, only the more general types can be discussed in an article of this nature.

Forty-five degree lighting. Probably the most easily duplicated, the 45-degree light is produced by simply holding the tandem flash above to the right or left and slightly in front of the subject. If properly placed, the auxiliary flash will cast a shadow at about 45 degrees with the plane of the nose. The on-the-camera reflector in this type of lighting provides the necessary balance.

Half-length semiprofile. The age-old Rembrandt illumination is one of the simplest to use with multiflash. The main or stronger light source is placed on the extreme right or left of the camera, and the subject turned partially toward the key source. The synchronizer bulb should be held about two feet above the camera.

SPECIAL PORTRAIT LIGHTING

An interesting variation in flash portraiture may be obtained by using Hollywood's famed style of backlighting. A deep reflector is placed behind and above the sub-

The Starliter 400 electronic-flash outfit includes two modeling units (one with barndoors), a variable beam spot on boom arm, and a background flood.

Thomas strobemeter, used to take direct exposure readings of subjects illuminated by electronic flash.

ject and directed toward the back of the head, glamorously highlighting the hair and setting the subject off from the background. The backlight can be used in conjunction with practically any type of front- or sidelighting. However, care must be taken to prevent any light from striking the camera lens directly.

In many instances, it is not desirable to use a light at the camera because broad faces are made still wider by such flat lighting. In this case, tandem flashbulbs may be placed both to the right and the left of the camera, and balance achieved by locating one of the bulbs slightly nearer the subject. Both lamps should be well above the level of the lens and the subject's head.

Frequently advantageous in drama photography, photojournalism, and salon work is the highly dramatic and eerie atmosphere created by beneath-the-lens illumination. Tandem flash reflectors directed upward toward the subject cast long, dark shadows which are tremendously effective in dramatic photography.

Background control in portraiture can be accomplished by direct-

ing flashbulbs toward the background, as in home flash photography. A pleasant and interest-centering effect in flash portraiture may be obtained by placing a flashbulb, without the reflector, between the subject and a plain black surface. A gradual modulation of white at the center to gray at the corners is achieved by this multiflash treatment.

MULTIFLASHING GROUPS

In photographing groups with single-flash technique, those nearer the camera are bound to get more exposure than those in the rear. Also a larger aperture must be used to accommodate the reduced light on those farthest from the camera. This results in "burning up" the foreground and in less depth of field.

Single-flash lighting especially handicaps the photographer who is taking a group which extends in a narrow line from the front of the lens almost to infinity, such as at a long table. Here it is virtually impossible, even with the latitude

Here one light gives the effect of multiflash because of the small space and high reflection from the bathroom walls. Good modeling is kept in the figures without overlighting the foreground. (Photo: Edward Lettau)

of modern films and with considerable dodging, to obtain detail and sharpness in both foreground and background.

Multiple-flash lighting can be utilized to solve all these group lighting problems and to add beauty and human interest to a prosaic assembly of persons. Placing auxiliary flash reflectors at intervals above or to the side of groups permits a much smaller aperture, because the foreground and the background are evenly illuminated. The subjects immediately in front of the lens require no less exposure than those farthest away.

For even illumination of a small group of persons, numbering up to 25 or 30, only two or three bulbs are required. For broad lighting, the tandem flashes may be placed about 15 feet to the right and to the left of the camera. These auxiliary lamps, in combination with the at-the-camera bulb, will provide ample illumination for a wide spread of persons and are particularly useful in outdoor night photography.

The knotty problem of photographing a long table extending away from the camera can best be solved by placing auxiliary flashbulbs every 20 feet, directed away from the camera down the group. These should be located as high above the group as possible. With this method the camera aperture can be extremely small and a great depth of field obtained.

There is nothing difficult about calculating the exposure for a picture made this away. Simply assume that each lamp is lighting only its own part of the scene, and ignore any light that spills over from one lamp into the field of the next. Simply space out your lamps (Figure 2) in such a way that each is as far from its part of the scene as the main lamp on the camera is from the front of the subject. Now, calculate your exposure for the one lamp on the camera, and that is all. Make no allowances for the other lamps.

PHOTOJOURNALISM AND MULTIPLE FLASH

Historians of journalistic illustration have noted a definite and growing demand for top quality in news pictures. Formerly, if a press photographer secured a fairly sharp picture, he was considered a good photographer. Today, however, with the advent of perfected flashbulbs, fast films, and fine-grain developers, editors have raised their standards and are demanding sharp pictures combining action, quality lighting, and perfect darkroom treatment. In reply to this demand, multiple-flash photography is being used by more press photographers every day. It has proved one of the most valuable aids to good reproduction in recent years.

Portraiture is one of the most frequent assignments given to news photographers and photojournalists. For crisp reproductions, the features of the face must be in sharp contrast. To best accomplish this hold the auxiliary flash in the left hand and release the synchron-izer with the right. By combining the single hand-held tandem flash with the bulb in the synchronizer, the majority of regular portrait lightings can be duplicated with a minimum of time and effort.

The most valuable use of multi-synchronization for the press photographer is the elimination of retouching and the control of backgrounds. The main difficulty in all newspaper arts is to make subjects stand out from their surroundings, whether in group shots or portraits. This is particularly noticeable in winter when men wear dark suits and are photographed against black backgrounds.

The easiest way to make a subject stand out is by placing an auxiliary lamp behind him, thus highlighting the edges of his figure. This gives a more natural effect than retouching with white paint, and also eliminates the dark outline shadow formerly on the background.

The background may be eliminated altogether, by overexposing it to the point where it burns out. To do this, we use a relatively small lamp—a No. 5 or Press-25 on the camera, and a rather large one in a reflector placed between the subject and the background and aimed so all its light falls on the background. Depending on the color of the background, this auxiliary lamp may be a Sylvania No. 2, a GE No. 22, or only a medium-size lamp like the Sylvania Press-40 or GE No. 11.

Frequently the natural lighting of a scene is a vital part of the story, and only by duplicating it exactly can the true feeling of the subject be given in news pictures. Illustrations of this are numerous—industry, the home, about campfires, theatrical productions, and hundreds of others. The majority of these natural, storytelling light setups are easily and quickly duplicated. In interiors, it is usually a matter of substituting photoflash bulbs for regular AC bulbs and connecting the lamps with the synchronizing unit. In industry, tandem flash often can be employed to reproduce the effect of blast furnaces, molten metal, etc.

MULTIFLASH IN COMMERCIAL USE

The small commercial photographer is beginning to awaken to the possibilities of multiple-flash photography in his field. Previous discussion has shown how multiple flash can be employed to produce more natural portraits, better group recording, and highly lucrative dramatic studies. With multiple-flash photography, the commercial illus-

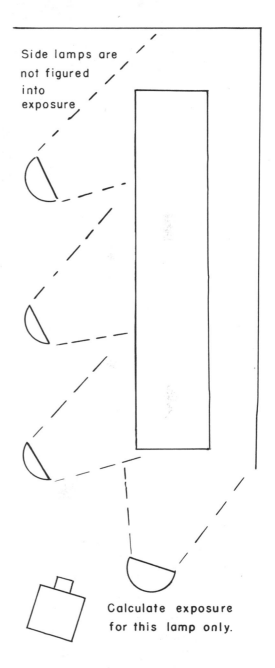

Side lamps are not figured into exposure

Calculate exposure for this lamp only.

Figure 2. *Lighting a deep space may call for using booster illumination along the side. Calculate the exposure from the frontlight only, as shown in the diagram.*

trator has been able to give balanced lighting to the largest of groups, and has advanced his income considerably by making wedding, anniversary, and industrial photographs much more easily and quickly.

One trick of combined flash is taking pictures of large interiors by stopping the lens way down and walking about the interior flashing bulbs about every 20 feet from the camera. The result, if the light has been evenly spread, is a well-lighted interior photo.

Multiple-flash lighting preserves the nice details as well as the humor in this domestic scene. (Photo: Bob Taylor)

MULTIFLASH WITH COLOR FILMS

Naturally, everything we have discussed so far applies as well to color as to black-and-white photography. But we have not, perhaps, emphasized sufficiently the fact that multiflash is even more valuable in color than in black-and-white. The reason is simple—color film has a limited contrast range, and if only a single flash is used, either a frontlight is essential, or else we must cope with "empty" black shadows. But, with multiflash, we can easily set up a balanced light that will produce even, smooth lighting over the entire scene, without flatness.

Furthermore, the trick we mentioned previously, lighting a long, deep banquet hall with a number of equally spaced units, is an even more valuable device for lighting large areas in color pictures. Color films are "hungry" for light. Even the new faster films do not approach the speed of ultrasensitive black-and-white emulsions. So, for a large factory interior in color, or perhaps only to light up your living room for a color record shot, several well-placed lamps will make a better picture than anything you can do with one big lamp on the camera.

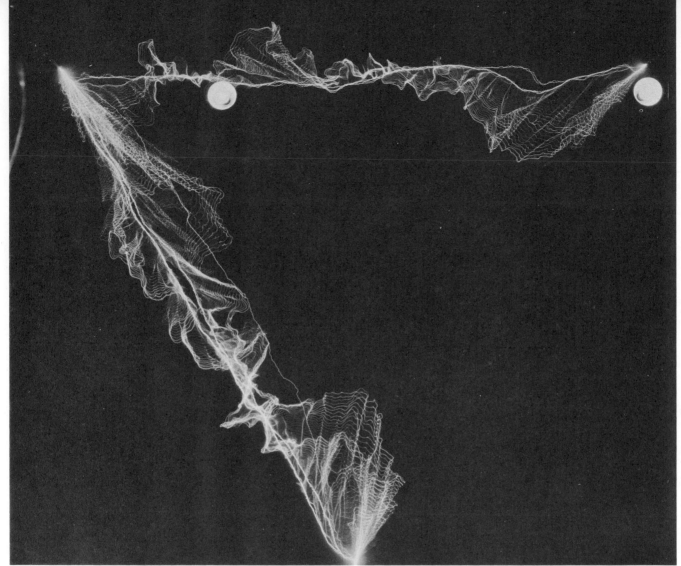

Three-phase, 60-cycle power arc of one million volts. The third phase had not struck yet. Exposure was a half second at f/22. Picture was taken with the camera lying on the laboratory floor, lens pointing upward with the shutter remotely operated. The two large white circles are ceiling lamps.

LIGHTNING PHOTOGRAPHY

J. H. HAGENGUTH

High Voltage Engineering Laboratory, General Electric Co., Pittsfield, Mass.

[The photography of lightning has long been fascinating to the amateur and important to the electrical engineer. In this article its more scientific aspects are explained by two experts who have helped, with the use of the camera, to answer many questions about lightning and the mechanism of the lightning stroke.]

All illustrations from General Electric unless otherwise noted.

TO THOSE WHO ARE NOT AFRAID of lightning, the sight of lightning strokes between cloud and ground and within the clouds themselves is not only a source of awe but also a pleasure. There are, however, relatively few photographs of lightning, despite the fact that any camera, including simple models, can be used to photograph a lightning stroke. The illumination provided by the stroke itself is so great that even using the smallest stop on the camera, the stroke will be considerably overexposed if it occurs within a few miles of the camera.

FINDING LIGHTNING STROKES

Lightning strokes are a random phenomenon; it is usually not possible to predict where and when they will occur. For that reason, the camera shutter should be set on "time" and should remain open for considerable periods of time. The photograph has to be taken at night at a location where the illumination from street lights, houses, and the reflection of city lights from the clouds is at a minimum, otherwise the film will have to be changed frequently.

By observing a number of storms, it will be noticed that certain sections of the cloud mass seem especially productive of strokes. These stroke centers travel along with the clouds and, by watching the approach of these centers toward the camera, it is frequently possible to be prepared for some good strokes. It is usually not advisable to take photographs of strokes which are farther than ten miles from the camera, although some good cloud effects may be obtained from a violent stroke center at greater distances.

After a stroke is photographed, its distance from the camera can be roughly measured by noting the number of seconds elapsing between

STILL CAMERA
PHOTOGRAPH
OF STROKE

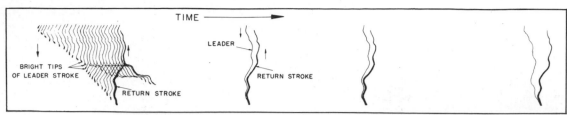

CLOUD TO EARTH

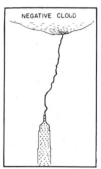

STILL CAMERA
PHOTOGRAPH
OF STROKE

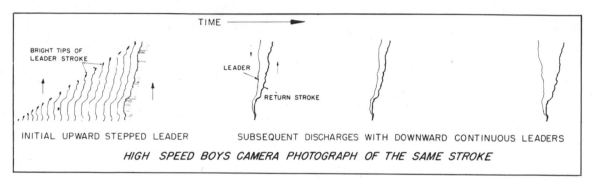

CLOUD TO TALL CONDUCTING STRUCTURE

Figure 1. *Graphical representation of the mechanism of a lightning stroke. The cloud is negative, while the ground or building is positive.*

the time a stroke is seen and the time thunder is heard. Light travels at 186,000 miles per second and the lightning illumination is perceived almost instantly by the eye. Sound waves travel more slowly, at approximately 1000 feet per second. Therefore a count of ten seconds indicates a distance of 10,000 feet, or roughly two miles.

The best place to take photographs is a location which has a free view in all directions. Good photographs probably can be obtained from your home. An automobile offers the chance of finding a vantage point from which photographs can be taken, and at the same time the steel body of the car will protect the photographer from lightning and rain. The danger inherent in exposure to lightning strokes should always be kept in mind.

The average person, looking at a lightning stroke, sees a bright streak connecting cloud and ground by a twisted and tortuous path, followed by a tremendous noise which we call thunder. At times the lightning stroke will flicker. The color of different strokes will vary from a a bright, almost white light to a reddish glow. The observer will note that there are differences during the length of time the illumination persists. The stroke forms at a cloud and advances in short steps— 30 to 200 feet per step—with a bright tip at its end, until it reaches the ground (Figure 1). The illumination given off during this period is extremely small and usually only the bright tips can be seen on the negative. At the instant the stroke contacts the ground, a bright illumination is observed spreading rapidly upward from earth to cloud. This process may be repeated several times.

Only during succeeding discharges does the weakly illuminated leader traverse from cloud to ground nonstop. (There is strong evidence that small currents flow continually between the separate peaks.) If these discharges are rather large, the color of the stroke will assume a reddish glow, and fires may be ignited in trees or unprotected houses. The highly illuminated portions of the stroke produce the explosive effects of thunder.

The bottom part of Figure 1 shows the mechanism of a lightning stroke to very tall structures, such as the Empire State Building in New York City. In most cases the initial discharge starts from the building toward the cloud, continuing for fractions of a second with low current. Later discharges initiated from the cloud follow the same pattern as the succeeding discharges of cloud-initiated strokes. At the same time, while the visible phenomena described occur between cloud and ground, similar progressive discharges occur in the clouds, resulting in background illumination often seen in photos.

All these discharges occur within about a second and a half. Most strokes have a duration of less than a second. The time it takes for the brightly illuminated portion of a stroke to progress from ground to cloud is only a few millionths of a second. It is clear that special equipment is required to photograph different discharges and to obtain time measurements.

LIGHTNING CAMERA

The camera used to photograph the short-time separations of the stroke is shown in Figures 2 and 3. The principle of its operation is shown in Figure 4. A lightning stroke *A-B* is photographed by means of two lenses simultaneously on a rotating film on which are traced the lines *a-c* and *a'-c'* as the illumination progresses from *A* to *B*. With the film velocity known, the separation between lines *a-c* and *a'-c'* gives the measure of time. In the camera

shown, the film rotates at 3600 revolutions per minute. This allows measurement of time intervals as short as 20 millionths of a second. By enlarging the original, considerably shorter times can be measured.

The high speed of this camera does not permit ready identification of the sequence of the strokes. For this purpose, a slower speed camera is used (Figure 5). Here the film is stationary. The center lens gives a still photograph of the stroke, while the outer lens revolves at 120 revolutions per second (7200 per minute).

The type of photograph obtained with this camera is shown in Figure 6. This corresponds to the bottom drawing of Figure 1, where the stroke initiated at the building, moving toward the cloud, continues with rather low current values and therefore low-intensity illumination, as seen at the bottom of Figure 6. This is followed by several current peaks of greater current amplitude

which are initiated from the cloud.

The high-speed photograph of this same stroke is shown in Figure 7. At the top are shown the initial stepleaders, indicated by the bright tips. The lower photographs show the subsequent leaders, followed by the upward-moving return stroke with much heavier illumination.

The light given off during the different intervals of a lightning stroke varies from approximately one ampere in the continuing discharges between illumination peaks to probably 200,000 amperes for the most severe upward-moving illumination of the return stroke. This wide variation of illumination results in many problems in properly photographing the single portions

Figure 2. *The General Electric High-Speed Boys Camera, designed by C.V. Boys. The camera has an elevating mechanism and multiple exposure notching device; film width of six inches; drum diameter, eight inches; drum speed of 3600 to 7200 rpm; lens, 35 mm, f/2.3.*

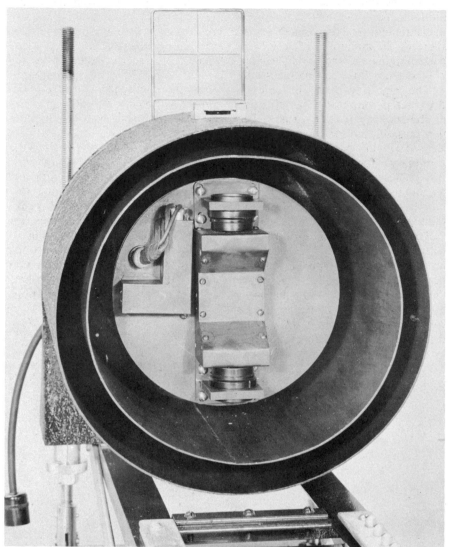

of the components of a lightning stroke (Figure 8). Or it is possible to make a simple oscillating table which permits motion of the camera over several degrees of the horizon, allowing separation of the several illumination peaks.

When the rate of motion is known, the time interval can be computed. Similar effects can be obtained by simply moving the camera back and forth by hand. When operating with an oscillating camera, however, the photographer should be careful not to mistake the moving image of a street light for a peculiar and new type of lightning stroke.

Very high resolution is required to secure definite separation of multiple strokes, and this leads to an examination of a fundamental principle of lenses. According to Rayleigh's criterion, the resolving power of a lens, if it has no aberrations at all, cannot exceed 2000 divided by the *f-stop*. That is, a perfect lens at $f/8$ will resolve 250 lines per mm. But this statement contains nothing about the focal length of the lens, only the *f*-stop. This means that all lenses (if equally well corrected) will resolve 250 lines per mm at $f/8$, and this resolution is measured at the film, not at

Above: Figure 3. *Lens assembly of the Boys camera, showing prism mount and shielded neon tube for recording timing pulse.*

Right: Figure 4. *Diagrammatic sketch of the Boys camera, showing the principle of resolving the progression of illumination in lightning strokes.*

of a discharge. Photographs of the type shown in Figures 6 and 7, coupled with other information obtained with oscillographs on the ground end of the strokes, permit the extension of our knowledge of the lightning stroke and result in improvements of the methods of lightning protection.

EQUIPMENT

The majority of photos of lightning probably will be taken with the camera in a fixed position, which will give a composite photo of all

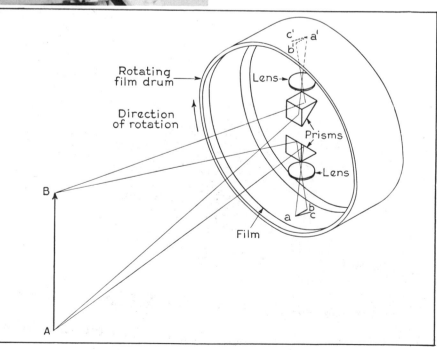

the subject.

But the longer the focus of a lens, the larger the image produced on the film. Therefore the $^1/_{250}$ mm detail on the film will represent a smaller part of the subject with a long lens than with a short one. This leads to the general rule that for photography of distant objects, there is no adequate substitute for focal length—greater detail will be rendered by a long-focus lens than by a shorter one.

However, long lenses are seldom as sharp as normal lenses for 35 mm cameras. Only testing will show if the larger image is actually sharper. Often, for the best rendition of distant lightning, a large view camera and a lens of 10- to 12-inch focus is preferable to a 35 mm camera whose lens is of only 2-inch focus. A long lens can be used on the 35 mm camera, but its effect will be to restrict the field, and only a small area of horizon will be covered in a single shot. Very often the result will be that a given lightning stroke will occur just outside the picture area, but with the 12-inch lens on an 8×10 camera, there is much more film area and larger subject field.

As for film, since speed is not essential, you will do best with a fine-grained, high-resolution film, though the very thin emulsion films are lacking in latitude and may lose detail in the image if only slightly overexposed. Probably the best film for the purpose would be a pan film such as Ansco Versapan or Kodak Panatomic-X. A compensating developer, such as Kodak D-23, will probably produce the best negatives.

Color films can be used, but unless the exposure is very accurate, the lightning flash will burn out to white. However, a blue sky background may be obtained, and if the photo is being made in the city, neon lights, auto tail lamps, and other light sources will give some color to the picture which will add to its pictorial interest, if not to its scientific value. If an oscillating camera mount is used, and the lightning flash is broken up into its components, the different colors may be well rendered on the film.

Figure 5. *General Electric Boys camera auxiliary, Model 11, 129 rpm. Front view, showing elevation mechanism, stationary center lens, and rotating lens. Film is stationary. Lens is a Kodak Anastigmat f/4.5, 78.95mm, equivalent focus.*

ELECTRICAL ARCS

When a small current at very high voltage leaps a gap in an electric circuit, it is known as a spark. It is possible to use a lower voltage and heavier current, and by touching the poles together and separating them, a continuous discharge, known as an arc, takes place between the two electrodes. The current-carrying medium in this case is either ionized air or a vaporized material from the electrodes themselves.

Lightning has the characteristics of both types of arcs. The initial discharge is a spark in air; the energy released ionizes the air, forming a conducting path through which the subsequent arc discharge flows. The discharge ends when the current stored in the atmosphere has been exhausted (usually in a frac-

Figure 6. *Multiple lightning stroke to the Empire State Building, taken with the camera shown in Figure 5. Center lens (f/15) shows composite picture of the complete stroke; rotating lens (f/8) shows the resolution of the stroke into its several components on fast pan film. Arrow at lower left indicates where oscillograph started to record.*

tion of a second).

In the laboratory and for industrial uses arcs can be produced which burn continuously as long as current is supplied. Such arcs are used as illuminants in motion-picture projectors and as a heat source in high-temperature furnaces. On the other hand, there are uncontrolled and unwanted arcs, such as those which occur when an electric switch is opened; these may result in severe damage to equipment.

These arcs are much too bright and usually last too short a time to allow their study by mere observation. Still pictures, stereo pictures, or motion pictures taken of such arcs and later observed and properly interpreted, are invaluable to the engineer.

ARC COLOR

Since these arcs are extremely intense and since their color is almost entirely toward the blue and ultraviolet end of the spectrum, photographic records can be made very easily without the aid of special lenses or special films. In fact there is always so much light accompanying such arcs that small diaphragm openings have to be used to prevent overexposure. This, in turn, aids in obtaining fine definition.

Where there is a flame there is

also heat. When the arc jumps through air, it will cause intense heating of the air around it, which will cause the arc to be rapidly carried up and fanned out. It would therefore appear necessary to use a quick exposure for a clear-cut record of an arc.

But the basic nature of an alternating-current arc introduces into this exposure question an interesting complication. What appears to the eye as a continuous sheet of flame is really a rapid succession of individual tongues of flame with total absence of fire in between. On a

standard 60-cycle power system, 120 flashes will dart along the arcing path every second. It is like

Figure 7. *High-Speed Boys photographs of the same stroke as in Figure 6, showing the initial leader progressing upward from the building and the subsequent downward leaders and return strokes.*

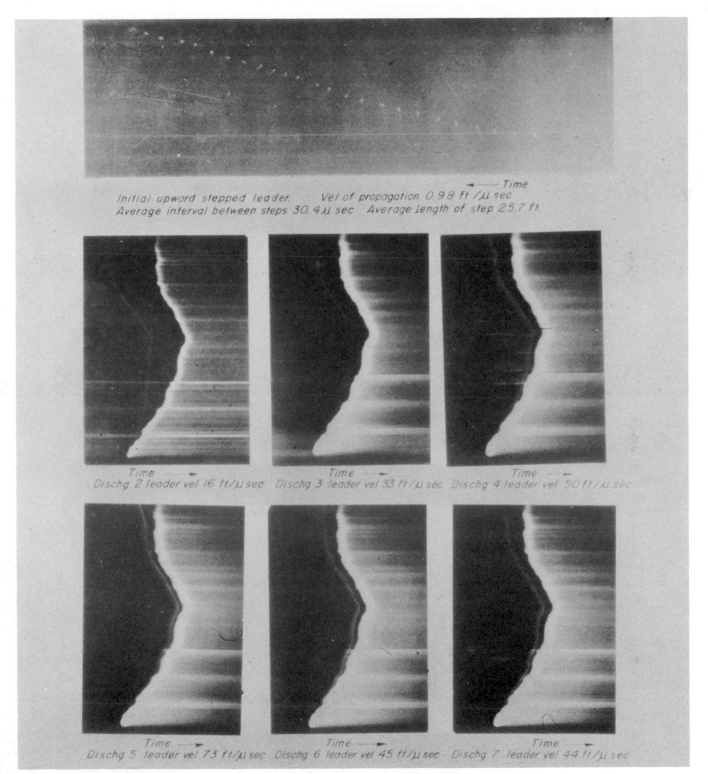

Initial upward stepped leader.   Vel of propagation 0.98 ft /μ sec
Average interval between steps 30.4 μ sec   Average length of step 25.7 ft.

Time →
Dischg 2 leader vel 16 ft/μ sec   Dischg 3 leader vel 33 ft/μ sec   Dischg 4 leader vel 50 ft/μ sec

Time →
Dischg 5 leader vel 73 ft/μ sec   Dischg 6 leader vel 45 ft/μ sec   Dischg 7 leader vel 44 ft/μ sec

The graphic pattern of an arc flame in relation to current. In general, an exposure of less than 1/60 of a second is apt to get only part of the flash, as shown, while longer exposures will record the entire flash.

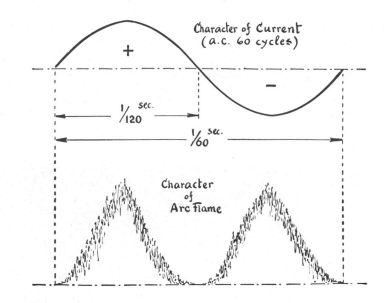

movie projection, where there is darkness of the screen between individual frames and where the eyes coast over these blind spots due to the persistence of vision.

An exposure of $1/120$ of a second may therefore show on the negative only one individual leap of the arc. I say "may" because only with perfect synchronization of the shutter with the periodically alternating current could you get one full leap. With synchronization a half beat off, you would get the declining end of one and the rising start of the next flash. With an exposure of $1/25$ of a second you would get about four flashes.

Upon development you may find not a "washed-out" effect like a waterfall picture, but four parallel streaks of the flash, like a lace pattern. This peculiar effect is due to the rising arc. Since no two flashes follow exactly the same path, each of them produces its own separate path on a spot of film not previously exposed. Since the direction of the rise is not in all places along the arcing path in a plane at right angles to the axis of the lens, the lace pattern will not be fully pronounced throughout the picture.

Depending upon the purpose of the study, arc pictures may have to be taken at shutter speeds of $1/50$ of a second to one second. Using high-speed films, openings of $f/8$ to $f/11$ will result in usable negatives.

Filters are of no value, except to avoid overexposure where the lens cannot be stopped down far enough for the speed of the film. An interesting experiment is to use a deep-red filter and infrared film; the resulting picture shows only the hot part of the discharge, the arc, and eliminates the colder parts which occur before ionization and the beginning of the main arc.

Figure 8. *Lightning near Radio City in New York.* (Photo: Kurt Severin)

SHADOWS

MICHAEL L. EDELSON

The problem confronting the photographer in this composition was to unite the bottom half of the photo with its wet and wrinkled newspapers to the top of the picture with the people's legs and their shadows. It is the shadow areas and darkened lines of the middle ground that bring the two halves of the picture together. Were there no shadows in the central area, the picture would split in half, despite the cobblestones. To prove this, the viewer need only place a piece of paper over the shadow areas in the middle ground to see the picture divide into two separate parts. The photographer, however, avoided this common pitfall, creating a composition that stands up as a whole.

LIVESTOCK PHOTOGRAPHY

J.C. ALLEN

J.C. Allen & Son, Rural Life Photo Service, West Lafayette, Indiana

[An important adjunct to farm photography is the picturing of livestock. The informal rural pictorial and the formal portrait are both covered here—with details given for the handling of sheep, hogs, dairy and beef cattle, and horses.]

•*Also see: Animal Photography; Farm Photography; Horse Photography.*

I LONG AGO DISCOVERED THAT ONE of the prime requisites of a livestock photography is patience and more patience—patience with the animals, patience with the animal handlers and owners, and patience with would-be helpers.

The subject of livestock photography covers the photography of common domestic farm animals including horses, cattle, hogs, sheep, and poultry. There are two general classifications into which this subject may be divided: 1) formal posed pictures of individual animals or small groups of animals, showing them at their best; and 2) informal pictures of the animals under natural conditions, running loose in the barnlot, down the lane, along the old rail fence, out in the pasture, or along the creek. The informal poses are more interesting and lend themselves to pictorial photography with much greater possibilities for artistic effects. They therefore have the

Left: *Sheep cross a creek along one of their regular routes from pasture to barn. Notice that the photographer is high enough to look down on most of the group and that the sun, coming from the side, gives good modeling.* (Photo: J. C. Allen & Son)

Right: *Feed is used to draw the animal's attention. As it moves, it will probably take a correct position with its feet. Notice that the legs are directly under the animal, except the rear foot near the camera, which is slightly back. This seems to give added depth to the ham, a desirable feature. The head being down keeps the back up and makes it appear strong. For white animals like this, select a dark background.* (Photo: J. C. Allen & Son)

greatest appeal to one who takes pictures primarily for pleasure.

Spring is my favorite season for farm pictures, for it is then that new life is in abundance. Little pigs and lambs, young colts and calves are frisking about the pastures, and baby chicks fill every chick brooder house. Perseverence and close attention to the small details of these animals are very essential in all kinds of livestock photography. One should have some knowledge of the habits of farm animals and what they may do under certain circumstances.

EQUIPMENT

Before making informal pictures, the photographer should become familiar with the operation of the camera, so that he can take advantage of good poses quickly, after working and waiting for the animals to arrange themselves in the desired setting. He must always be ready to take the picture, because a good pose is seldom held more than a few seconds.

A 2¼ × 2¼ reflex is one of the best cameras for taking this kind of picture; it also has sufficient speed to stop action. Personally I do not favor the 35 mm camera except for making color transparencies for projection.

The first livestock picture I can remember taking was with a 4×5 camera and rapid rectilinear lens. It was a rather classy outfit for those early days. Later I secured a 5×7 Press Graflex fitted with an 8×10 f/4.5 lens having a focal length of about 12 inches. In my opinion no better outfit has ever been made for most kinds of farm and livestock pictures—with the exception that for close-up front or rear views there would be too much distortion. The focal length of the 12-inch lens is still not great enough for close-up shots of individual animals from the front or rear, when used on a 5×7 camera. Professional livestock photographers use about a 23-inch lens and a tripod view camera for close-up shots.

I bought three of these Press Graflex cameras many years ago and still prefer to use them for most livestock pictures. They are out of production now and it is almost impossible to buy one second-hand. The usual lens furnished with this camera has a focal length of 8½ inches, which is too short

when used on a 5×7 camera for many kinds of farm pictures. It does not permit one to get close enough to livestock in pasture, and for close-up formal poses gives too much distortion. The 12-inch lens gives a much larger image at the same distance and helps to eliminate distortion. The only drawback is that the depth of field is not as great as with the shorter-focus lens.

APPROACH TO ANIMALS

When photographing farm animals I prefer to do my work with the assistance of my son and with some help from the farmer or owner of the livestock—if we can make him understand the goal toward which we are working. The animals should always be handled slowly and with a minimum of excitement. If you attempt to hurry them, they may become scared and head off to the other side of the pasture.

Sheep are attractive farm subjects and are easily handled if one is careful. Being light in color, they fit nicely into attractive backgrounds. One of the difficulties in photographing sheep is gaining sufficient height so that the entire group may be seen. Select a high knoll from which to take the picture; on level ground you may find it necessary to stand on top of a car or use a stepladder.

For the best lighting for this type of picture the sun should be coming from an angle of from 45 to 90 degrees. Sheep, being light in color, need sidelight to make shadows, giving roundness to the forms of the animals and setting them off one from another. More experienced camera fans, by using a sunshade and larger opening of the diaphragm, may get lovely effects from backlighting—taking the picture almost directly into the sun being careful that the sun does not shine directly into the lens. With a reflex

A light background has set off the dark body of the turkey, and the feet are separated for a realistic appearance in the print. (Photo: J. C. Allen & Son)

The photographer had to move quietly to take this gentle shot of a horse at the pond. Taken with a Rollieflex camera on Ilford film.

camera, you can see this "flare" on the groundglass and correct it by shading the lens before making the exposure.

Morning or evening light with the sun to one side is preferable to noonday light with the sun directly overhead. The latter makes the light too strong on the backs of the animals and the shadows too heavy underneath.

Set the camera at about $f/11$ and $f/16$, depending upon the strength of the light and the speed of the film used, and make the exposure

from $1/75$ to $1/150$ of a second. If possible use a light meter to find the exact stop for a correct exposure. Take one or two shots as the animals graze, and then get set for an additional picture. If you have not already disturbed the sheep and caused them to turn away from you, make some sharp noise and watch the heads come up. Be ready to snap the picture.

Generally the flock will turn away immediately, and the rear shot

is not attractive. At some distance the sheep are sure to turn back again toward the object of interest, and you will have another chance to follow them, if you move cautiously. Often you will find paths across the pasture that the flock usually follows on its homeward journey. Take a position along one of these paths and have your helper disturb the sheep just enough to start them for home. But don't crowd or hurry them.

Above: *A bleak winter landscape and struggling horses combine to make an unusual livestock photo. Rollieflex camera, Tri-X film at f/11, 1/250 of a second.* (Photo: Maurice Horner / Des Moines Register and Tribune)

Left: *Percheron stallion "Koncarhope," Lynnwood Farm, Carcel, Indiana. This picture was taken a little from the rear with a long-focus lens. Note that the front feet are on higher ground than the back, the head is up with ears forward, and all feet are placed so that they show.* (Photo: J. C. Allen & Son)

FORMAL POSE

Sometimes formal posed pictures are wanted by the owners of individual sheep. When taking pictures of a single show sheep, place the animal squarely on its feet, except for the rear foot next to the camera which should be slightly back; have the front end slightly higher than the rear, and be sure the back is straight.

The light should come from the side of the camera at an angle of about 45 degrees, and from the rear of the sheep rather than the front so that the shadows from the ears do not show on the neck. Be careful not to have heavy shadows on the flank. Watch the background carefully and be sure it is dark enough to contrast with the light tone of the sheep.

The angle from which to take the picture will depend somewhat upon the focal length of the lens. For taking close-up front or three-quarter views, the professional livestock photographer uses a long-focus lens in order to get the correct perspective and avoid distortion. A picture taken from the front with a short-focus lens will show the head of the sheep much larger than its true proportion to the entire body; the body will have an elongated appearance. Conversely, too long a lens causes foreshortening, with the body appearing compressed and unnaturally short.

With the sheep posed and the camera set for immediate exposure,

Planning and patience made possible this birthday photo by Harold Revoir of the Chicago Tribune.

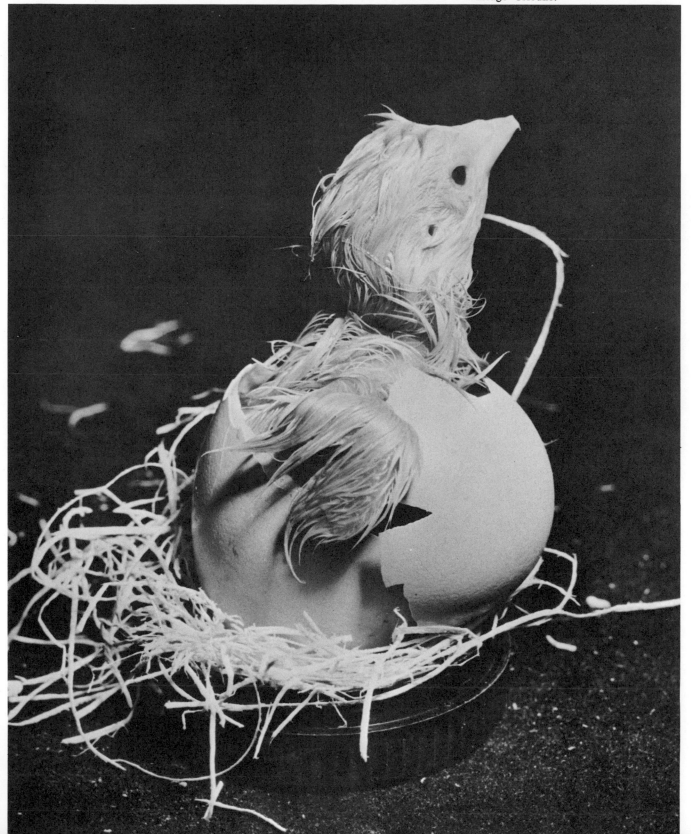

have someone make a noise or motion in front of the animal to get the ears forward, then snap the picture. If the sheep is fairly gentle, try having the shepherd turn the sheep loose just at the instant the ears go forward. If you are lucky and quick enough, you may get a perfect picture of the sheep alone before it moves out of position.

Groups of three or more sheep (show groups) are usually taken from the rear because, if taken from the front, the men holding the animals will show too prominently and be too important a part of the picture. Pose the front end of the sheep a little higher than the rear,

and have them at a slight angle to the camera so the side of the near sheep shows a little in the camera. Be sure the rear ends of the group are even and that the legs are fairly well apart, to give a blocky effect.

A slight elevation of the camera to see down on the backs of the sheep will improve the view. Check the background and lighting. Let the light come slightly from one side to give small shadows and separate the outline of one sheep from that of another. When the sheep are gentle, it is possible to hold them in line long enough for a picture by running a string or wire in front of them, providing a front view.

Probably no farm subject lends itself better to interesting farm pictures than do lambs. They are very inquisitive and, with patience, two or three of them may be photographed together looking at the camera or playing in the pasture. Lambs are easy to handle and, when posed with children, always make good subjects. Orphan lambs taking milk from a bottle have probably been pictured more than any other farm subject.

PHOTOGRAPHING HOGS

Making satisfactory photographs of hogs is quite different from photographing sheep. If you know in advance when you plan to take these pictures and can get the owner

Old Glory, a champion representative of the Highland Cattle class, poses for his photo. He was bred in Yorkshire, England.

An Arab horse shows its lines to the camera.

to hold the feed away from the hogs so they will be hungry, it will make the posing much easier, especially for the formal posed pictures. The individual brood sow or gilt is easiest to photograph because she responds more readily to feed and is usually gentle. Boars are most difficult to handle because they often will pay no attention to feed even when hungry.

When posing individual hogs, use smooth, slightly sloping ground and place the front part of the animal on the higher ground. All four feet should be seen from the camera. For a side view, the rear foot next to the camera should be back three or four inches more than the other, to give an appearance of added length and to square up the rear quarters. The front foot away from the camera should be back of the other just enough to be seen in the direct side view.

If a partial front view of the hog is desired, then the front feet should be even and the rear foot next to the camera just a little back to get a good view of all four feet and make them appear to be directly under the hog. The back of the hog should be up so that it appears strong. If the animal is a little low in the back, this will usually not show to disadvantage when the head is down feeding.

Place the feed in a narrow row two or three feet long, let the photographer take his place and be ready. As the hog moves slowly up this line of feed he is reasonably certain to get a good pose.

Distortion is not too objectionable in hog pictures. It may appear to add size, which is often desirable. The height of the camera from the ground has an important bearing upon how the finished picture will look. Styles of hogs have changed from time to time. Fifty years ago

the breeder and showman wanted his hogs to appear low-set and blocky. This effect was secured by holding the camera higher—about the height of a man. Later owners wanted their hogs to appear up-standing and large with very high arched backs. The photographer, to increase this effect, often used a medium-length lens and held the camera down on the ground to take the picture.

Today breeders prefer photos with the camera held about even with the animal. Remember that if the hog is a little off type, it can be made to appear larger and higher by holding the camera low, or it can be made to appear shorter legged and lower set by keeping the camera higher. The medium focal-length lens is suitable for hog pictures since breeders often want a slightly distorted picture that makes the hog appear larger. In all cases the tail

Close-ups of farm animals should show their personalities; ears should be forward for an alert appearance. The photographer must guard against distortion of the animal's features. (Photo: Bob Taylor)

head portrait has possibilities, especially of a Berkshire with its turned-up nose. It is usually best to have the background out of focus.

DAIRY AND BEEF CATTLE

The technique of taking informal pictures of herds or small groups of dairy or beef cattle is not much different from that of making pictures of groups or flocks of sheep. One should learn the natural habits of the cattle and be able to guess what they are apt to do under certain circumstances.

If the cattle are grazing, the first shots should be made before they have been disturbed. If the cattle are gentle and easy to handle, one may locate a picturesque setting of woods, creek, or lane and maneuver the cattle into position.

If the cattle are black or dark red, the setting should have only enough sidelight to make them stand out from one another. If they are white, the lighting can be handled much the same as for sheep—that is, a greater amount of sidelight to give roundness to the animals and separate one from the other. An unusual noise will make their heads come up and ears come forward.

Since the perfect dairy cow should have a "wedge shape" and a beef animal should be square and blocky, the problem of making individual pictures of them is entirely different. The dairy cow should be posed with the front slightly up hill; the picture should be taken slightly from the rear. If she has a good rear udder, then place the rear feet so that the one nearest the camera is slightly forward and the front feet squarely under her, head up and ears forward. If some slight distortion to show the udder and rear quarters more prominently is desirable, use a shorter lens. When making satisfactory posed photographs of individual animals, it is necessary to determine the animal's best qualities, which should be emphasized in the picture, and to hide the poor points. Before taking livestock pictures you should gain some knowledge of breed characteristics and what is judged desirable in a good show animal.

of the hog should be curled—and this is not a joke. A straight tail will most certainly ruin what might otherwise be a perfect pose. Usually driving the hog around will naturally curl the tail.

The most satisfactory background for a black hog is the sky, or a light-colored building. For a white hog, shrubs or bushes make an excellent background.

Groups of three to six hogs may be lined up in a row, with the aid of feed and patience. If they are a little wild and won't eat, a portable hurdle may be held in front of them until they are lined up against it. The hurdle is then quicly taken away, and the hogs are photographed before they move.

For informal hog pictures, sows and little pigs make the most interesting subjects. More mature hogs produce good pictures when grazing on alfalfa or clover pasture, or around the feeders. A close-up

Before taking close-up shots of individual animals, be sure they have been cleaned. The owners probably will have brushed or even washed the animal, cleaned the feet, trimmed the hair and sometimes curled it, and even placed ribbons in the mane and tail.

The photo location in relation to background and elevation of the front feet is of utmost importance in taking pictures of individual animals. It is best to decide this before the animal is brought out of the barn.

Pictures of individual beef cattle, if taken with a small camera and medium-length lens, should be made from the side. The feet should be placed much the same as for individual sheep—squarely under the animal with the rear foot nearest the camera slightly back.

Professional photographers often take beef cattle pictures from a three-quarter front view, using a fairly long lens to avoid distortion. The same effect may be had with a small camera by getting back some distance and making the image small on the film, to be enlarged later. In the finished picture the animal should appear square and blocky with a straight top line. A little sidelight should be used, but not enough to make heavy shadows in the flank or shoulder.

HORSES

When photographing draft horses, it is best to use the off-mane or left side which gives the animal a neater, cleaner appearance. The front of the horse should be elevated more than for any other class of livestock in order to make the back appear level.

Then comes the problem of

A difficult problem in lighting and focus. A slow shutter speed allowed moderately small aperture to gain depth of field. (Photo: Bob Taylor)

setting the feet in proper position, being careful that the horse does not appear stretched. A horse trained for the show ring will move his feet on command of the handler, but they may have to be moved several times to become correctly placed. The best position is with the front feet and legs squarely under the body. The leg farthest from the camera should be slightly back for a direct side view, and the rear foot nearest the camera should be slightly back.

The head should be up and the

ears forward. It is particularly important to have the ears forward in horse pictures, and it is sometimes very difficult to get draft show horses to put their ears forward. All kinds of tricks have been attempted. Probably an umbrella opened and closed at some distance comes nearest to getting perfect results.

The professional photographer with a long lens usually takes a three-quarter rear view of draft horses. For this view the front feet should be squarely under the animal with the rear foot nearest the camera slightly forward. The head should be up and turned slightly to the left so that both ears will show in the photo.

LOW KEY AND HIGH KEY

A low-key photograph is one whose tones are predominantly dark; a high-key photograph is one in which light tones predominate.

It is important to note that the key word is *predominate*—the proportion of dark to light tones is high in a low-key picture, with the exact opposite being true in a high-key picture. In either case, however, it is essential that the picture contain a full range of tones from black to white. Otherwise a key cannot be determined, and the picture will simply appear to be incorrectly exposed or printed.

This implies that the key of a photograph depends entirely on the subject matter and lighting, that it

A good action shot of gray Percheron mares stepping together. Taken with the camera low; shadows separate the horses from the sky and from each other. (Photo: J. C. Allen & Son)

cannot be produced in printing or developing. Variation in exposure may emphasize a key already determined by the subject and the lighting, but it alone cannot determine the key of the picture. A high-key photograph can be made of a white or a light-gray cat, but rarely of a black one. By the same token, a blonde model usually cannot be photographed effectively in low key, though by the proper use of lighting, props, and background, a low key may be approximated.

When working in this technique, a tonal scale point of reference should be included in the photo. In photographing a white cat against a white background, for example, the final print must be mostly white paper. Without a point of reference it will be hard to decide whether it is really a white cat and a white background, or whether both were gray and the negative was accidentally overexposed. To pin down the key of the picture, a tiny spot of black is needed somewhere to complete the scale. In one of the most effective pictures of this type, a white cat was illuminated very flatly against a white background; the fur blended into the background, with very little modeling, and the print was hardly more than white paper. But, the pupils of the cat's eyes were large, round, and black— jet black. These two intense black spots established the key of the whole picture, and definitely pinned the tone scale down so the viewer knew the cat was white and the background white.

The same principle applies to low-key photographs. Imagine a picture of an old man sitting near a table in semidarkness. So far the whole picture consists of dark grays and black. In order to indicate that this is not just an underexposed shot, a candle is placed on the table; its small flame produces a pinpoint of pure white, completing the scale, and putting the dark grays and blacks in their correct tonal relationship.

It is possible to have a high-key photograph in which the whole print is in the middle grays, such as a fog scene. If there is one small spot of black somewhere in the picture,

This high-key photo is dominated by white and light-gray tones. Note that the tonal point of reference can be taken from the pupil on the rooster's eye. Rolleiflex with Tri-X film exposed at f/8 for 1/100 of a second. (Photo: Philipp Giegel)

it is a high-key scene. Omit the black spot and substitute a white one, say a street light, and the same fog picture is now low key, though its over-all tone is still the same middle gray as before. Put in both black and white, a parked car and a street light, and it becomes a normal-key picture with the gray in the middle of the scale.

MAKING THE HIGH-KEY PHOTOGRAPH

For a high-key effect, the lighting must be full and soft. Fill lights for the shadows should be as strong as the key light, in some cases even stronger. Backgrounds will require separate lighting, or they will be

too dark. With such a limited range of tones, exposure is not critical; the black areas will be too small to require much detail, and the exposure for such a picture should be fairly short. From two to four times the normal film speed rating may be used for a high-key scene. Development should be full to maintain good separation of the few tones which are essential to the picture. The print must be carefully made

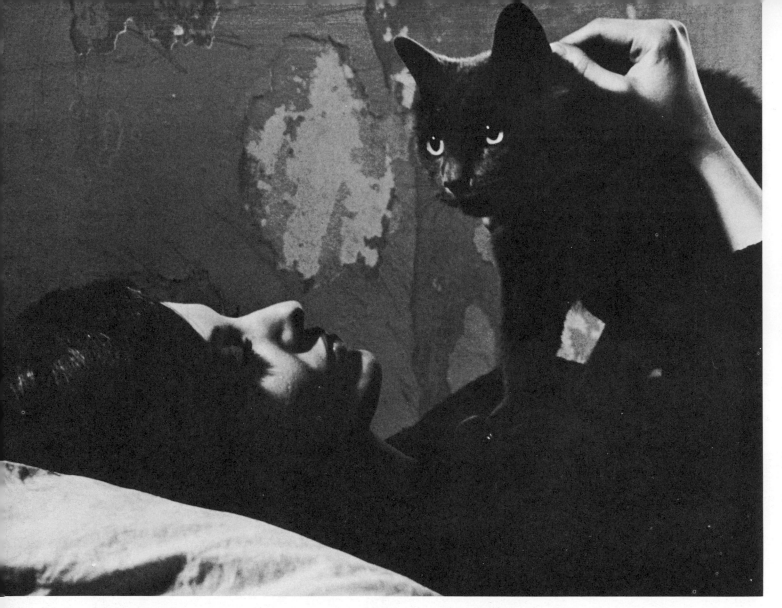

The low-key mood of this haunting photograph is established by both the unusual subject matter and the predominantly dark tones. The tonal range is pinned down by the pure white catchlights in the cat's eyes. Pictures of this type are most effective when printed on a glossy paper to obtain the deepest blacks possible. Leica M2 and 90mm Elmarit f/2.8 lens. Tri-X exposed at f/2.8 for 1/60 of a second. (Photo: Michael L. Edelson)

to assure that full detail is present in highlight areas, but without excessive grayness. At the same time the black accents must be fully and solidly black.

MAKING THE LOW-KEY PHOTOGRAPH

The low-key photograph is lighted in much the same way, except that no attempt is made to fill the shadows completely. Highlight areas, except for the necessary white accent, should not be lighted much above the background level. The lighting must be just about the same as for high key, except that the background itself should be of darker tone and the subject matter

likewise dark. Again, exposure should be on the minimum side, and development rather full. If the accent—a catchlight in the eyes, in a glossy object, a candle flame, or whatever—is burned out to pure white in the final print, no harm will be done, provided its actual area is quite small.

PRINTING HIGH- AND LOW-KEY PHOTOS

If the lighting, exposure, and development of the negative are correct, the printing of a high-key or low-key photograph presents no particular difficulty. The high-key negative will be quite dark; the low-key negative will appear quite

thin. Strangely enough, both will print with practically the same exposure. This is as it should be, since the density of the high-key negative is no different from the density of the highlight areas in an ordinary negative. The only difference is that the highlight areas are larger.

The essence of printing either high- or low-key negatives is simply to assure that the complete scale of tones is present. The black accent in a high-key picture must be fully black when the principal parts of the picture are white or light gray. In the low-key picture, the white accent must be white while the shadows are as black as the paper can make them, or as the photographer desires. Unless this condition is fulfilled, high- or low-key prints will simply look like bad prints from normal negatives.

The color photographs appearing on these eight pages were selected from the pages of a powerfully visual and very special book, *Creative America* (THE RIDGE PRESS, New York 1963). These pictures serve to point up the book's theme—that man's life is enriched and affirmed through his creativity.

Inspired by the controversial National Culture Center for the Performing Arts in Washington, D.C., and conceived by publisher-editor Jerry Mason, *Creative America* contains essays by President John F. Kennedy; former Presidents Truman and Eisenhower; poet Mark Van Doren; naturalist Joseph Wood Krutch; critic Louis Kronenberger; novelist James Baldwin; and poet Robert Frost.

All photographs in *Creative America* and those reproduced here are from MAGNUM.

DENNIS STOCK / *The Book of Job*

Following two pages: ERNST HAAS / *Utah*   DAN BUDNICK / *New York*   ELLIOTT ERWITT / *Virginia*

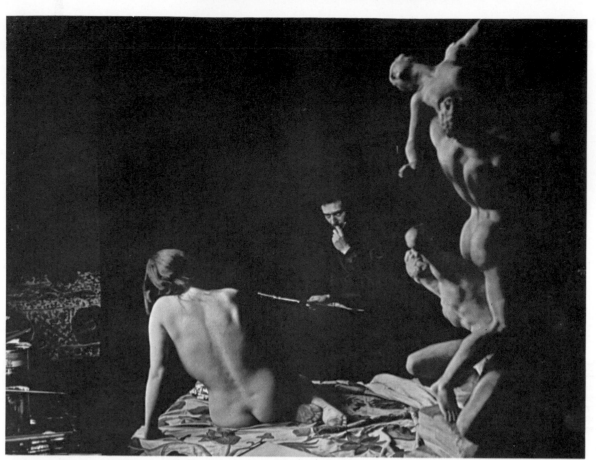

ELLIOTT ERWITT / *Painter Paul Resika*

BRUCE DAVIDSON / *New York Philharmonic*

DENNIS STOCK / *Soprano Anna Moffo*

ERNST HAAS / *New York City Ballet*

MAGIC-EYE CAMERA

The magic-eye camera is widely used by newspaper and magazine photographers in photographing sports events and other subject matter involving rapid and unpredictable motion.

Basically, the magic-eye is a type of motion-picture camera which has been adapted to still photography by adjustments to the shutter. In the conventional motion-picture camera, the shutter angle is about 180 degrees; if the camera is run at 24 frames per second, each frame is exposed for $\frac{1}{2}$ of $\frac{1}{24}$ of a second, or $\frac{1}{48}$ of a second. This is adequate for motion pictures since an object in motion need not be shown sharply on the film; but for still photography, $\frac{1}{48}$ of a second is too slow.

For still work the camera is modified to provide an adjustable shutter which can be set at various openings from 180 degrees to 18 degrees, producing a range of exposures from $\frac{1}{48}$ of a second to $\frac{1}{480}$ of a second, with the camera making 24 pictures per second. If the speed of the camera is increased, say to 48 frames per second, then all shutter speeds are doubled, and the range is from $\frac{1}{96}$ of a second to $\frac{1}{960}$ of a second (roughly from $\frac{1}{100}$ to $\frac{1}{1000}$ of a second). This is adequate for almost any kind of sports work. Naturally fast film and lenses are required.

The camera itself is a 35 mm movie camera, holding a roll of 100 feet of film—this is enough for 1600 separate 24×18 mm pictures (just half the 24×36 mm size of the usual 35 mm still camera). The normal lens is of two-inch focal length, but wide-angle and telephoto lenses can be fitted as with any other camera. Tri-X Pan and other high-speed films are generally available on spools for these cameras.

James Northmore of the *Detroit Times* is generally credited with developing the magic-eye camera. Early versions of the instrument were made by modifying the shutter of a standard DeVry spring-wound 35 mm newsreel camera. This camera was convenient for the purpose because it held 100 feet of film and would run through nearly 55 feet on one winding of the spring motor. However, certain mechanical changes had to be made in the spring drive to assure the camera stopping with the shutter closed after each burst of pictures. Moreover, the camera had but one running speed.

Later on, National Cine Laboratories of New York developed a special camera for news still photography. The camera takes 100-foot spools of film and has a fully adjustable shutter from $\frac{1}{50}$ to $\frac{1}{1000}$ of a second with running speeds from 12 to 64 frames per second. This camera is still in use by many newspapers and magazines. Other manufacturers have

The magic-eye camera—motion-picture techniques adapted for stills.

Double play. Here is a fast-action sports sequence taken with the magic-eye camera. The runner slides into second, as the shortstop takes the ball and throws it to first for the double play. (Photo: International News)

built magic-eye cameras, either from the ground up, or by using one or another type of hand-held movie camera as a basis.

Magic-eye cameras can be hand-held when the short focal-length lenses are used. For telephotos, sharper pictures are obtained with a tripod. A pan and tilt head on the tripod is essential for quick aiming and centering of the action.

□

MAGNESIUM

Before electricity became generally available, magnesium was used as a source of light for contact printing. First a ribbon of magnesium was made to a very precise thickness. A specific length of this ribbon was then burned, producing a certain amount of light. Exposures for contact printing at one time specified, for example, that for an average negative, with a certain paper, the correct exposure would be obtained by burning three inches of magnesium ribbon at a distance of one foot from the printing frame.

Attempts were made to use magnesium as a steady-burning light source in slide projectors by means of a simple clockwork mechanism which slowly fed the ribbon from a container as it burned. For short exhibitions, the burning ribbon provided a fairly good projection light source, but the problem of getting rid of the smoke, and the cost of burning magnesium in quantity, prevented the system from ever becoming much more than a curiosity.

Magnesium was used extensively up to a fairly recent date in the form of flash powder. Fine magnesium powder was mixed with other chemicals that provided a source of pure oxygen during burning; this made the powder burn with a short sharp flash of light, usually lasting about one tenth of a second for small quantities of p o w d e r. Larger amounts burned longer, and since exposure was always by open flash, greater exposure resulted even

Erich Lessing / Cardinal Mindszenty, Budapest, 1956.

though the flash was actually no brighter.

This mixture of magnesium and oxygen-producing chemicals was highly explosive. Numerous accidents resulted from carelessness in pouring the powder from the bottle onto the pan of a flash gun where a few sparks still lingered from a previous exposure. The use of this flash powder diminished rapidly and disappeared completely with the introduction of flashbulbs.

The salts of magnesium are rarely used in photography. They are more expensive than the corresponding sodium or potassium salts, and many of them are highly deliquescent—because they absorb moisture from the air, they have poor keeping qualities.

Magnesium metal has one very valuable property: it is extremely light. Alloys of magnesium and aluminum (Magnalium, etc.) are used for castings in camera parts where light weight and strength are required. One alloy in particular, known as Duralumin or Dural, is lighter than aluminum and as strong as a mild steel. It is used in making tripods, lamp stands, and other similar items. One special studio-type 35 mm motion-picture camera was made with a body of magnesium, enabling it to be hand-held for special photographic problems.

MAGNUM

ARTHUR GOLDSMITH
Editor, Famous Photographers School, Westport, Connecticut
[This article recounts the colorful history of Magnum and points up the importance of this unique picture agency in the field of contemporary photojournalism.]
All photographs by Magnum photographers.
• *Also see: Agencies, Photographic.*

MAGNUM PHOTOS, INC. IS AN international cooperative picture agency with offices in New York and Paris. It is wholly owned and controlled by its members. Founded in 1947 by a small group of photographers, it has grown in size, prestige, and influence to become a vital force in contemporary photojournalism.

Today, Magnum's 26 members, associates and contributing photographers roam the globe in search of pictures. Their efforts have resulted in thousands of published pages in the world's major magazines, in more than 40 books, and in hundreds of other publications in-

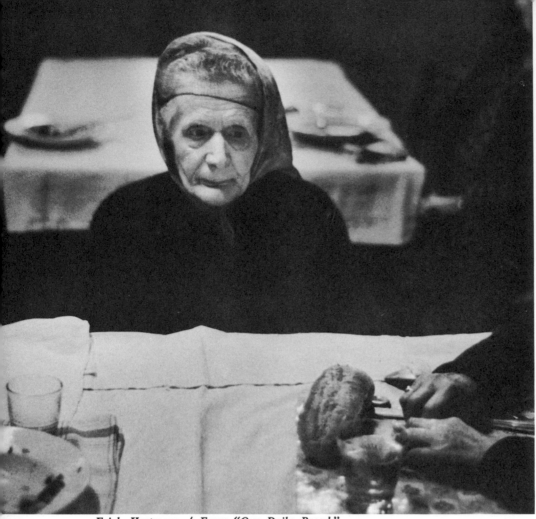

Erich Hartmann / From "Our Daily Bread."

cluding calendars, advertisements, textbooks, movie publicity and annual reports. Magnum has created and circulated distinguished photographic exhibitions and experimented with large-scale picture reports-in-depth. Also it has nurtured new talent and aided members in completing personal projects that would have been difficult or impossible for them to do on their own.

Along with Magnum's material success has grown a legend—an aura of glamour and excitement that is unique among picture agencies. It is due in large measure to the creative achievements, personal charm, and adventurous careers of its member photographers. Magnum has never been short on colorful personalities who might be lovable, insouciant, stimulating and at times exasperating, but who were almost never boring.

Magnum photographers have produced picture books, been honored with one-man shows, and won top awards from many organizations, including the American Association of Magazine Photographers, the Overseas Press Club, and the Art Director's Club of New York. Yet it is not only what Magnum photographers have done, but the style and dash with which they have done it that has helped create the legend.

The very founding of Magnum has a story-book quality that set the tone for much that followed. It began at World War II's end in liberated Paris where three old friends met unexpectedly in an atmosphere charged with elation and uncertainty. They celebrated their reunion—and began to brainstorm some tenuous plans for the future.

The trio included a young Hungarian-born American named Robert Capa. A man of great charm, wit, and personal courage, he had won a reputation at the age of 22 with his close-up coverage of the Spanish Civil War. As a *Life* war correspondent he followed the cutting edge of combat from North Africa across Sicily and up the Italian peninsula, then landed with the first wave to hit the beaches at Normandy, and accompanied the first American troops across the Rhine.

Another member of the group was a shy, intense Frenchman named Henri Cartier-Bresson. Once a painter, he had discovered a new universe of vision through the viewfinder of his Leica, and became a distinguished photojournalist before the war brought his career to a temporary halt. Captured by the Germans during the Battle of France, he later escaped from prison camp to join the underground as a Resistance leader in Marseilles.

The third man was David Seymour, widely known by his nickname of "Chim." Born in Poland, he had studied at the Sorbonne and worked on photojournalistic assignments with Capa and Cartier-Bresson before the war. Becoming an American citizen, he entered the U.S. Army as a private and later was promoted to a lieutenant. Now he too was restlessly looking ahead to a future in which photographers might once again roam the world freely.

As a happy result of their meeting these three men decided to form a new kind of photographer's association that would give them the support of a group, yet allow the utmost possible individual freedom. Aptly enough for the time and place, they decided to name the group "Magnum"—after the two-quart bottle of champagne—and agreed to meet again soon in New York.

In the spring of 1947 Magnum was formally incorporated. It included Capa, Cartier-Bresson, and Seymour, plus an Englishman, George Rodger, and a former *Life* staff photographer, William Vandivert, with Maria Eisner as business manager.

Long on talent, dreams, and energy, the little group was short on capital (the initial investment amounted to about $400 each).

Wayne Miller / Peter, from "The World is Young."

Dan Budnick / Willem de Kooning.

Miraculously enough, it survived those first critical years and began to grow. Other talented free lance photojournalists were attracted by the promise and atmosphere of the organization. Werner Bischof of Switzerland and Ernst Haas of Austria both joined Magnum in 1949. Eve Arnold, Erich Hartmann, and Dennis Stock of the U.S., and Erich Lessing of Austria became members in 1951.

Others soon followed. John Morris, a former *Life* editorial staffer and Picture Editor of the *Ladies Home Journal,* became Magnum's Executive Editor in 1953—a post he held until 1962, when he left to set up his own photographic consultant service and handle Magnum's newly created newspaper service.

The spectacular personal successes of various Magnum photographers and the rapid growth of the organization in the early 50's gave rise to the phrase "Magnum Luck." Then, in 1954, the agency was dealt a shattering double blow. First, Werner Bischof was killed when his truck plunged off a mountain road in Peru. A few days later in Indo-China a land mine exploded and killed Robert Capa, who was covering the war in his usual fashion —as close to the shooting as possible. Tragedy struck again two years later when David Seymour was killed while on assignment covering the Suez crisis. But however bitter the personal loss of these key men to the rest of Magnum, the organization was strong enough to survive.

ORGANIZATION AND POLICIES

Magnum has been called "a miniature United Nations," a "mutual aid society," and "a state of mind." All three descriptions are apt.

Magnum is international in more than one sense. It might be said quite literally that the sun rarely sets on this organization. Somewhere, at any given moment, the sun is likely to be shining on at least one

Elliott Erwitt / Buckminster Fuller, 1960.

member photographer. They cover the globe, with usually a majority of members away from New York at any one time. You might find one aboard a trans-Atlantic jet heading for Paris, another covering a launching at Cape Canaveral, and another in Hollywood working on a color assignment for a movie. Somebody else may be doing a travel story in Hong Kong, covering elections in Rome, or photographing riots in Guatemala.

Some members are practically shuttle commuters between New York's West 47th Street Magnum headquarters and the European branch at 125 Faubourg St. Honoré in Paris. The agency also has offices in London and Zurich, and representatives in Amsterdam, Antwerp, Copenhagen, Helsinki, Milan, Oslo, Stockholm, and Tokyo.

Marc Riboud / Ganges 1956.

Magnum members themselves are a cosmopolitan, multilingual group, continuing the tradition set by the founders. Current members include Eve Arnold (U.S.), Brian Brake (New Zealand), René Burri (Switzerland), Cornell Capa (U.S.) Henri Cartier-Bresson (France), Bruce Davidson (U.S.), Elliott Erwitt (U.S.), Burt Glinn (U.S.), Ernst Haas (Austria), Erich Hartmann (U.S.), Sergio Larrain (Chile), Erich Lessing (Austria), Wayne Miller (U.S.), Inge Morath (Austria), Marc Riboud (France), George Rodger (England), and Dennis Stock (U.S.). Associates are Ian Berry (France), and Dan Budnick, Charles Harbutt, Ken Heyman, Constantine Manos, and Andrew St. George (all U.S.).

As a business organization, sole ownership and control of Magnum is vested in its members. It elects a new president and executive committee each year at an annual board

Inge Morath / Mrs. Roosevelt and Adlai Stevenson at U. N. Session, 1960.

meeting with Cartier-Bresson serving as permanent chairman. Overall policies and plans for the coming year are set at this time, with the president and executive committee acting as a kind of watchdog to see that they are carried out.

The day to day operations of Magnum as a picture agency and a business enterprise are conducted in New York by Bureau Chief Gideon de Margitay, Editor Inge Bondi, and associate Editor Lee Jones, and in Paris by European Editor and Bureau Chief William de Bazelaire, and Associate Editor Joseph Morhaim.

Running a cooperative picture agency in the fiercely competitive area of publishing and advertising is a little like piloting a ship through dangerous seas on the New

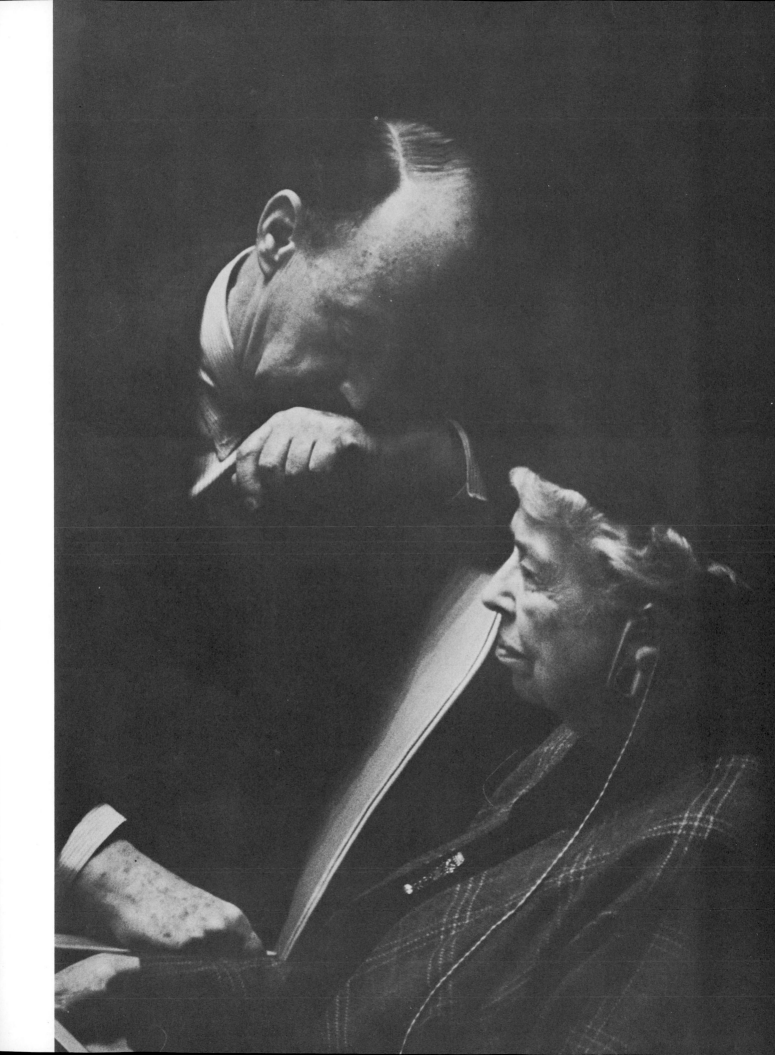

England town-meeting plan. A certain loss of efficiency is bound to result. Yet despite the system, or perhaps even because of it, Magnum has not only survived but thrived.

WORKING PROCEDURE

Each photographer contributes a percentage (currently about 45 percent) of any income received from assignments or stock picture sales. In return, the photographer receives the support of the organization with its prestige and contacts, and is able to draw necessary advances. The aim of the organization is not to make a corporate profit but to increase services and reduce the percentage.

However, cooperate ownership is only one part of the Magnum concept of what a photographer's agency should be. From the very beginning the photographers who founded Magnum envisioned it as a kind of critical forum and clearing house for new insights, techniques, and creative ideas. "I believe creative work demands communication," Henri Cartier-Bresson has said. "So it is extremely encouraging to be with a group who form a community and to know you're not isolated."

In its pooling of intellectual resources, sharing of craft skills, setting of standards, and the frank, mutual appraisal of each other's work, Magnum bears some similarity to a medieval guild. Like a guild too, it sometimes uses a kind of apprenticeship system with a younger, less experienced photographer put under the guidance of a veteran member of the group. All this is usually done in an informal, even off-hand kind of way (Magnum is nothing if not informal), but has a real impact, as many Magnum photographers past and present will attest.

Magnum's goal is to abolish the worst perils of isolation and insecurity that threaten a free lance photographer while at the same time protecting and stimulating his independence and creativity. In practice, the organization seems to have achieved considerable success in realizing this goal. Many Magnum people feel that the criticism and guidance they got from other members was a crucial factor in achieving personal and professional growth. On the other hand, some photographers have tried Magnum, not found its particular brand of individualism plus group therapy to their liking, and left.

Not that Magnum lacks for new applicants. Members have deliberately limited the size of the organization for fear of losing the personal, intimate quality that is one of its most endearing and fruitful characteristics. They have set high standards before accepting newcomers, and getting in is difficult.

First, the prospective member's portfolio of pictures must be seen by all members present in New York. If his work looks promising enough, he is encouraged to get to

David Seymour / Bernard Berenson.

Cornell Capa / Pasternak, 1958.

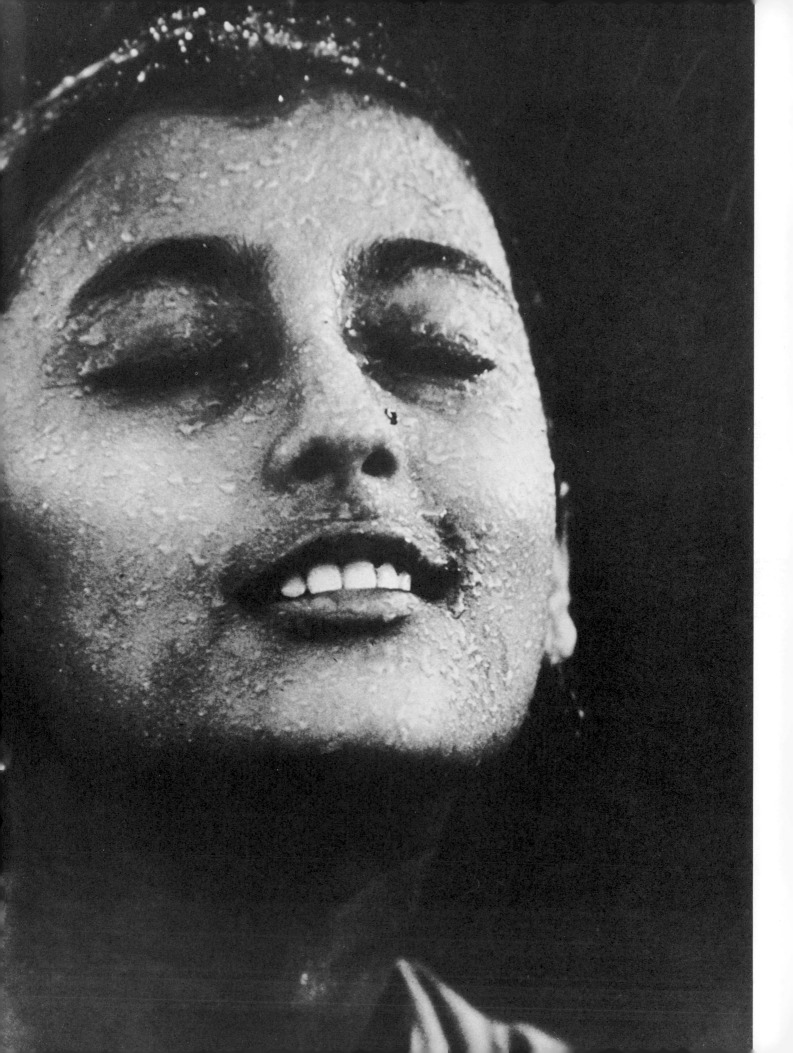

know the members personally and become familiar with their ideas and methods. If after a period of time, he seems acceptable, he is elected to associate membership. If this relationship works out to mutual satisfaction, he may then be elected to full membership at an annual meeting of the Board.

MAGNUM AND PHOTOJOURNALISM

Most Magnum photographers are primarily photojournalists who prefer the small-camera (usually 35 mm), candid, available-light approach to picture reporting. However, the organization represents no one school of photography. Styles vary among its highly individualistic photographers, including the fantasies of color, reflections, and blurred motion by Ernst Haas, the poetic realism of Bruce Davidson, and the geometric precision of Henri Cartier-Bresson.

What Magnum photographers have had in common over the years is a preoccupation with the human aspect of events. In their best work they have revealed the concrete, personal meaning of contemporary happenings, trends, and states of existence. Famine is no longer an abstract word but a piercing reality in the faces of the starving Indian peasants photographed by Werner Bischof. The emotions that knit together a teen-age gang were sensitively explored by Bruce Davidson. Wayne Miller turned his camera on his own children for a rich and subtle study of modern childhood that eventually appeared as a book, *The World is Young.*

The capacity of Magnum photographers to dig behind the surface of the news and find pictorially striking images filled with human meaning was perhaps best demonstrated in its ambitious "The World as Seen by Magnum Photographers" exhibition. A huge show—it includes 400 running feet of aluminum panels on which the pictures are mounted—the exhibit is both a cross-section of the best work of Magnum photographers and a trib-

Right: *George Rodger / Africans.*

Left: *Brian Brake / From "Monsoon."*

ute to photography as an art of visual communication. With the agency's usual capacity for colorful showmanship, the exhibition first opened in Tokyo, then toured major U.S. cities, and then was shipped off to Europe.

Other Magnum projects have included picture reports on a grand scale. The first of these, organized by Robert Capa, was called the *Youth of the World*. Its purpose: to examine through photographs the new post-war generation. Eventually sold as a series to *Holiday* magazine, it repaid in prestige if not in money the thousands of dollars and months of research and shooting invested in its production.

Another example of Magnum's capacity to generate unusual ideas and carry them out was *The First Hundred Days*, a picture book documenting the first months of the Kennedy Administration in 1961. Various member photogra-

Eve Arnold / Baby's Birth.

phers were deployed to cover different aspects of the Washington scene, and the book was completed and on the stands in about three months. Like many another 90-day wonder, it suffered from too-hasty preparation and got somewhat mixed reviews. However, it paved the way for possible future publishing projects. One of these, *Creative America*, is currently in production for the National Cultural Center.

Magnum's archives are a likely source for picture books. It has a collection of prints by the late Dr. Erich Salomon, and acts as exclusive agent for Ansel Adams, Philippe Halsman, Hiroshi Hamaya, and Dorothea Lange. As the picture files proliferate with the continuing global reportage of 20 photographers, Magnum's photolibrary becomes increasingly important as an income producer for the agency and a mine for picture researches.

In the best of all possible worlds, Magnum photographers probably

Bruce Davidson / Teenagers, 1959.

would accept nothing but photojournalistic assignments. However, the fall of giant magazines and the shrinking of some photojournalistic markets have made it economically unfeasible to follow this course. Magnum photographers, in common with many other photojournalists, have turned to other markets.

Today a substantial percentage of Magnum's income is derived from advertising, motion-picture publicity, and industrial assignments. One of the challenges facing it in the future is whether or not it can adapt to the current demands and pressures without losing its identity. However, Magnum has found solutions to difficult problems in the past and it seems likely that as long as people want photojournalism Magnum photographers will continue to explore the world with honesty, compassion, and imagination.

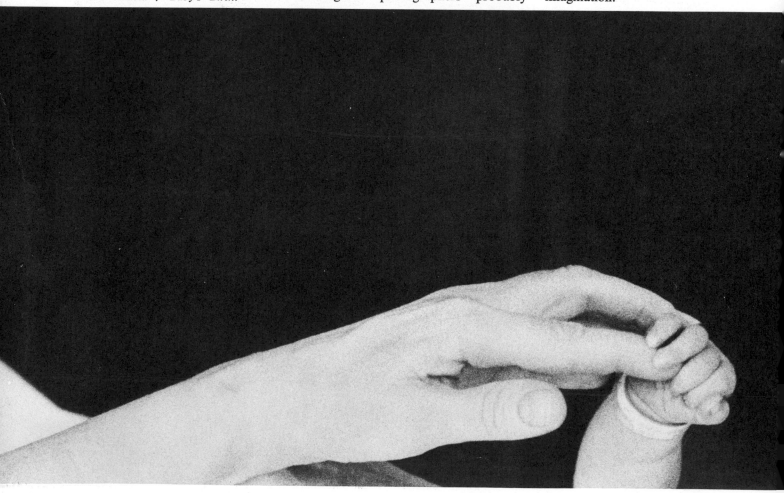

Left: *Sergio Larrain / Peru 1957.*

Below: *Werner Bishof / Famine in India.*

Andrew St. George / Cuba 1960.

Henri Cartier-Bresson / Srinagar, Kashmir, 1948.

Ernst Haas / Return of Austrian Prisoners of War.

Charles Harbutt / Blind Boy, Copyright 1961.

Robert Capa / *Mothers of Naples, 1943.*

Dennis Stock / Billy Crow.

Burt Glinn / At Berlin Wall, 1961.

René Burri / Cuba 1963.

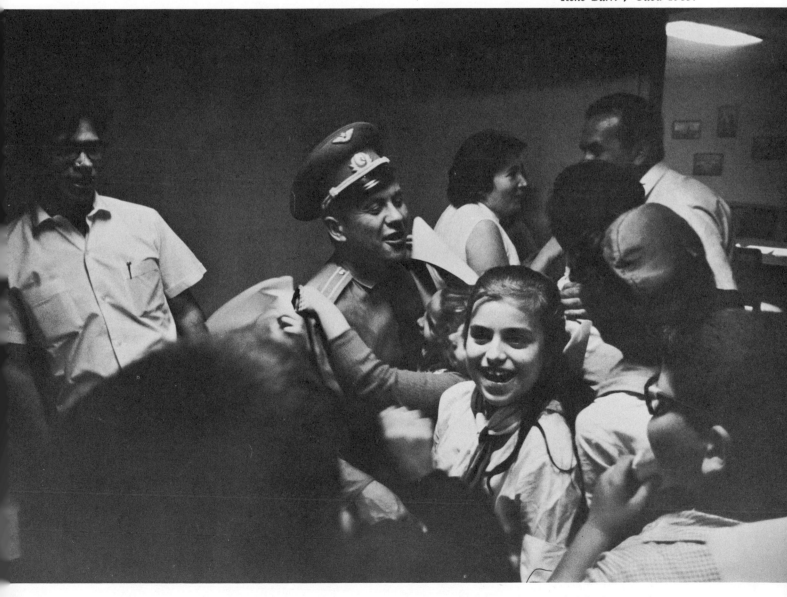

Ian Berry / Congo 1960.

David Seymour / Bernard Berenson.

Ken Heyman / From "Willie," 1963.

Constantine Manos / Charles Munch.

MAILING PHOTOGRAPHS AND FILM

The postal regulations applying to the mailing of photographs and films are relatively simple but because of frequent changes, it is best to consult your local post office for rates and classifications.

DOMESTIC MAIL

First class. First class mail must be sealed and may contain written matter, photographs, negatives, printed material, or all mixed.

Second class. Second class mail is a special classification for newspaper and magazine mailers. It is not of much interest to the photographer, since it can be used only on special occasions. For instance, when mailing a complete copy of a magazine or newspaper to some other town, the transient second-class rate may be used with certain limitations.

Third class. Third class is for printed matter, photographs, and small parcels of merchandise up to, but not exceeding one pound. Written matter may be enclosed under certain restrictions. The rate is based on weight.

Fourth class. Fourth class is popularly known as "parcel post," and is intended for packages of merchandise, printed matter, or photographs weighing more than one pound. The rate varies not only with the weight of the package but also with the distance, which is calculated on a zone basis. Weight limits are 40 pounds to zones 1 and 2, and 20 pounds beyond, except in certain special cases, such as packages traveling between second- and third-class post offices (small towns). Written matter may be enclosed under certain conditions. Packages may be sealed or unsealed; no special notice is required on a sealed package, as the post office takes the payment of fourth-class postage as indication of permission to open and inspect all such packages.

Air-Mail. Domestic air parcels may include written matter or merchandise without extra charge.

ENCLOSING WRITTEN MATTER

Third- and fourth-class rates are intended for merchandise, pictures,

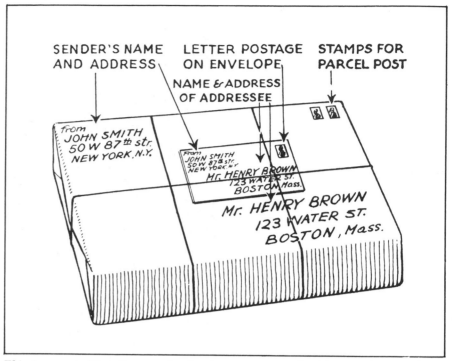

This is a post-office diagram showing how to wrap and address a double package —with the written matter going at the first-class rate and the package at the parcel-post rate.

and similar items and not written matter. However, if it is necessary to include a letter of instruction, picture captions, or similar material, such a letter may be enclosed directly in the package. On the outside of the package, directly beneath the stamps, must be written: "First-class mail enclosed; postage paid." An additional stamp (first-class postage) is placed on the package, above the postage required for third- or fourth-class handling.

The size limit of fourth-class packages is 72 inches, length and girth combined. To calculate this, wrap a tape measure around the package the short way; to this measurement add the length of the package (not completely around, only length). The total of the two measurements must not exceed 72 inches. Your local post office can inform you as to the various other size limits for air mail, and for foreign mailings.

MOTION-PICTURE FILMS

Motion-picture films must be packed in spark-proof metal boxes or cans, and are governed by Interstate Commerce regulations for shipment of dangerous articles. Short motion-picture films, not exceeding

25 feet in length, may be sent in tightly closed metal cans and outside containers of corrugated strawboard or other material. Motion-picture film not exceeding 1000 feet may be sent in tightly closed metal cans lined with asbestos, in outside fibreboard or corrugated containers—with a yellow caution label.

Nonflammable motion-picture films are accepted without other restriction when packed in strong containers; each container must be plainly marked "Motion-picture films—not dangerous." Mailing of photographs is limited in subject matter by Section 124.4 in the Postal Manual, which prohibits the mailing of obscene, lewd, lascivious, or filthy publications or writings, or mail containing information concerning where, how, or from whom such may be obtained. Also prohibited is matter which is otherwise mailable but which has on its wrapper or envelope indecent, lewd, lascivious, or obscene writing or printing.

PACKING

Always pack photos with stiff cardboard or a similar material to prevent any accidental bending. Take special care of the corners, which are easily bent during transit. Indicate that easily damaged photographs are enclosed. If the contents are fragile, the parcel must be labeled "Fragile." Pictures which are framed with glass fronts must be protected on both sides with stout material, preferably boards, and enclosed in a wooden or strong fibreboard box with cushioning material. When unframed and flat, cushioning material is not necessary, but photos should be protected by strong stiffening material. When rolled, they must be enclosed in a strong mailing tube or carefully rolled around a strong smooth stick of greater length than the article itself.

FOREIGN MAIL

Foreign mail often requires the attachment of customs declarations, statements for the disposal of undeliverable mail, and other forms. Regulations vary from country to country, and it is essential to check with the post office for the specific rules for each package. The post office will supply customs tags, special stickers for disposition, and other necessary forms.

Foreign air-mail regulations vary between countries. Current rates can be obtained from the post office.

EXPRESS

Packages which are too large or too heavy for parcel post, as well as packages containing certain unmailable materials (such as explosives) can be sent by express. There is a rather large minimum charge, which varies with distance, making it seldom economical to send small packages this way. Written matter cannot be sent by express, though a sheet of caption material can accompany photographs. Packaging of film, being a matter of Interstate Commerce Commission regulation, must be followed for express as well as for parcel post.

There are certain advantages to express shipment, one of which is that the shipping charges are not prepaid, but are paid by the recipient. This makes it unnecessary to weigh the package or to have to estimate shipping cost in advance. However, the recipient must be available to receive the package and pay the charges on delivery. Insurance coverage up to $50 is automatically applied to all express packages; higher insurance is available at additional cost.

There is a special rate which is useful to motion-picture photographers: the return of a package of film is at a lower rate than the original shipment.

Where speed is the most important consideration and cost no object, air express provides not only fast transportation en route, but immediate messenger delivery on arrival. The same service can be had with parcel post by using air mail and special delivery. Compare the rates of the two services to determine which is most useful.

□

The author is pictured above as he appears in real life, and below made-up as an arrogant Nazi general with the aid of latex rubber mask, artificial moustache and eyebrows, and collodion scar. (Photo: Barry Kramer)

MAKE-UP FOR PHOTOGRAPHY

ROBERT O'BRADOVICH
Director of Make-Up Department, NBC-TV, New York City
[As the senior make-up artist on an eight-man staff, the author is a veteran of many years in professional make-up work, as well as having had acting experience in television productions. This is a definitive article about straight, corrective, and character make-up procedures for color and black-and-white photography, including information on fundamental equipment needed and step-by-step instructions for its use.]
All photographs courtesy NBC-TV.
• *Also see: Character Studies; Lighting in Portraiture; Portrait Photography; Portraiture—Elementary Technique; Psychological Portraiture.*

SINCE THE EARLIEST DAYS OF THEATER, artificial methods have been used to enhance the effectiveness of the human face as an instrument of dramatic expression. These methods have varied in each society and in each era according to the prevailing theory of drama.

In ancient Greece and Rome, where drama was a very highly stylized and non-naturalistic art, the human face was covered entirely by a mask which was a caricature or radically conventionalized representation of a human attitude or type. These highly formal and exaggerated characters were in perfect accord with the style of drama being performed at that time. Other extremely stylized dramatic traditions, such as the No drama of Japan, have left the human face exposed but have used make-up in a manner which gives the face a mask-like quality.

The Western dramatic tradition has developed mainly along more naturalistic lines since the Elizabethan era. The over-all aim has been to make, within certain conventions, the characters represented on stage, screen, and television appear as lifelike as possible. Even when special effects are being created, such as making up of a young actor to portray a very old

Julie Harris, at the beginning of Victoria Regina, *acts the part of an 18-year-old in straight make-up.* Center: *As the 27-year-old queen, Julie Harris begins to show signs of age in the skillfully drawn (lining pencil) lines of the make-up artist.* Right: *A more complicated character make-up starts with 42-year-old impersonation of Queen Victoria. Here the cheeks, jowls, and nose tip were latex rubber appliance pieces fastened to the face with spirit gum. Lines and wrinkles were accentuated by highlights and shadows made with a lining pencil.*

person, the result generally must be as natural as life itself.

It is even necessary to use artificial methods to achieve the natural image of life. A person appearing on television needs the make-up artist if he wants to appear on the viewing screen as he does in everyday life.

The dramatic medium, no matter which one, is essentially artificial and requires the aid of artifacts to render a real-life image; the artifacts needed and the techniques of facial make-up vary according to the dramatic medium. Make-up technique for the screen is different from that used for the stage; television make-up differs from the other two. The following are some basic rules of make-up work for the film and still photographer.

FACIAL QUALITIES

One of the most essential elements of still and film photography is the proper application of make-up. Since the greatest concern of the cameraman is to obtain a pleasing, natural look, he must consider the three basic qualities of the face—photogenic coloring, skin texture, and facial contours. At infrequent intervals, more the

exception than the rule, nature produces flawless beauty. But facial beauty is lacking or needs modification or correction in most instances, emphasizing the need for a professional make-up artist. The make-up department of any film-producing company is one of its most important areas; in still photography, the photographer relies on the model's ability to use make-up or brings in a free lance make-up artist.

The chief division in make-up is between the materials used for black-and-white and those used for color photography—this is more a matter of choosing the right cosmetics than of technique of application. Under each of these two divisions, there are subdivisions—straight, corrective, and character make-up. Each of these uses the same basic techniques, but each requires progressively complex handling. We will start with the application of make-up in its simplest form and work toward the more intricate applications.

MATERIALS NEEDED

The foundation which is used as a base for make-up is available in two forms—grease and pan cake. The choice is up to the person

doing the make-up. I use Factor's Pan-Stik or Pan-Cake for almost everything. The Pan-Cake foundation is easier to apply and remove, but the grease foundation has slightly superior qualities. These and other cosmetics may be obtained from many drug and department stores.

The basic make-up kit should contain these items: 1) foundation, 2) sponge for applying pan cake, 3) powder, puff, and complexion brush, 4) eye shadow, 5) moist and dry rouge, 6) lip rouge and brush, 7) eyebrow pencil, 8) mascara and brush, 9) liner and brush, 10) towels and facial tissue, 11) cleansing cream, and 12) smock or apron.

The dressing room is an accepted necessity for both still and film photographers. It can, in many cases, also serve as the make-up room, though a make-up stand with proper lighting is really essential. All materials needed for a particular make-up job should be neatly arranged and handy before the application begins. A quantity of clean towels, a working smock or apron, and some form of covering or protection for the subject should be provided. Towels or hair nets can be used to protect the hair-do and keep hair off the face.

All equipment such as brushes and powder puffs should be kept very clean; individual powder puffs which can be discarded after use will eliminate this problem. Brushes can be sterilized by washing in soap and water and rinsing in an anti-septic solution for a few minutes. This is one part of the make-up procedure that should never be neglected.

It will probably be necessary to work under artificial light, so be sure it's available. If you cannot arrange the standard ring of bulbs around the mirror as seen on most professional or company make-up tables, then at least arrange the lighting so there is even illumination.

PAN MAKE-UP

The purpose of the basic straight make-up for monochrome photography is to provide a photographically satisfactory coloring and texture of the face. The problems have been solved mainly by the chemists who have compounded the modern panchromatic make-up materials. These products are balanced chromatically to photograph under any commonly used type of lighting, including daylight, ordinary tungsten, photofloods, and flash.

To achieve this end, no less than five pigments are blended to provide each given shade of make-up. The result is, in the case of the foundation and powder, a neutral brownish color which is photographically correct for panchromatic materials and reasonably natural visually.

To suit the needs of different complexions, a range of ten different shades is provided in pan make-up. The lightest is a delicate tan or beige; the darkest a dark brown, like a good tan. Each cosmetic company has its own system of numbering, but for all of them the low numbers designate the light shades; as the numbers increase, the shade becomes darker. All are based on roughly similar chromatic values.

A few general principles should be mentioned about the application of straight make-up. First, a blonde uses a darker make-up in relation to her skin coloring than a brunette, and a man's make-up is considerably darker than either. In each case, a natural effect is achieved by making the face tone a definite contrast to the hair color. If, on the other hand, you want to decrease the contrast, use a darker make-up with the brunette and a lighter on the blonde, thus shifting the contrast between skin and hair. All such changes must be made carefully, for if they are altered drastically the natural unity of the face—eyes, brows, lips and coloring —will be poorly related.

It might be well to say here that most of our discussion will concern make-up for women. Very little make-up is used for men and children, other than a slight coloring of the lips to accentuate their form. Men usually look best without make-up, unless they have skin blemishes or a dark beard—which is exaggerated by the lens even when a man is freshly shaven just before camera appearance. Usually these difficulties can be minimized by applying a foundation, then toning it down with powder until it is scarcely noticeable.

Skillfully applied make-up should smooth out shadows (less contrast between lights and darks), give an even tone to the skin, and reflect light. It should cover minor defects, improve the contours of the face, make the eyes seem larger and sparkling, and softly brighten the mouth.

APPLYING STRAIGHT MAKE-UP

One basic principle in using make-up properly is to start with a clean face. Be sure the subject's face has been washed with a mild soap and warm water, followed by a cleansing lotion or cream. If the skin is oily, use a skin toner or a mild astringent after cleansing.

Now we are ready to apply make-up. Remember to work so

Left: The author carefully adjusts a latex rubber forehead piece as Julie Harris is prepared for portraying Queen Victoria at the age of 58. The appliance pieces for the neck, jowls, and chin are already in place. Center: Miss Harris is ready for her appearance as the 58-year-old queen. Age make-up has been applied over the latex rubber; artificial eyebrows have been added. Wig and costume complete the illusion of age. Right: The Diamond Jubilee scene, in which Victoria is 78, required a complete latex rubber mask. The hands were also covered with latex rubber pieces molded and made-up to show aged veins and wrinkles. It took more than three hours to do the full make-up—starting at six in the morning. It took another hour, after the filming, to restore Miss Harris to her normal appearance. Photographs of the real Victoria were used as guides during the stages of making up. (All Julie Harris Photos: Fred Hermansky)

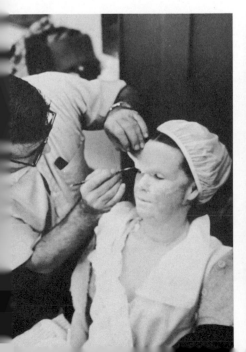

the result will be natural looking. If the model has strong shadows in the laugh lines, under the eyes, or in the nostril curves, spot make-up can be applied with a brush. Powder these shadow areas lightly so they will not smudge when the foundation is applied.

Cream foundation in the desired shade should be applied sparingly over the entire facial area. Use only as much as will cling to the fingertips and spread it so lightly that it is hardly seen. Work toward the neckline, blending thoroughly and patting well to avoid heavy spots or areas. This is very important because thicker areas absorb more powder which, even if not notice-able to the eye, will photograph as a smudge or skin discoloration. Keep the foundation out of the brows, lashes, and hair, but otherwise cover the face and throat. If the foundation matches the skin tone, a sharp contrast or line of demarcation where make-up ends and natural skin begins will be avoided.

The pancake foundation is applied with a moist, fine-grained sponge, preferably one which is unbleached. The sponge should be just moist enough to take up the powder without thinning it out. Usually it is best to begin by applying make-up to the forehead and nose, working to the cheeks, and blending down to the neckline. Take care that pancake make-up goes on evenly; let it dry and then go over it to work out any uneven-ness.

Liquid foundations are applied either with a pad which is supplied with the foundation or by a pad formed of fine cloth. As with the other foundations, use caution in applying. Avoid excess in any step, for overdone make-up will be picked up by the camera.

Next, the rouge is applied, either moist or dry. If I am using Pan-Stik, I use moist rouge; otherwise, dry rouge. Rouge should be a rosy tint, not too red or orange in hue. Start application of the rouge with fingertips or a sponge at the heaviest or fullest part of the cheek, and blend it carefully outward over the desired area. It should taper off gradually toward the hairline. Cheek

Seldom is such an array of make-up creations seen at one time as in this group from **The** Catholic Hour. *The actors were transformed with the aid of latex rubber appliances, artificial hair, wigs, plastic caps, and a full assortment of make-up materials.* From left to right, *the make-up man's creations are: Alexander The Great, Napoleon Bonaparte, Julius Caesar, the priest, Adolf Hitler, Joseph Stalin, and Genghis Kahn.*

Top: *Any production of* Cyrano de Bergerac *centers on the nose. For the* Hallmark Hall of Fame *production, the author fashioned four latex rubber noses for Christopher Plummer to choose from.*

Bottom: *A contrast in the use of make-up for the production of* Cyrano de Bergerac *broadcast in color. In the foreground, Hope Lange's (Roxanne) beauty was enhanced with straight make-up, while Christopher Plummer is disguised by many artifacts.*

rouge should be applied in a subtle way, never visible as a heavy spot or blotch but so that it seems to vanish at the edges as it would in a natural blush.

We are ready now to apply the eye shadow. The color should be only a hint, for when subtly applied, eye shadow does flattering things. The color gives depth to the area around the eyes, and if there is any flatness or puffiness below the brow, this seems to be softened. Neutral shades such as bluish turquoise and grayish brown are good.

Apply the shadow to the upper lid only. Do not extend it to the eyebrow area. Shadow can be fanned outward slightly toward the temple at the outer edge of the lid. The softest effect is achieved by applying the shadow with a brush. Powder lightly over the eye shadow and then, to give an added glow, remove the excess powder with a damp sponge.

At this point, the make-up is about half completed, so it is a good time to check its appearance. Make certain it has a smooth look and is well blended. Smooth out with the fingertips any spots that seem bumpy on the forehead, under the eyes, and around the nose and corners of the mouth, before starting the important phase of powdering.

FINISHING STRAIGHT MAKE-UP

Work with a neutral-shade powder having no reddish or orange tones. Pat the powder generously over the entire face and throat, using a clean puff to apply it gently. Remove any excess by patting the powdered area with a damp sponge. This sets the powder and gives the skin a glow.

While the model looks upward, powder the lower lid and around the eye. Then have her look downward so you can powder the upper lid. After that, start the general powder application, beginning at some naturally recessed point such as a hollow cheek, a receding chin, or a thin neck. Pat the powder on firmly, applying it rather plentifully over the rouge. Remove all excess powder with a soft powder brush, making sure it is brushed off lashes, eyebrows, and the hairline.

A soft, medium-brown pencil is good for lining the eyes. If you want a light line, apply with delicate touch; if you want it dark, use a firmer touch. Start at the outer tip of the eye with a little upward stroke that elongates the eye line and gives a lift to the face. With the eye shut, draw this line at the outer tip, starting almost at the corner and moving upward and outward for a quarter of an inch or so toward the tail of the eyebrow.

Next draw the line on the upper lid. This should be drawn exactly on the lash line so there is no white area between the line and the lash roots. Starting about one quarter of the way across the eyelid, draw the line so that it merges with the upward line at the outer tip. The line on the upper lid may be widened slightly as the outer tip of the eyelid is reached, but a hard dark line is unattractive. Soften a harsh line by tapping it lightly with a brush.

To bring out the beauty of the eye, the "line" on the lower lid should be made in little dots. This "line" should be started just below the line on the upper lid and continued to the outer corner.

In applying mascara, coat the upper lashes from roots to tips, so it is backed up by the eye line to present an appearance of a thick, dark fringe. Brush the lashes well after applying the mascara so they will not stick together. It helps when applying mascara if the model tries to keep the eye closed while you pull gently upward so the lid is held firmly. The same method can be used in applying mascara to the lower lashes by placing the fingers on the cheek and pulling gently downward as the model tries to keep the eye closed.

Now work on the eyebrows. The brows should be brushed upward before drawing the eyebrow. I like an arched eyebrow, but there sometimes is a question of where to put the arch. Usually it is wise to go two thirds of the way across the brow before arching. Don't bring the tail of the brow down so far that it seems to droop, or make the downward turn overly abrupt. Keep the penciling in the upper line of the brow and slightly above the natural hairs. Use a medium-brown pencil and hold it lightly, making feathery touches, not long hard lines.

Be careful to start the brow away from the nose. When plucking the brows, widen the space between them by removing the excess hairs that grow between the brows. Don't pluck the rest of the brows too much.

Now to the all-important make-up for the mouth. If the model's lips are naturally full, follow this lip line. The upper lip can be built-up slightly if it is thin, but if the color goes much beyond the natural lip line, the lip appears distorted.

The lip line should have an upward tilt at the tips for a pleasant look. This can be achieved by carrying the color on the lower lip all the way out to the corners and by not bringing the line of the upper lip down too far at the corners. The application on the lower lip and that on the upper lip should meet exactly at the corners.

The best lip contour and the effect of fullness are made by shaping with a lipstick brush. If a mistake is made, correct it by wiping away the unwanted stroke with a bit of foundation cream on a fingertip and then powdering the area. Do not apply lipstick so heavily that it rubs off on the teeth. After coloring, blot the lips with

Peter Ustinov being made up for his part as Sam Johnson on the Omnibus *show. Ustinov refused to shave his beard for the show; it had to be concealed with latex rubber appliances.*

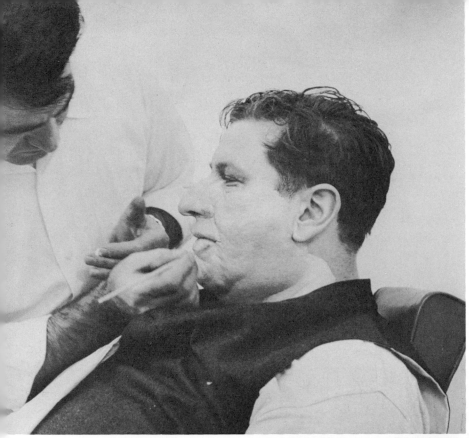

using the same technique as for women. However, no eye shadow or cheek rouge should be used, and unless the lips are very pale, no lip rouge should be applied. The object of make-up for men is to reduce the prominence of skin blemishes and to give the skin a natural, healthy appearance. If it seems necessary to use lip rouge, face powder should be put on as the last step. This reduces the emphasis of the rouge and, at the same time, makes heavy eyebrows less noticeable.

The objective of make-up is to show a person as attractively as possible by subduing defects and enhancing natural beauty. The best way to judge the effect of make-up, aside from actual camera tests, is to view the subject from a distance of about three feet. Any crudities in shading, lining, cheek rouge that

Above: *After the rubber latex appliance or mask is firmly in place, a special foundation of rubber-mask grease paint must be used before the final touches of character make-up are applied.*

Right: *The complete make-up with wig and costume makes the appearance of Sam Johnson believable as he waits on the set for his entrance cue.*

tissue. If more luster is desired, use a little lip salve.

As a rule this completes the straight make-up. Remember that in using any make-up for photography, the final result should look smooth. The inexperienced person is likely to fall into the habit of applying it too thickly, giving the face a mask-like appearance.

MAKE-UP FOR MEN

Cosmetic companies provide preparations especially made for male make-up, even though men, as a rule, use it sparingly. A man having a smooth skin, a light beard, and flesh of normal color—that is, not red or very tan—should require little more than an application of powder. A man should be freshly shaved or the stubble will be very noticeable. If the eyebrows are very light, an eyebrow pencil may be used to improve the line.

For men who require it, a more complete make-up may be applied,

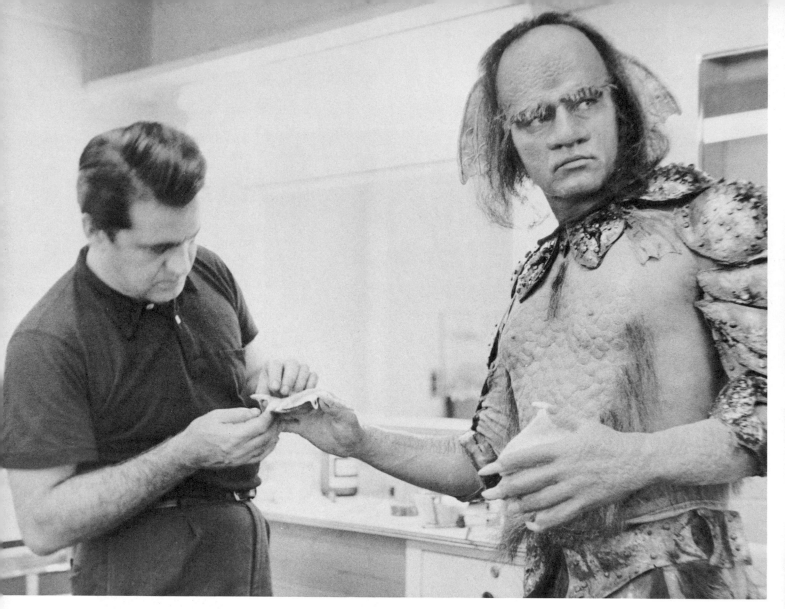

*For the production of Shakespeare's **The Tempest**, the author had to make latex rubber appliance pieces for the forehead, nose, arms, shoulders, back, legs, hands and the top of the head of Richard Burton who played the role of Caliban, the beastlike slave of Prospero.*

are visually disturbing at this distance will be evident on the screen or in a print.

CORRECTIVE MAKE-UP

There are seven basic types of faces: oval, round, square, oblong, triangular, inverted triangle, and diamond. Of these, the oval shape (classic Greek) is usually designated as the most nearly perfect. Make-up, properly applied, can be used with remarkable effect to correct the contours of the face so it will appear, especially photographically, more like the ideal oval. The same methods are applicable in correcting slighter defects, such as sunken or protuberant eyes, hollow or too-full cheeks.

The principle of this type of corrective make-up is basically simple. The cinematographer or still cameraman uses highlights and shadows to correct defective contours when he places the lighting on the set or in the studio. When he throws more light into a concave area, by properly placed highlights, he is trying to eliminate or minimize the effect of hollowness. In the same way, a slight shadow, or a lessening of light, will minimize an area that bulges.

Similar effects can be achieved with make-up. Sunken or receding areas are accented with a make-up highlight—the local application of make-up in a lighter shade than that used on the surrounding area.

Darker shades of make-up are used to shadow the protruding areas so they are less noticeable.

The first step in applying corrective make-up is to determine which of the seven types a particular face resembles. Then the cosmetic highlights and shadows can be used to bring it into closer photographic conformity with the ideal oval. Shadow the areas that are too broad and highlight those that are too narrow. By following this procedure, you can lessen the rotundity of a round face, shorten and broaden the effect of an oblong one, diminish the square jaw line and forehead of a square face, widen the forehead and narrow the jaw of a triangle type, narrow the forehead and widen the jaw of an inverted triangle, and broaden the forehead and chin while narrowing the cheek bone width of a diamond-shaped face.

First, determine the correct foundation color for the over-all make-up. Suppose the model is a woman who will look best with a medium-light shade of foundation. To reduce the roundness of the face, apply a base that is three shades darker than the basic foundation—at the temples and down over the fullness of the jaw line, extending it halfway between the nose and the center of the cheek. Blend this area and the lighter foundation very carefully. The cheeks are not in the shadow so the face tends to reflect the illusion of an oval contour. The same general method is followed for the square face and the triangle. In the case of the triangle, the narrowed jaw line can be widened by highlighting with a lighter shade.

For the oblong face, the same areas are shadowed as for the round face, and the cheeks and cheekbones are highlighted by applying a foundation two shades lighter than the basic one. In correcting the inverted triangle type of face, the same general method is used. To reduce the width in the upper part of an inverted triangle, use a foundation one shade darker than the color on the forehead, which will offset overhead light and minimize forehead width. The high cheekbones of a diamond-shaped face will be less noticeable if you use a foundation two shades darker on the cheekbones, and two shades lighter on the cheeks and the lower half of the face, down to the chin. Use this same lighter shade in the hollows of the temples and up and over the forehead.

CORRECTING SPECIAL FEATURES

A highly arched eyebrow diminishes the size of the eye. It should not be higher above the eye than the normal opening of the eye itself. As a rule, it is better to follow the normal eyebrow line quite closely for a natural look. To enhance small eyes, lower the line under the eye a bit and use mascara only on the tips of the lashes. For deep-set eyes very little shadow should be used and none at all in the extreme hollows of the eyelid. It often helps to use a foundation shade considerably lighter than the basic color between the upper lid and the brow. The opposite, or a darker shade, helps to minimize the effect of bulging eyes.

If there are dark circles under the eyes, use a foundation that is very light, almost white, on them. For puffs under the eyes, use the foundation in one shade darker on the puff itself. To create width between the eyes, add false lashes to the outside corner, but do not pencil or line the inner corners near the nose. Pale blue eyes which normally photograph with a washed-out appearance will look much better if a tiny spot of red is placed in the corners of the eyes causing small, dark catchlights in the iris.

A double chin may be de-emphasized by using a foundation two or even three shades darker than the over-all color used on the face. In some instances, it is also advisable to use a dark shade of dry rouge on the chin after powdering. This treatment throws the chin into a shadow, tending to conceal it. A receding chin, on the other hand, would be helped by using a foundation two shades lighter. You might try, too, a tiny amount of light-toned dry rouge, after powdering, to highlight the chin, making it seem more prominent.

A wide, flat nose can be made

In took the author more than four hours to transform Burton into Caliban. The mottled effect was made by stippling the cream foundation with a sponge. After rehearsal, Burton decided the fangs were overdoing the part, discarded them. (Photo: Vincent J.R. Kehoe)

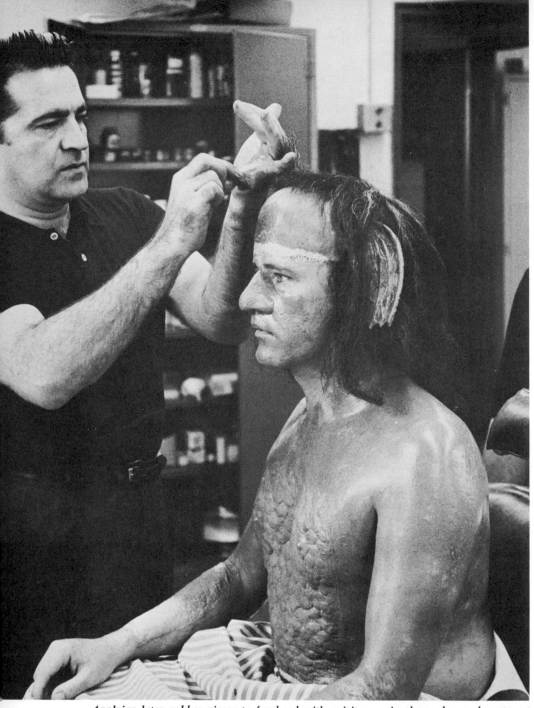

Applying latex rubber pieces to forehead with spirit gum in the make-up department at NBC-TV, New York. The victim is Richard Burton being made up for his role as Caliban in The Tempest. *(Photo: NBC-TV Studio)*

to look thinner and higher by running a highlight down the bridge, using a foundation two or three shades lighter and shadowing the walls with a darker shade than the basic tone. To make an overly thin nose seem wider, reverse the procedure by shadowing the bridge and highlighting the side walls. If darker foundation, possibly three shades darker, is applied over the tip of the nose and around the nostrils and blended up to the tip, the shortening effect will be quite pronounced. Be careful of any hard line spoiling the effect.

If a thin nose is accompanied by lips that are normal, the nose can be further shortened by decreasing the weight of the lips. If, in such a case, the bridge of the nose is rather sharp, be sure to avoid any highlights. Powder applied to the nose has a tendency to reduce the natural highlight of the bridge, and of course makes the nose less conspicuous; on the other hand, very often the mere appli-

cation of a highlight extending from a point between the eyes to the extreme tip of the nose is all that is needed to increase its length.

If a short nose is also wide, further corrective treatment may be done by applying to the sides of the nose a foundation two shades darker than that used for the whole face. Begin by applying from the corner of the eye to the tip of the nose, and blend very carefully to the cheek beside the nose and along the bridge. A narrow line of the basic make-up on the bridge of the nose should be noticeable, and to this can be added a highlight after powdering.

The appearance of a narrow mouth, which is usually accompanied by thin lips, can be greatly improved not only by increasing the width of the lip line, but by extending the lip line slightly beyond the natural corner of the mouth. The lip line can be drawn slightly heavier than normal and also much wider at the corner of the mouth.

It is well to avoid highlights on a mouth with thick lips and to avoid dark lip rouge. The use of a light lip rouge has a tendency to make the lips somewhat less conspicuous. To reduce thick lips, it is sometimes necessary to carry the basic foundation slightly over the natural lip line and to follow the new line with lip rouge. A very light application of powder will reduce highlights and, as a result, make the lip line less noticeable.

It is sometimes necessary to minimize an overly deep dimple, cleft chin, or hollows at the corner of the mouth. This is done by highlighting the hollow with make-up that is two shades lighter than the surrounding area. In reverse, to accentuate a dimple, create a shadow with foundation two shades darker than the adjacent area.

If the jaw line is full the mouth should be made up to its fullest width because a smaller, narrower mouth outline would only accentuate the width of the face. To make a mouth appear smaller by increasing the appearance of width in a narrow jaw, do not make up the mouth to its fullest extent.

MAKE-UP FOR COLOR PHOTOGRAPHY

The correct make-up is very important when using color film of any type. Just as you cannot use identical filters for black-and-white and color photography, you cannot use pan make-up when shooting in color. The same companies that manufacture pan make-up also have complete kits for color photography, including special preparations for negative color.

Good make-up technique is necessary for successful color portraiture because facial blemishes are more noticeable on film than they appear to the eye. When working with color film, they cannot be removed easily, if at all, by retouching. Some corrective work can be done, but only at premium prices by a very small group of trained specialists.

One of the paramount reasons for the keen interest in color make-up is the fact that color is being used far more widely than ever before. The photographer who produces illustrations for advertising and editorial publications now spends the majority of his time with color. Films, for both movies and television, are now more often shot in color than in black-and-white.

Television filmers have additional problems, since color broadcasting and receiving is not at maximum use; in anticipation of increased use of color broadcasting and to satisfy the present demands, many television productions and commercials are made on negative color film so prints can be made available in both color and black-and-white. Because this is a prevalent way of working, it has become necessary to have make-up designed specifically for use with negative color.

After you have obtained the proper cosmetics for use with color

film, their application and use is the same as for pan make-up. Since this has been thoroughly treated previously, I will not repeat the methods here.

CHARACTER MAKE-UP

Character make-up is primarily a matter of creating a new personality over the actor or model's personal features. As the actor assumes the personality of a real or fictional person in gesture and voice, the make-up provides facial reality and the costume completes the illusion. The make-up man's work is governed by two factors: the character to be impersonated and the personal facial structure of the model or actor. This type of make-up is much more exacting than either the straight or corrective methods, because it can be so easily overdone.

In my work as director of make-up, I have to plan, devise, and execute many characterizations. Some of the most valuable lessons I've learned have been from working on my own face—this may be a

Roddy McDowall as Ariel in The Tempest. *In character make-up of this type, the make-up man can let his imagination have full play—it took O'Bradovich four hours to translate his ideas into concrete form. Each of the wave-like strands had to be placed individually, the sparkle carefully clustered, the pointed ears created and the wing-like eyebrows fashioned from crepe hair.* (Photo: NBC-TV Studio)

good tip for photographers who are interested in developing make-up technique. I frequently try out ideas for facial changes on myself before using them on an actor.

PREPARING CREPE HAIR

There the nothing that changes a man's appearance quite so much as a beard. In some productions, the actors actually do grow beards, but this takes time. Using artificial hair (crepe, wool, or yak) to produce beards, moustaches, sideburns, bushy eyebrows, unshaven stubble, and so on, is a much faster and convenient method. It is not a difficult procedure, but it must be done carefully.

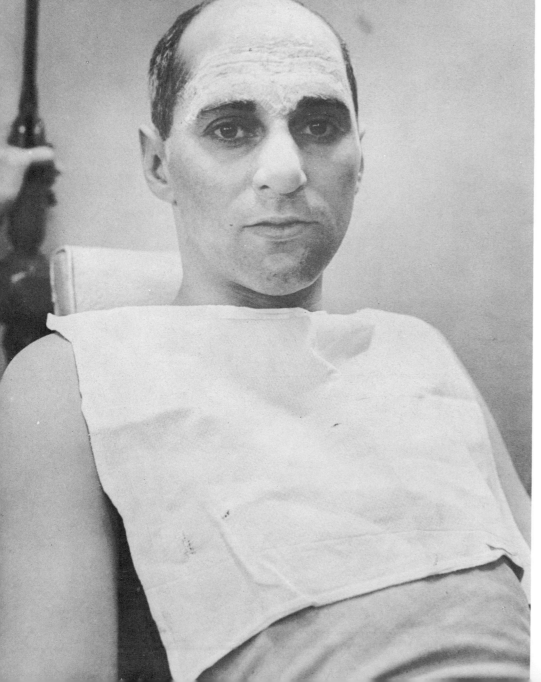

Crepe hair, usually the wool variety as this is easier to use, comes in braids sold by the yard. It is a good idea to have several shades on hand (light, medium, and dark brown; light, medium, and dark gray; blonde, red, and auburn are available; black and white are rarely used), for normal beards are rarely the same color throughout. Also, some roles call for a pepper-and-salt effect.

The string entwined in the braid is discarded as the hair is unbraided. It is now too curly for use unless the character calls for this type of hair. One way of straightening it out is to wet it thoroughly (only the amount you are using), letting it dry while stretched out taut between the legs or arms of a chair. I prefer to place it in boiling water for 15 or 20 minutes. After this treatment, it can be hung up to dry without stretching. Don't make the mistake of putting more than one shade in the same pot, or you will have rainbow-colored crepe hair.

Next the dry hair is combed. Professionally this is done on a hairdresser's hackle, but an ordinary wide-tooth comb is quite all right. A sufficient quantity of each shade (a full beard takes 15 or 20 lengths, cut two to three inches long) should be combed and stacked within easy reach. A thin coat of spirit gum is applied to the area where the beard will sprout; do this carefully so a natural-looking hairline is created. Take one of the lengths of hair, hold it between thumb and forefinger so it hangs straight down, then place it on the sticky spirit gum.

The most important single step in making a convincing beard is to lay the hair on the face in the direction of natural growth. The hair must be placed in position a small section at a time. Resist the temptation to rush or you may spoil the entire effect. Start with the first layer under the chin to establish a base, then add three layers beneath this one. After that, work upward on the face. As each layer is placed, push down on it with a finger of the left hand. If your fingers get sticky from the spirit gum, powder them. Never allow the hair to adhere sidewise, for the outer layers will not conceal this unnatural effect.

Follow the natural growth pattern of a beard of the desired style, using a lighter shade to finish off the edges. When all the hair for the length and thickness desired is in place, press it down firmly, holding it for a few seconds. If you do this to every section as the hair is applied, it will stick firmly. Now the beard is roughed in and can be

Robert Ellenstein waiting for the surgical adhesive (forehead) to dry so it will produce the wrinkles of age for his role as Albert Einstein. A latex rubber nose is also in place.

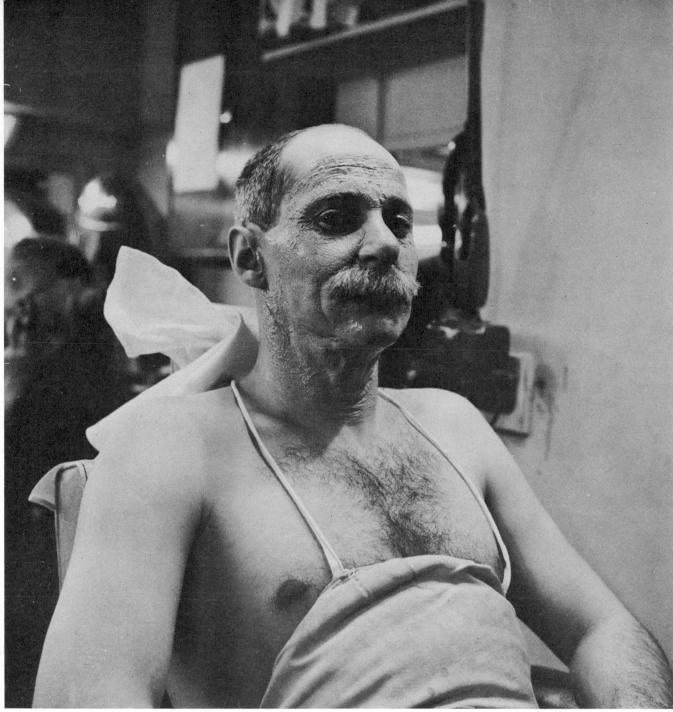

The second stage of the Einstein make-up. Old-age wrinkles on the face and neck, and the fold on the side of the nose have been produced with surgical adhesive. A cream-type foundation is used so that the highlights and shadows may be blended better. A neutral shade of powder is used on old-age make-up so that the accentuated areas will not be subdued.

combed, brushed, and trimmed like a real beard. Use tweezers to remove hairs which make the beard look untidy. After shaping the beard, apply hair spray so it will keep its shape.

MOUSTACHES AND STUBBLE

Building an artificial moustache is done in a similar manner. The upper lip is coated with the spirit gum in an outline of the desired shape. The hair is then applied a little at a time, beginning at the outer corner of the lip and working inward—most natural moustaches

have a part in the middle. Press your finger against the hairs so they will adhere firmly; then, holding the hair in place, comb it gently to remove any loose hairs. It can then be trimmed into the desired contour or style. To finish, spray it lightly with hair spray to set the hairs. Finally, shape the moustache with wax, if needed. The same method is used for the application of sideburns, bushy eyebrows, hair

fringe, and receding hairline.

An unshaven effect can be produced by either of two methods. If not much stubble is needed, smear a gray-blue or red-brown lining stick over a porous rubber sponge. The sponge is then used in a stippling motion over the foundation in the area of whisker growth. This must be done before powdering.

The second method is much more realistic and should be used

Comparing this portrait with an actual picture of Albert Einstein, one might be fooled. It is a much more painstaking feat of illusion when the make-up man starts with a young person. (All "Einstein" Photos: Paul Bailey)

if a noticeable stubble is desired, especially if close-ups are to be taken. Spirit gum is applied over a two-inch-square skin area. Then very short lengths ($^1/_8$ to $^1/_4$ inch) of hair are placed evenly on it. Pick up the hair with a moist sponge (natural) or the fingers and push it against the sticky area. Extra hairs which may fall into a clump can be brushed away. Continue the application in two-inch patches until the area is covered. When finished, if there is a harsh, sharp line at the edges, the moustache will look unnatural. Soften this edge by using

eyebrow pencil of dark or medium brown to make a blending shadow.

If the character calls for gray or white hair, use hair whitener according to directions. This may be used for either natural or artificial hair in any areas of growth.

AGE MAKE-UP

If the actor or actress is somewhat near the age you want to portray, the aging effect may be accomplished with applied make-up. For more intricate roles where a young person impersonates an old one, or a character grows in the

role from youth to old age, a latex rubber mask is used.

In applying make-up for an aged look, my method is to use surgical adhesive (Duo), painting it on the areas while the skin is held taut. Warm air from a hand hairdryer is convenient for drying the adhesive. As the facial skin relaxes, very realistic wrinkles will appear. The area is then stippled with a rubber sponge coated with foundation. This will accentuate the facial wrinkles— the first touch of old age. Repeat the taut skin procedure during powdering.

If the character is to age only slightly, I use a lighter than normal foundation to give the skin a sallow look. The cream type of foundation is best, for highlights and shadows can be blended better. The age lines noticed first are the ones running from the nostrils to the corners of the mouth, and those downward from the corners of the mouth, with an outward curve. Crow's feet around the eyes, pouches under the eyes, sagging cheeks, and flabby throat are other signs of age.

The No. 6 or No. 7 (Stein's) lining stick may be used to create shadow areas with the 1-W Pan-Stik, No. 21 Pan-Cake, or No. 22 Stein's lining stick used for highlights. Remember that a wrinkle should never appear as a sharp line, as this is most unnatural. We see wrinkle lines because the shadowed area beneath one line meets the highlighted top of the wrinkle below. It is very important that these areas are highlighted just outside the shadowed part.

Every shadow requires a highlight next to it. These must be blended with great care so there are no definite edge lines between. A firm jaw line can be broken up in the same manner as can indented temples, labial folds, and wattles under the chin. Use a neutral shade for the powdering, so the accentuated areas will not be subdued.

Very old characters need highlights on the bony structure of the cheek, jawbone, nose ridge, and frontal bone, while the natural hollows of the temples, cheeks, and eyes should be shadowed. Use make-up on these areas in combination with the procedures accentuating wrinkles. The shadows thus produced should be of a lighter tone than the accentuated lines and wrinkles.

NOSES

To make minor changes in the shape and size of a nose without casting one of latex rubber, use nose putty or Derma Wax. Small pieces of cotton or sponge rubber, cut to the desired shape and then covered with spirit gum, are also effective. Coat with flexible collodion before the application of the foundation. Highlighting and shadowing with make-up, as explained

Because Frank Scofield is a young man, his impersonation of Lincoln started with a plastic cap which blocked out his own hairline and created the high, wide forehead of Lincoln. A latex rubber nose and mole were used to create these familiar characteristics. Skillfull use of a liner stick produced the wrinkles, sunken cheeks, and circles under the eyes.

in corrective make-up, is often used to change the apparent shape of a nose.

Be sure the nose is free of grease paint before applying any nose putty. Knead a small amount of the nose putty and then apply to the nose, shaping it with the fingers from the cheek to the center and back. Do not let it spread out on the cheeks. The edges of the putty should be thin so they blend into the skin. The foundation is then applied to the entire face, including the newly shaped nose.

BURN AND WOUND SCARS

There are really three types of scars—the raised or welt scar, the indented, and the old flattened-out surface scar. A raised scar or welt can be fashioned of nose putty. In modeling such a scar, be sure that the center is thickest and that the rest tapers off gradually to blend with the skin. The top of such a scar can be highlighted by applying foundation cream. The old, flat-surfaced scar can be created with make-up by highlighting and shadowing to simulate the natural discolorations of the skin. Any scar shape should be irregular as it would be naturally.

Burn scar tissue can be made quickly and effectively by spreading spirit gum over the area, large or small, where the indication of injury is to show. Spread a good amount of cotton on the sticky gum, pressing it down firmly. Leave the cotton for 30 or 40 seconds, and then pull the bulk of it away so that only a thin film remains on the spirit gum. With a brush apply a thick layer of nonflexible collodion. Any thickness can be built up, but each layer of collodion must dry before the next is applied. The collodion should be applied quite heavily and beyond the area of cotton and spirit gum. The drying of the nonflexible collodion creates the scar tissue by puckering the skin. You can leave the finished scar the natural transparent color of the collodion, or you can color

A complete foam-rubber latex mask was modeled to Marissa Pavan's specifications for the aged-lady scenes in Hallmark's production of Shangri-La.

it with moist rouge or make a discolored effect with red and blue lining sticks.

A very thin make-up material called fishskin can be used next to the skin to prevent ether burns from the collodion. Professionally this is seldom used unless the actor has a very sensitive skin, or a scar must be created in the same place several times, such as might occur if filming sessions last for more than one take.

Do not try to peel off the collodion, especially from a man's hairy skin. The collodion can be removed very easily with acetone—which is highly flammable and should be kept in a plastic bottle and never used near open flames or burning cigarettes. Such materials used in make-up should be stored in their own special area, either in plastic bottles or in bright-red containers. As a further precaution, steel fireproof cabinets are used in our make-up department for all such materials.

Raw or bleeding wounds of almost any type, as well as dripping blood, are made with the application of a make-up product called Panchromatic Blood.

EARS AND BALD HEADS

If you want to create the impression of a cauliflower ear, bend a hairpin around behind the ear until the top of the ear is forced out from the head, at an angle. Fasten it in

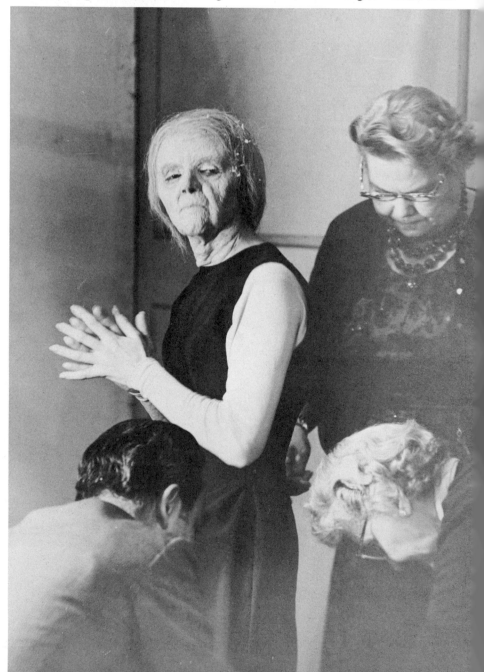

place with adhesive tape. A more natural cauliflower ear can be achieved by using nose putty on the inside of the ear, modeled so it will give a puffy appearance. The tape or putty is covered with make-up foundation before powdering. Protruding ears are often sealed back against the head with liquid adhesive. Allow the adhesive to dry before pressing the ears back.

To achieve the effect of a missing front tooth or teeth, use black tooth wax or enamel over the tooth. Since the appearance of teeth in pictures is very important, any prominent gold display or unevenly colored teeth may be improved in appearance by the use of ivory or cream tooth enamel.

The professional make-up man uses a plastic cap to achieve a bald-headed appearance or to cover the actor's natural hairline if a higher or wider forehead is needed for a character part. The cap is made on a standard hat block by applications of plastic liquid. It takes about 27 layers, with a setting period between each layer, to build up a suitable covering. After the cap is finished, it is left on the block for several days of curing. When it is ready for use, it is fastened to the head with spirit gum. If you need a partially bald head, artificial hair can be applied to the cap and trimmed.

CREATING A CHARACTER MASK

The rubber face masks, usually grotesque or fanciful, which are such favorites for Halloween and Mardi Gras are in construction about the same as those we create for various productions. The difference is that ours are custom-made for a particular character to the individual specifications of the actor playing the role. These latex rubber masks are very flexible. Since they are fitted to the form of the individual wearing them, they move easily and naturally with any gesture, motion, or expression of the actor. Latex masks have largely replaced other methods of making drastic changes in the physical appearance of an actor.

One of our most successful productions (it received a special Emmy Award for make-up) was

that of *Victoria Regina,* photographed and broadcast in color on the *Hallmark Hall of Fame.* It was a monumental undertaking for the make-up department, for we had to create convincing physical changes through a span of 60 years.

We not only went forward in time, but backward as well, for 32-year-old Julie Harris, playing the Queen, had to appear as an 18-year-old who in the course of the play ages to 78 years. It took a fantastic assortment of latex scraps, masks, and wigs to accomplish this.

In transforming the slender Miss Harris into a dowager queen, I spent a total of 360 hours designing, casting, and piecing together an intricate array of rubbery noses, eye bags, jowls, nose tips, forehead and neck pieces, and a full face mask. For the climactic Diamond Jubilee scene, in which Victoria is 78, I had to work with the actress for more than three hours, starting at six in the morning.

RESEARCH

In creating any type of mask, the first step is research. Whenever possible, we obtain photographs of real personalities or illustrations of fictional ones.

The actual production of the rubber appliance or mask starts with a face mold of the person—a life mask. This is done with impression cream, a preparation used for denture impressions. It is a powder which, mixed with water, is applied to the entire face or parts of the head and neck or hands with a brush.

It sets in a short time in a firm but flexible form. To eliminate the risk of spoilage when it is peeled from the face, the form is reinforced with a shell of plaster bandages which are soaked in water before application. The shell is then removed from the face in a perfect replica. This negative mold shows the face inside out; a positive is made by pouring a plaster of Paris mixture into the negative and letting it harden.

This positive mold or cast is a solid model on which needed changes and corrections are made

with modeling clay. We may need to build up or widen the nose, pad out the cheeks, put in bags under the eyes, create moles or other skin disfigurations. We model the new character right on the face form of the person who will recreate the personality for the screen. A constant check is made with whatever visual material is at hand so that a faithful and authentic likeness can be made. After all possible changes have been made with clay, another plaster of Paris cast is made. This produces another negative mold, but with the additional changes.

CASTING THE LATEX MASK

The next step is the casting of the latex rubber mold. The foam-rubber latex is a thick liquid rubber which must be mixed with a forming agent, a curing paste, a setting agent, and a dye. Each must be measured accurately to the gram. The dye (red, orange, or black) is added for special skin-pigmentation color. The ingredients are then put in a kitchen-type blender and thoroughly mixed.

The completed mixture is poured into the negative plaster mold. The positive plaster mold, with modeling clay removed, is pressed firmly into the negative mold, causing the latex to be forced into contact with the hollows and projections of the negative mold. The latex sets in about 15 minutes and is baked in a kiln for about four hours. The molds, at this stage, frequently weigh from 5 to 40 or more pounds.

The mask is removed from the molds after baking and at this stage resembles a Halloween rubber mask. It is often necessary to make duplicate masks if filming lasts for more than one session; masks are seldom re-used for they become soggy and dirty from contact with skin and make-up.

The mask is fitted to the actor's face and fastened with spirit gum or surgical adhesive, especially around the eyes. A special preparation of rubber-mask grease paint must be used as a foundation, for ordinary make-up would destroy the latex. The mask is then made-up as if it were ordinary skin. Powder-

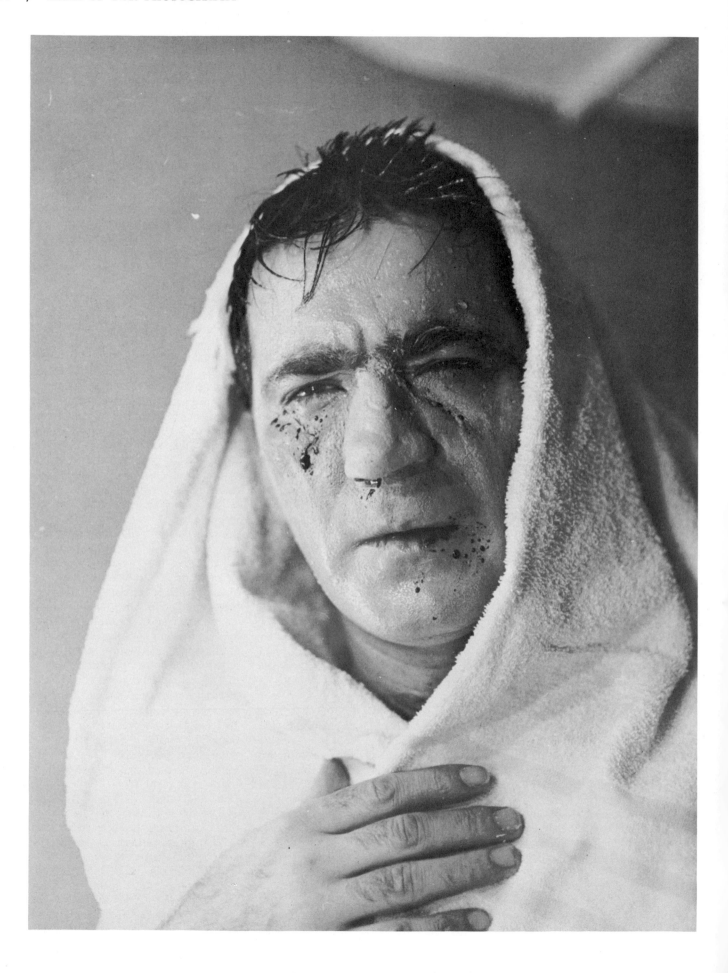

ing is heavier than normal, but shadows and highlights are applied with lines, as usual.

Any character make-up consists of more than facial changes, so masks also must be made for smaller areas. These are called appliance pieces and might be for arms, legs, backs, noses, ears, or puffy cheeks. In *The Tempest,* for instance, I made casts of Richard Burton's shoulders, arms, legs, and the top of his head for his role as Caliban. For *Cyrano de Bergerac,* it was the famous nose which was cast in four versions. In *Victoria,* the nose tip, eye bags, jowls, and wrinkled forehead were all separate pieces, cast for each age portrayed.

All modern make-up is easily removed by liberal application of cleansing cream. After working the cream in a bit, make-up can be wiped off with facial tissues. The face then should be washed thoroughly with hot water and soap. If you use the cream or grease type of foundation, it is necessary to cut it with cleansing cream. On the other hand, the pancake type of foundation comes off easily with hot soap and water.

All character effects involving the use of spirit gum, such as beards, moustaches, and scars, as well as latex rubber masks and appliances, must be removed with acetone or Deo-Base, which is easier on the skin. After removal of the character devices, the cleansing cream plus hot water and soap treatment is advisable. A mild astringent, such as witch hazel, completes the restoration. Fortunately, not many character make-ups are as tedious to remove as Victoria's—it took a full hour to peel away the aged queen so Miss Harris could emerge as herself.

Left: *Here the author takes a dose of his own treatment in making-up himself as a battered prizefighter. A rubber latex nose built up with putty, dabs of Panchromatic blood, a collodion scar, and a mixture of water and glycerine (perspiration) were the materials he used.* (Photo: Barry Kramer)

Right: *Exercising his experience in make-up and acting, the author poses in make-up consisting of a latex rubber nose, crepe-hair stubble, burnt cork, and lining-pencil smears.* (Photo: Barry Kramer)

A list of basic make-up materials follows.

MAKE-UP MATERIALS

Acetone—Solvent used for removing spirit gum, cleansing lace of toupees, wigs.

Adhesive tape—For making dressings, holding ears.

Artificial hair—Made of crepe, wool, or yak; for creating artificial beards, moustaches, sideburns, bald-head fringe, stubble.

Barber shears—For trimming crepe beards, cutting false eyelashes.

Brushes—A variety of sizes for applying lipstick, mascara, eye shadow, old-age make-up with highlights and shadows; a Chinese brush for applying spirit gum to wigs and toupees.

Burnt cork—For dirt effects on hands and face.

Blade—Single-edge type, used for sharpening eyebrow pencils.

Cleansing cream—For removal of make-up; sometimes used for perspiration effects.

Collodion—Flexible and nonflexible; a substance made by dissolving pyroxyline in a mixture of ether and alcohol. Used for creating scars and burns (nonflexible); wrinkles (flexible).

Cotton—For cleaning face; used with liquid rubbers for creating extreme old age on face and hands and with collodion for scar tissue.

Combs—Used for combing out

beards, moustaches, hair fringe.

Derma wax—For creating artificial noses, making scars, building up facial parts.

Duo—Surgical adhesive for applying false eyelashes, latex rubber appliances; used with cotton and spirit gum for old-age wrinkles.

Eyebrow pencil—For eyebrows, lining the eyes; brown eyebrow pencil sometimes used for making wrinkles in old-age make-up.

Eyelash—False lashes are used to make eyes seem larger, to augment natural eyelashes; a curler is needed for curling natural lashes.

Eye shadow—Enhances appearance of eyes.

Fishskin—Protection for skin under some types of make-up materials.

Foundation—Panstick, pancake, and liquid are three types. Used to provide a base on which the make-up is built.

Glycerine—For making artificial tears and perspiration.

Hair whitener—For graying and whitening of hair and eyebrows in old-age make-up.

Liners (Stein's)—These lining color sticks come in practically every shade and may be utilized in many ways. The reds, maroons, blues, and white are used for various clown make-up; the No. 6 and No. 7 are used for the shaded areas and wrinkles; the No. 22 stick is used for highlighted areas.

Lipstae—A product used for setting lipstick so it will not smear, especially for kissing scenes.

Lipstick—To contour and color lips.

Mascara—To enhance attractiveness of eyes, making them seem larger and more brilliant.

Nose putty—For creating artificial noses, making scars, building up facial structure.

Panchromatic blood—Product for creating artificial cuts, bruises, gunshot wounds.

Powder—Specially blended for make-up use, comes in various shades; used to set the foundation when using cream-type base, also for eliminating face shine.

Powder puff—For use in applying powder.

Rouge—Moist and dry. For highlighting cheekbones, supplying pink tinge to cheekbones for color photography.

Scalp masque—Brown and black. To touch up bald spots on male performers.

Spatula—For mixing colors, such as eye shadow.

Spirit gum—An adhesive used to fasten beards, toupees, sideburns, rubber appliances.

Sponge—Rubber sponge for stippling on rubber mask grease paint, to make old-age stipple wrinkles; fine-grain sponge is used for application of pancake foundation.

Tooth enamel—For blacking out teeth, concealing gold or discolored teeth.

Toupee tape—For anchoring down hairpieces to the bare scalp; also used for temporary adhesion of moustaches.

Witch hazel—Used as an astringent before applying make-up and after removal.

Make-Up for Black-and-White (Pan) Film

COSMETIC	PRODUCT NAME	WOMEN	MEN
FOUNDATION	Factor's Pan-Stik or Pan-Cake	#3N-6N	#6N-9N
POWDER	Stein's Neutral Shade Factor's, with Pan-Stik	Neutral	#C-3-238
ROUGE	Factor's Technicolor	Light or moist flame	Dark (optional)
EYESHADOW		Neutral, blue-gray, or grayish brown	None
LIPSTICK	Factor or Mehron	#3	None
EYEBROWS		Black, dark brown, light brown—depending on hair color	Brown

Make-Up for Color (Reversal) Film

COSMETIC	PRODUCT NAME	WOMEN	MEN
FOUNDATION	Stein's Velvet Stick	#3-C to 6-C	#6-C to 9C
POWDER	Factor's C-3-238 with Pan-Stik	#3-C-328	Same
ROUGE	Factor's Technicolor	Light or flame	Dark (optional)
EYESHADOW		Blue-gray	None
LIPSTICK	Factor or Mehron	Rose red medium Rose red light	None
EYEBROWS	Eyebrow pencil	Black, dark brown, light brown	Brown

Make-Up for Color (Negative) Film

COSMETIC	PRODUCT NAME	WOMEN	MEN
FOUNDATION	Factor's Pan-Stik	7-25B—7-25C	7-25E or F
POWDER	Factor's	C-3-238	Same
ROUGE	Factor's	Moist flame	None
EYESHADOW		#6, 8, 16	None
LIPSTICK	Factor's	#7-22	None
EYEBROWS	Eyebrow pencil	Brown	Brown

This famous action picture of the Out-Island Regatta, in the Bahamas, was made by Jarvus Darville. A fast powerboat, a keen eye for action, actors, and excitement —these are just the starting point. Most marine photographers make many exposures to get an outstanding one. (Photo: Bahama News Bureau)

MARINE PHOTOGRAPHY

John R. Whiting
Publisher, "Popular Science Monthly"; Author, "Photography Is a Language"

[Anyone who has tried to picture an exciting moment in a yacht race or to shoot a power boat in rough water will know the fascinations and trials of marine photography. Here an experienced marine photographer tells about the variety of subjects, the equipment necessary, and the special techniques involved.]

• *Also see: Telephotography.*

If you want subject matter that is dramatic, challenging, always changing, and full of opportunities—look to the sea. Skill with your eyes, a sense of timing, an ability to see all scenes as though they were in squared-off frames— this is one half of marine photog- raphy. The other half is a know- ledge of the subject matter itself.

Let us first take a panoramic view of the scope of marine pho- tography. There are the action shots of fast-sailing racing yachts —the beautiful "landscape in ac- tion" upon which photographers like the Rosenfeld family and Frank and Keith Beken of Eng- land have built reputations. But the remainder of the panorama is more difficult to describe, per- haps because the greatest marine photographs are yet to be made. Only a handful of fine pictures of the water itself have ever been made —waves, breakers, storm-lashed oceans, great tide rips. Even the places where water meets the land, described so well in Rachel Carson's book *The Edge of the Sea,* have been hardly touched by the cam- era. Will Connell photographed the rocks and pines of Point Lobos in California, Samuel Chamberlin the coast of Maine and Massa- chusetts, Aubrey Bodine the Chesa- peake's beauty. But most great harbor pictures, most close-ups of sand, breakers, seashells, have yet to be made.

The great steamships and motor ships, the effect of weather on the sea (water, sky, clouds, squalls, fog, great storms), underwater pic- torials, the occupations of the sea —the list of opportunities for the many variations in marine photog- raphy is a long one. Many cam- eras today are aimed at the small boats, the informal scenes that have come alive with the great growth of recreational boating. In this area of marine photography, there are many ideas for everyday pictures, and considerable informa- tion on how to get the most out

of available equipment.

SEEING THE PICTURE

Most people can learn to think in terms of pictures. They see the light on the water, put a mental viewfinder in front of their eyes,

Left: *The bright sun on the water and along the shore makes it easy to stop down the lens for greater depth—showing two related things in one photograph.* (Photo: Marjorie Dietz)

Below: *Foggy days are no excuse to put the camera away, although some care is needed to keep it from getting wet. Here a small dinghy sails across Montauk Harbor, with the fog so thick the shore cannot be seen. The light on the water is usually bright, even on hazy days, but sometimes it is of a low intensity.* (Photo: John R. Whiting)

and begin to plan a way to turn the scene into a picture. They are always practicing seeing—and indeed this can be fun even without a camera.

Some people are shocked at the word "imitate." But imitation is valuable in developing the ability to see photographically. Painters, writers, and photographers are not brought up in a vacuum—they all do some imitating as part of their education. In any event, seeing a good published photograph—a sunset scene in a pleasant harbor, action on the deck of a racing boat, a fisherman's happy face as he lands the big one—can be part of learning to take a good photograph. Where was the photographer standing? Did he wait for that moment of action, or did he miss something because he took too few pictures?

Color slides taken by your seagoing friends, pictures in boating, photographic, and outdoor magazines, scenes on television—all of them are rich photographically. Your enjoyment of reading will be greater if you practice reading the pictures too—and your own picture taking will also improve.

ANTICIPATE THE SHOT

Anticipating the shot can be as elaborate as planning for a particular picture, or as simple as

Above: *Looking down, yet photographing against the sun, is part of the secret of the drama of this picture taken by Roland Rose. Timing, knowing how to be in position, and a watchful eye at the viewfinder were other important ingredients.* (Photo: Bahama News Bureau)

Left: *Gala events, such as the Fourth of July, or Going Into Commission Day at many yacht clubs are celebrated by "dressing ship" with all possible flags hanging in the rigging. If the wind is blowing it can make a striking picture.* (Photo: John R. Whiting)

having your camera loaded all the time.

If you are going ashore with your family for a beach cook-out, plan to do more than toss the camera in the duffle bag. Plan to set aside 15 minutes for picture taking while the light is still good. Get someone else to build the fire, salt the steak, open the beer, watch the children. Assign yourself a quarter of an hour to roam around with your camera, looking through the viewfinder to develop a handful of ideas you hope will turn into pictures.

As for planning: it may be that you're about to sail into a harbor, to drop sail, to anchor. Ordinarily this is a busy time that makes picture taking impossible. But today you notice the wind is light, the harbor isn't crowded. You can divide your crew up to do the work (or get permission from your skipper to let everyone else work) and concentrate on pictures. You may even arrange to be dropped off in the dinghy, and thus photograph the whole operation from a distance of 50 feet.

As you go about your boating, learn to think in terms of smaller things, symbols, details—not merely the long shots of the sound or lake on Sunday afternoon. A pile of duffle on the dock, a close-up of an anchor, a newly polished winch or cleat—all these are fun to photograph, and doubly good if there is a special significance for your family.

LONG SHOTS

To the person with a sensitive soul a beautiful seascape four miles wide creates a subconscious feeling of pleasure. So he points his camera at the scene—and wonders why it is a dull picture a week later.

There is a way to capture these scenes on film. If you really have a picture eye, you see the big

wide scene with a frame around it—so you shoot it with something to help hold it together—a part of a boat in the foreground perhaps. Or, if you are in an imitative mood, you see a way to get four boats alike—each one further away, repeating the scene over and over. Or, if your strong point is foresight, you may arrange to look down on your scene from a bridge, or other appropriate vantage points.

Somewhere in between the close-up, the still life, the story telling detail, and that great wonderful long shot there is another class of pictures—medium shots of people. Perhaps no part of photography is more natural—we are all family-album snapshooters at heart. But of all the aspects of boating photography that are wide open with opportunity, really good pictures of people enjoying their happy sport are just waiting to be made.

TECHNIQUE AND EQUIPMENT

Most people seldom use the full range of even the least expensive cameras. Try using a simple flash camera on a boat at night—inside the cabin, on deck, on the dock, in the harbor. You may waste a few flashbulbs, but you'll get more good pictures than most people do on a roll of film.

Usually there is an abundance of light on the water—even on overcast days. The meaning of all this light is important. If you do not use a meter or an automatic camera, remember to stop down more than you would in most land situations. Also you can switch from fast film (often desirable ashore) to slower emulsions that give you extremely fine grain for enlarging and better control of gradation. With slower emulsions you can use color more often than you can ashore—late in the day,

Above: *This picture was not taken from the masthead, but you have the exact feeling of that almost-impossible view. Low-level airplanes, bridges, and tall parts of other boats are excellent vantage points for marine photography. On a rough day the work is hard, and even dangerous, if you try it the "masthead way." But it is possible to get aloft, to the spreaders on a medium-size boat, or much higher on a large sailboat. Ask the crew to send you up in a bosun's chair; use an extra line around your waist and around the rigging to keep you from swinging.* (Photo: Bahama News Bureau)

Right: *It takes boating skill, or a friend with a fast boat and the know-how, to be in position for action shots in sailboat races. The Rosenfeld name on a marine picture usually means it was taken from "Foto," their powerboat, and the whole family knows how to get into the right places.* (Photo: Rosenfeld / Du Pont Co.)

on very "dark" days.

There is one important caution: beware of heavy shadows on sunny days. Indeed, take advantage of the excellent modeling that is possible with softer light of cloudy days.

If you walk far enough, know your seacoast, and wait for the light and weather to be right, all you need to add is skill in framing a picture. (Photo: Minor White)

Although almost any camera equipment is usable on the water, a long focal-length objective, even a telephoto lens, is a great help. In black-and-white photography, use filters to bring out clouds and skies. If you don't know what to buy or where to start, follow this simple rule: get a medium-yellow filter, and open the lens diaphragm one stop.

In many cases, the techniques used in other photographic work are helpful. Fill-in flash for pictures of people, for example, adds a great deal. Reflectors for sun are difficult to use on boats; often light-colored decks, white sails, and the water itself do a good deal of "no extra charge" reflecting.

Many picture ideas seem to pose technical problems—reflections on the water, night shots in a harbor, interior shots in the cabin. Each one of these situations requires some ingenuity, and each can easily lead to an outstanding photograph.

1. When photographing against the sun, with reflections on the water—take plenty of exposures, and try a variety of *f*-stops.

2. From a dock or a beach, a tripod shot of a harbor is easy. It is worth the effort to get into the best position.

3. Pictures inside the cabin of a boat are more difficult than room interiors, because of the cramped quarters. Lighting problems are easily solved if you use bounce flash. Open the diaphragm two or three stops more than for the same picture with direct flash.

UNUSUAL ANGLE SHOTS

Getting into position for good boating pictures is very important—and very often difficult. Almost every good idea for being in the right place at the right time has its drawbacks.

1. Try getting someone to take you up the mast in a bosun's chair, for shots looking down on the deck. You'll have to hold on and find a way of freeing your hands to use the camera. Usually a spare hallyard is not available for this high work when a boat is under sail—but you can have yourself hoisted to the spreaders before the boat starts sailing. You can sit there, preferably with a safety rope around your waist, and work with some convenience.

2. Sitting in a dinghy or rowboat, low to the water, works well on a day when the water is smooth. It's better to have someone else managing the oars.

3. A bridge over a river or inlet, if the highway police will allow it, provides another way of looking down on boats.

The best professional marine photographers work from power boats that are capably operated by people who know where the good pictures will be—and also keep out of the way.

Finally, to return to the art of seeing the pictures and capturing them with your camera: Look for variety in long shot, medium shot, and close-up; look for light and shade, for essentially photographic qualities; look for the storytelling picture, the imaginative documentation of the sea and the rivers, and for things involving water in all its infinite and memorable variety.

Even a dramatically simple marine photograph with one center of interest has certain complexities worth noting. In this view there are two levels of action—the people on the boat and the boat against sky and water. Then there are three main elements—the dark water, the completely separate and distant sky, and the sailboat.
(Photo: R. P. Van Steenburgh)

THE INDIANAPOLIS STAR

Top Left: **OUTLINE OF DISASTER.** Fiery blaze eating through roof silhouettes firemen as they scramble for safety. Minolta Autocord with Tri-X film exposed at f/3.5 for 1/10 of a second.

Bottom Left: **SPLASH SPECTATORS.** Even the elements are insufficient to deter Indiana University students from football. Nikon F with Auto-Nikkor Zoom lens set at 250 mm. Tri-X film exposed at f/8 for 1/125 of a second. (Photo: Frank H. Fisse)

Top Center: **HOW IT WAS DONE.** Proprietor demonstrates to camera how he shot stick-up man through plate-glass window as he left store. Rolleiflex on tripod with Tri-X film exposed at f/22 for 1 second.

Top Right: **ON THE SIDELINES.** Not all spectators are paying ones at the Indianapolis "500" Mile Race. Pentax H-3 with 200mm Komura lens. Plus-X film exposed at f/8 for 1/100 of a second. (Photo: Bob Daugherty)

Bottom Right: **DEATH.** Victim where he fell after his car collided with a train. Mamiyaflex-C with Tri-X film exposed at f/22 for 1/50 of a second. (Photo: Frank H. Fisse)

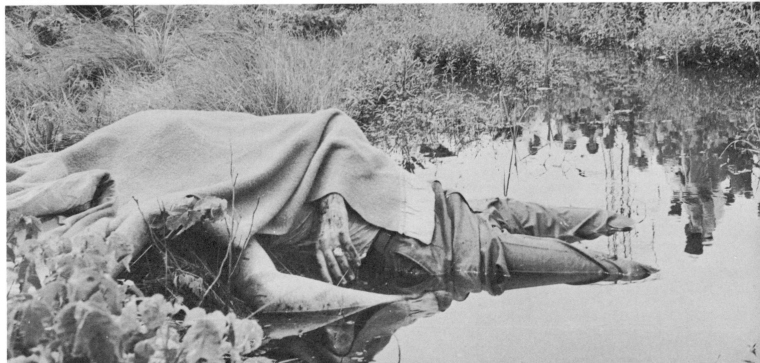

MASERS AND LASERS

The word maser is an acronym for Microwave Amplification by Stimulated Emission of Radiation. The maser itself is a solid-state or crystal device which can be shocked into emitting extreme shortwave radiation by the application of energy to the crystal; it is set into oscillation and emits a burst of energy several times as strong as the one which first excited it.

From the maser was evolved the laser (Light Amplification by Stimulated Emission of Radiation), which does for light radiation what the maser does for microwaves. In its simplest form, the laser consists of a ruby rod or crystal with polished end faces, surrounded by an extremely powerful light source such as a coiled electronic-flash or strobe-light tube. When "pumped" or pulsed with a flash of light from the surrounding tube, the crystal is set into oscillation and emits a short flash of light of considerably increased power.

The main point of the laser is not merely the increase in light output, but the fact that the emitted light is coherent—that is, it consists of waves of but a single frequency (or color); all the waves emitted are in phase, vibrating exactly in unison.

LASER USES

The primary value of the laser lies in the fact that its light is completely monochromatic—there is little or no need for chromatic correction in lens systems designed for use with it. The freedom thus gained can be used to attain higher correction in other directions; the result is a beam of light that can be focused to incredibly small dimensions. This makes it possible to project a light beam from a searchlight with almost no beam spread whatever—a laser beam, sent to the moon, was only a few feet in diameter when it arrived.

The use of the laser has been limited to some extent by the fact that its light is emitted only in short pulses. However, this is adequate for photomicrography and similar uses. Newer lasers, using materials other than ruby crystals, have been built. One recent development is the gas maser (or laser) which can operate continuously instead of in pulses. The output of the gas laser is much less than that of pulsed versions, but it promises a good deal with future development.

LASER LIMITATIONS

Because the light is coherent (monochromatic) there is no immediate prospect for lasers in projection or in color photography, both of which require sources of white (mixed or incoherent) light. In addition, most lasers emit somewhere in the infrared range, though one or two do put out visible light, usually of a deep-red color. Experiments with materials such as cadmium fluoride, doped with europium, show a strong laser action at 5893 Ångströms, which is in the border between green and red. The light would appear yellow in color. The continuous gas maser, so far, emits only in the infrared.

Other uses of lasers include a possible application to communications systems utilizing a modulated light beam to carry signals. The laser beam has a frequency range 10,000 times as large as microwave radio beams. It is theoretically possible that using a laser beam as a carrier, a single laser channel could carry all present coast-to-coast communications. In principle, a system such as the helium-neon laser could provide transmission of 10,000,000 television channels simultaneously on a single carrier. For interplanetary communications, a laser operating at 25 kilowatts could be detected at distances up to ten light years using a 200-inch telescope as a detector.

MEDICAL PHOTOGRAPHY

H. Lou Gibson, FBPA, FPSA
Eastman Kodak Company, X-ray Sales Division

[An authority on all phases of medical photography discusses its uses in case histories, diagnosis, surgery, research, visual materials, cinematography, color, and related subjects. There is a thorough coverage of equipment and photographic technique. Here an important science is explored for the still and motion-picture photographer.]

• *Also see: Copying and Close-up Photography; Dental Photography; Infrared Photography; Radiography; Science Photography; Ultraviolet Photography; Visual Teaching Aids: Production and Use.*

DIRECTLY OR INDIRECTLY, MEDICAL photography effects the life of everyone in the world, from the head of a great state to a small child in an obscure tribe serviced by a medical clinic. The teaching, dissemination, and practice of modern medicine would be impossible without one of its most potent instruments: the camera.

Medical photography challenges those who want to practice it and intrigues those who may never wish to do so. It is our aim here to discuss the field from both the applicational and the basic technical viewpoints. With this in mind, four avenues will be explored; their signposts can bear the simple words: Where, Who, What, and How. In this way, purposes, personnel, types of records, and techniques can be examined in turn.

The ring light can be detached and hooked onto an improvised bracket to form the general arrangement for simple lighting. It is also possible to alternatively run a sidelight or an ophthalmic light from the power pack of this ring light.

WHERE

The first place in which the physician experiences the specific impact of medical photography is in the classroom of the medical shool. Most medical schools in the U.S.A. and, in an accelerating fashion, all over the world have departments of photographic illustration. These are run by staffs of three or four up to about eighteen. They produce the numerous slides for the teaching staff and furnish material for static displays and student and library notebooks.

Through a photographic program, a collection of slides and prints covering numerous clinical phenomena is developed. Rare and unusual cases are naturally recorded. Such records have an important teaching function because patients with pertinent conditions are seldom accessible for observation just when needed.

Even when it is possible for physicians and students to see suitable patients, the full significance of the conditions presented for visual examination can best be understood after previous briefings illustrated by photographs. When the student knows what to look for, he grasps the significance of the actual superficial manifestations more readily. The study of photographs does not supplant clinical examination; it augments it.

Day-to-day hospital routine is frequently photographed as a matter of record. These photos can also be used for instruction, public relations, and fund-raising programs. This one illustrates a hospital's elaborate X-ray equipment in use.

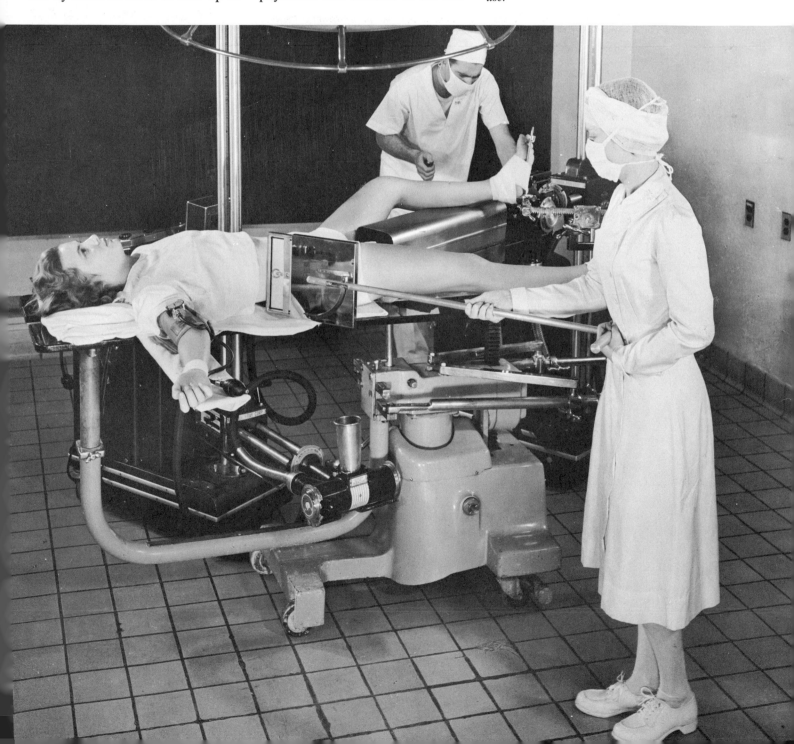

Preparing students for studying microscope slides by showing them photographs of typical microscope fields is an efficient teaching procedure. These subjects present a maze of detail to those unfamiliar with microstructures.

In medical schools, research men implement their work with the camera. It is generally accepted that funds for a research project or grant are less effective without an allocation for photography. Many research techniques make the camera the main instrument—for example, time-lapse and high-speed photog-raphy which reveal what the eye or other apparatus cannot disclose.

Photographic documentation pro-vides clear notes. There are many occasions during the course of med-ical research when a transient phase or step supplies important in-formation. Not only can photog-raphy make the writing of tedious descriptions unnecessary, but it can also provide a safeguard against the overlooking of details. A photo-graphic program is indispensable for recording the progress of research. At the climax of an experiment, the subject is usually destroyed for microscopic or other examination. In many instances, a series of photo-graphs is the sole remaining result of an investigation.

In the realm of treatment, photog-raphy makes record keeping more informative and reliable. With a heavy patient load it is impossible to remember the condition of each on previous visits, nor is there usual-ly time to enter lengthy written no-tations in the case histories. In addi-tion to serving as visual notes in such histories, photographs provide a most valuable reservoir of illustra-tion for teaching, publication, and research.

Unlike radiography or laboratory test procedures, photography can

The medical photographer must be able to make many photomicrographs because there are numerous uses for them in the medical field.

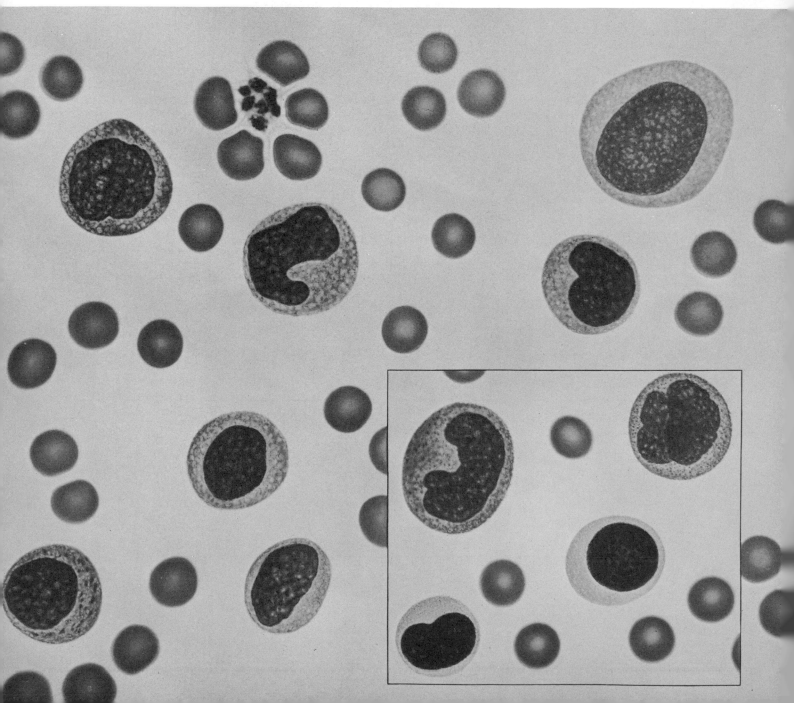

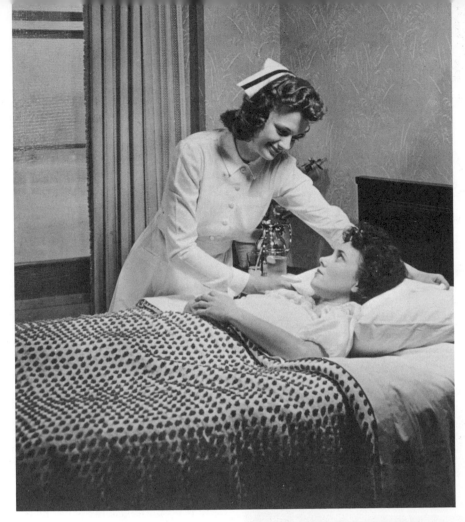

to encourage patients when their conditions manifest only slow improvement. When a patient is shown photographic evidence demonstrating progress that he cannot notice from day to day, he is stimulated to continue treatment. Sometimes pertinent photographs of other patients can be shown to sufferers in order to prepare them for improvements they can expect from the prescribed measures of treatment. Photographs have also been given to the families of patients needing home nursing, for the purpose of illustrating methods.

WHO

Under this heading, the kinds of people who make medical photographs can be presented. First there are those whose entire work

Left: *Hospital photography encompasses more than clinical and laboratory recording. This type of photograph is valuable for activities in public and donor relations.*

Below: *Laboratory photography includes exacting subjects like growths in culture dishes.*

rarely be used for diagnosis. A patient might well wonder why he is photographed—especially if he has to pay for the work. However, photographs advance medical knowledge, and the patient gains on an over-all basis since he is receiving the accumulated benefits of the many millions of medical photographs already made. His own photographs are often the subject for group discussion at a staff conference or scientific meeting. Thus his particular case is given further consultative consideration that it might not otherwise receive.

Again, as will be illustrated in the section describing types of medical photographs, many records serve as valuable working tools for the doctor in the management of a course of treatment. A large percentage of such medical photography is done by physicians in their private offices. Photographs in case records help them follow the progress of patients. (This is particularly true of the dermatologist, X-ray therapist, and ophthalmologist.)

Photographs are frequently used

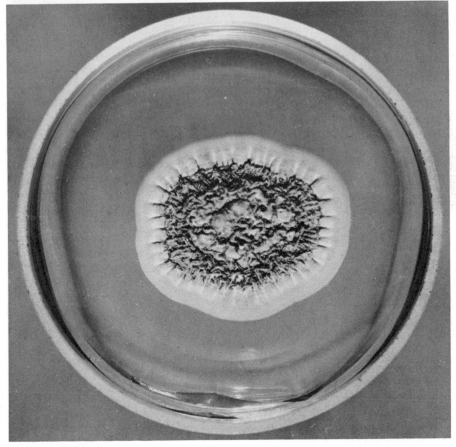

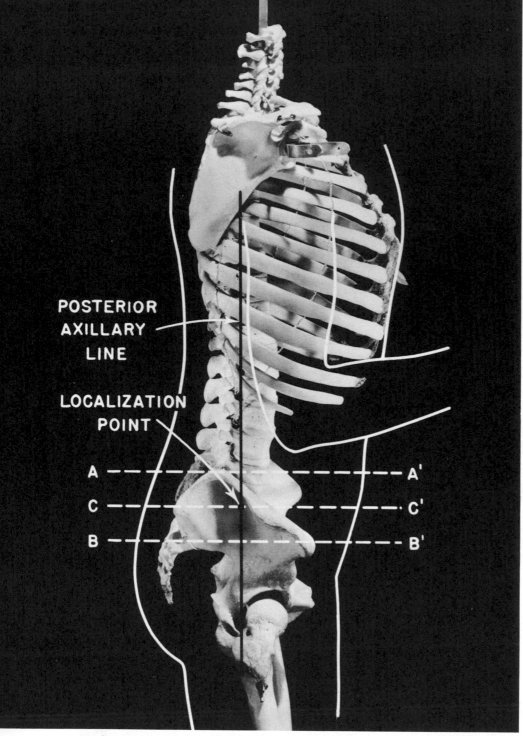

POSTERIOR
AXILLARY
LINE

LOCALIZATION
POINT

A -------- A'
C -------- C'
B -------- B'

Applications for photography are only limited by the imagination, skill, and energy of the medical photographer. This composite chart, and others like it produced by copying methods, serves for slides, wall charts, and notebook inserts.

graduates of this school. The only other such school in the U.S., conducted by the U.S. Navy, is still operating.

The second category is occupied by a certain number of commercial photographers who have taken up medical photography. They have a good basic knowledge and often become good illustrators. There is a great need for training hospital photographers in the U.S., and the best method at this time is that of apprenticeship in photographic departments already established. Apprentices may be requested to have a good grounding in general or commercial photography, because most medical photography department heads have neither teaching experience nor the time to study teaching methods. They are capable, however, of imparting the medical aspect to standard photographic technicians.

Finally, there are technicians, educators, and others who have taught themselves medical photography. They work mainly in their own offices or in hospitals where there is no photographic department.

Hospital medical photographers have varied prestige and status. They cannot all be classed as technicians because some have advanced university degrees. These are educators, because they can plan and direct efficient use of visual material, and are often considered as staff members. Their grade can be called "Professional." The next grade is "Senior Technician." They also may be university graduates, and have expert technical skill plus the ability to head an illustration department. Senior technicians all have the skill, but not always the personality or opportunity, to be the heads of departments. Finally, there is the "Junior Technician," the beginner in medical photography.

The quality of the work turned out by medical photographers varies. There is no examination or other method of evaluating the ability of a medical photographer in the United States, although there is such a facility in England. Of course, once the photographer has obtained a position his work can be evaluated, but in many cases those who use his

is medical photography. They can be called "medical photographers," although "hospital photographers" might be a better name for some of them. Many have obtained their training in a formal school of medical photography. The Rochester (N. Y.) General Hospital conducted such a school for several years after World War II. It accepted students who had been photographers in the

Armed Forces or who had other formal photographic training. These students were given 18 months of specialized education in medical photography. However, the school had to close because it could no longer find students with the proper backgrounds, and did not have facilities for intensive basic photographic training. Many of the leading medical photographers in the U.S. are

work do not always understand the requirements of quality.

The Biological Photographic Association (BPA) is composed of about 800-1000 medical and scientific photographers. They have committees working on methods for raising the standards in medical photography, and publish a quarterly journal that disseminates technical and applicational information. A similar publication in England is *Medical and Biological Illustration,* and in France, *Revue Médicale Internationale Photo Cinéma Télévision.*

WHAT

Medical photographic subjects can be broadly classified on the basis of camera techniques as: patients, gross specimens and apparatus, pho-tomicrographic slides, and radiographs or other originals for copying.

Patients

Most common in patient photography is the report illustration. It depicts the facts, saves words, and clarifies descriptions. Think how much would have to be written to describe the conditions of size, location, extent, tone, and texture shown in Figure 1.

The popular concept of medical photography is the common "before-and-after" pair. However, many serial photographs are also made to be used as "tools," such as gait records (Figure 2) and in the treatment of orthopedic problems. Many different views are made at each session. The value of such records can often be increased by indicating anatomical landmarks. For some applications the photographs can be made into photodiagrams.

It should be realized that the orthopedic department is not the only one to use the photographic tool; photography is widely employed in plastic surgery for the same purpose. Other fields, such as dermatology, radiation therapy, ophthalmology, mycology, and pathology are among the disciplines commonly adopting this aspect of medical photography.

Somatotyping is one highly specialized field in which photography is an indispensable part of the technique. Here, photogrammetric methods are employed to produce highly standard photographs from which measurements can be made. Consistent lighting is employed and a string reference grid is placed behind the subject. A rotating turntable is utilized for obtaining precisely posed front, side and back views. Many subjects can be recorded in a few

In photographs made as working tools for the plastic surgeon, perspective must be taken into account. The left-hand record was made at a subject-lens distance of 60 inches, which provides satisfactory delineation. Note the distortion (right) introduced by making a record of the same subject at 15 inches. The distance between the eyes is the same for both renditions, but foreshortening has altered the image size and appearance of the other features.

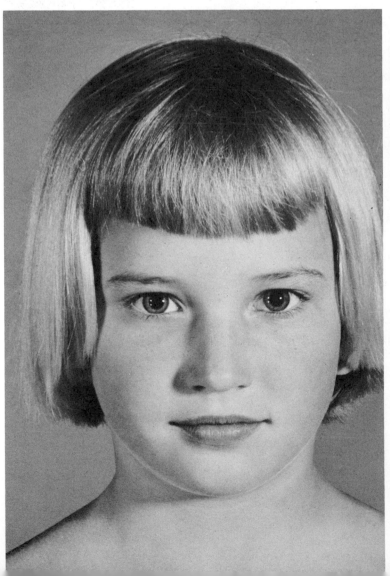
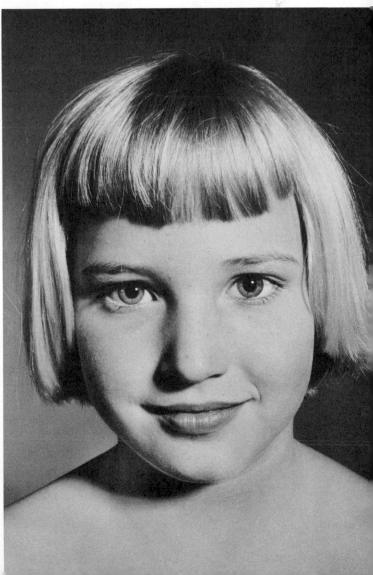

days, after which analysis of the photographs can be done over several years. This would be impractical to do from the subjects themselves. Careful standardization makes comparison of studies from all parts of the world valid. This is done, for example, in research on child development by the International Children's Center in Paris. Here the work from eight stations is corre-

lated: London, Paris, Zurich, Brussels, Stockholm, Dakar, Kampala, and Louisville.

Standardization is obviously the keynote in such photography. While this is not as crucial in other fields, the medical photographer can well

realize that consistency is practical and valuable.

Use of Infrared

Infrared rays have the property of penetrating the surface tissues further than light. Also, venous blood and various pigments present

Figure 1. *Medical photography is a graphic recording medium as well as a diagnostic tool. The left and center photographs show the limits of arm extension in an elbow condition; the right-hand photograph shows the limit to which another patient with the same condition can bend her arm.*

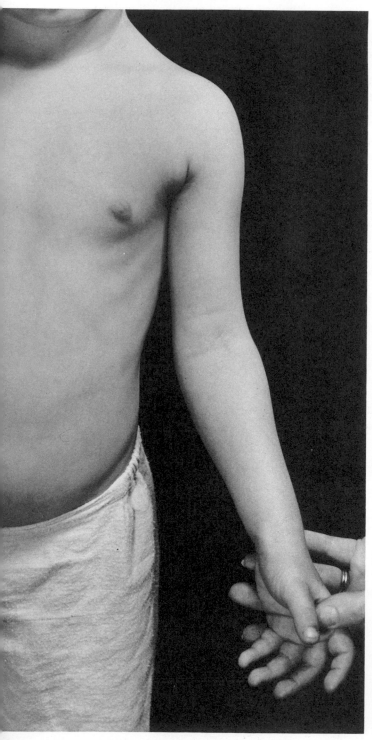
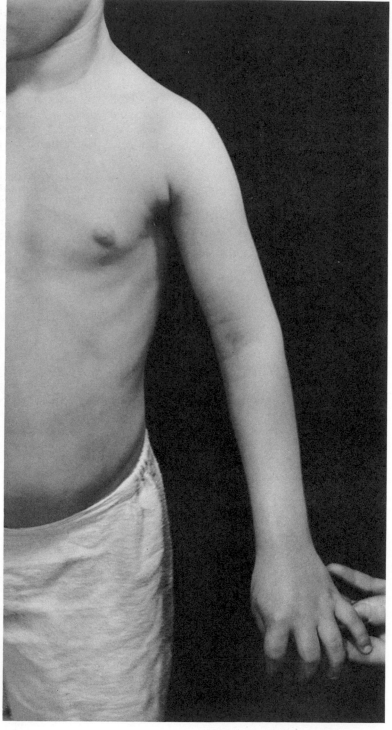

differing appearance in the pan-chromatic and infrared renditions. This has led to widespread applications in studying such conditions as varicose veins, cirrhosis of the liver, ulcers, tumors, breast cancer, corneal cataracts, and skin grafts.

Instruction

Sets of slides that teach such procedures as wearing a tracheotomy tube or colostomy bag, dressing

Right: Figure 2. *Gait studies are of great value and can be made with compact equipment in the studio.* (Photo: John A. Gaughan)

with one hand, and self-injection of insulin, can be made to accompany sound tapes of instruction. Before the patient is discharged, he and others concerned can run the set as often as necessary. The attending physician can introduce

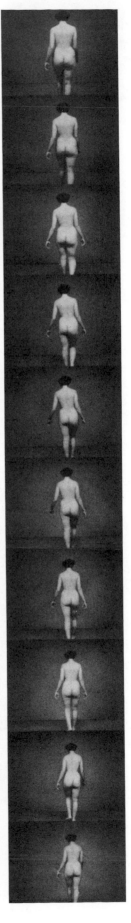

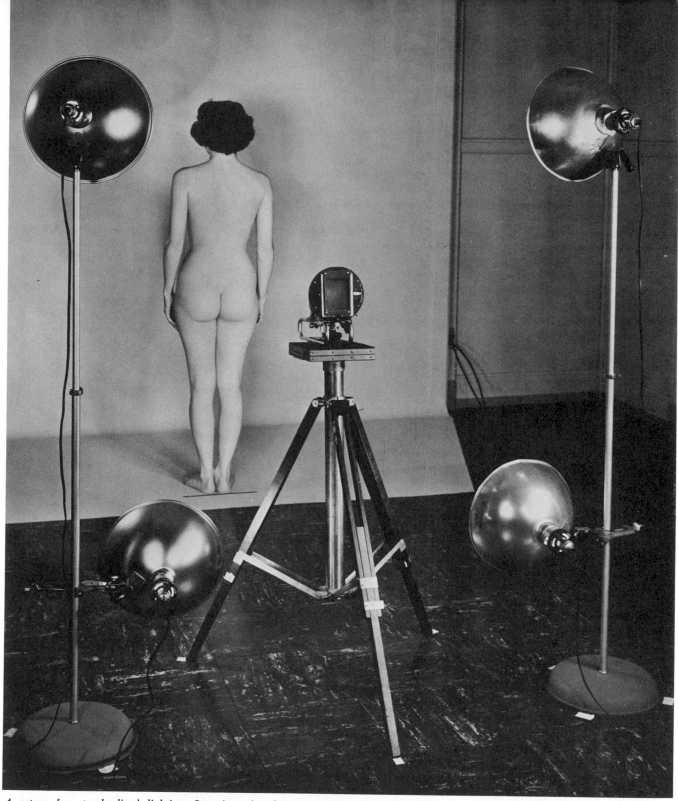

A set-up for standardized lighting. Locations for lamps, camera, and patient are marked on the floor. In this manner, those with only a little photographic experience can obtain good results. Although photoflood stand lights as shown here are practical, electronic-flash units are becoming widely used. They simplify medical photography because their exposure is instantaneous and of sufficient intensity to provide great depth of field. They cause no discomfort from heat.

the set by giving a brief "lecture" or demonstration the first time it is run.

Forensic Work

Medico-legal photography employs the techniques of patient photography and is an increasingly widespread field. When practiced by the hospital or school photographic department it affords safe- guards for the institution. Much is done outside hospital jurisdiction by photographers associated with law firms or by free lance photographers. The purpose of this type of picture is to record the condition of the patient, but it should not be looked upon as proof. It helps as evidence and aids those presenting testimony to give a clear and accurate story, but by itself can seldom be relied upon to prove anything.

This broad outline of patient photography cannot include every type. Patients are photographed in the operating room, in occupational-therapy situations, during psychiatric interviews, or while undergoing experiments such as sleep research. There are many new applications appearing each day.

Gross Specimens and Apparatus

Departments of pathology and surgery and laboratories need many photographs depicting gross surgical specimens, cultures, surgical instruments, and laboratory set-ups. This type of photography generally calls for close-up techniques. Shapes, tones, textures, and of course colors in color photography, have to be clearly shown.

A good file of gross-specimen photographs is often built up to release a large portion of the storage space occupied by the specimen museum. A few actual specimens are kept to impart such information as weight consistency, over-all morphology, and volume. A suitable gross-specimen photograph cannot supply such details, but in color particularly it has the tremendous advantage of depicting the fresh specimen.

Photography has many advantages in mycology and bacteriological studies. Obviously photographs are much safer to handle in teaching situations than the actual cultures. There are also many dish and test-tube subjects provided by precipitation and inhibition tests. Many of these are transient and self-destructive; thus photographs supply a permanent serial record.

Photomacrography

One of the challenging phases of medical photography is the making of extreme close-ups, from 1:1 to larger scales. This technique can cut across all the subject fields so far discussed. The work is done with a simple microscope arrangement—that is, one in which a lens of short focus (in itself, or made so with supplementary lenses) is used with a relatively long lens to film distance. This provides a degree of magnification. In other set-ups special photomacrographic lenses and cameras are provided which yield magnifications up to about 30×, which is near the practical limit for a simple microscope.

Photomicrography

About a quarter of the general medical photographer's work is likely to be photomicrography. This is done with the camera plus a compound microscope—one with an objective and an eyepiece. The department of pathology is the most frequent user of photomicrographs.

There is much research at present being done in normal and abnormal cell growth. Still photographs are important, but time-lapse cinephotomicrography has become indispensable in such study. An intriguing application of still photomicrography is in microsurgery.

Photomicrography requires the preparation of thin and carefully stained slides since it is more exacting than visual observation. The medical photographer should understand the preparation of microscope slides so that he can guide the laboratory technicians. He should also be familiar with various types of microscopes because phase, polarization, and interference instruments all have particular capabilities in disclosing needed information that has to be photographed.

Copying

Another large section of medical photography is concerned with the copying of the copious stream of graphs, charts, and tables used for teaching, publication, and conferences. Here too, the photographer can use his skill and ingenuity to extend the usefulness of the department by making composite illustrations.

The copying of radiographs is a challenging assignment. Slides and prints are made, the latter often calling for skillful dodging to record the long tone range of the originals.

Cinematography

The common concept of medical cinematography tends to limit it to films of surgical operations. This is only a small part of the actual and potential applications, however. Gait studies and time-lapse uses have already been mentioned. Even in the operating rooms, other procedures often have to be filmed.

There are many medical and hospital activities that have to be depicted in motion. For example, short "motion slides" on topics like bed-making and isolation techniques are invaluable in teaching. Their projection can be interspersed with that of the slides presented in the same session. When a more formal movie presentation constitutes the main visual feature, still slides can often be advantageously employed for briefing. For example, slides can be made of all the important steps in a surgical operation. The rate of their presentation can be adapted to the audience. Some can be repeated. Discussions of certain steps can be as thorough as needed. Then, to illustrate the tempo and flow of the action, the motion picture can be shown. Its information will thus be more readily and thoroughly grasped.

Magnetic sound stripping fills many of the special needs in the medical field. Sound tracks gauged to various audiences can be prepared for duplicate footage edited to suit such audiences. Also, there are many international conferences and functions, so that it is often necessary to prepare tracks in various languages.

HOW

Many phases of camera handling, film selection, processing, and printing are thoroughly examined in this encyclopedia. Accordingly, only those procedures of specific importance for medical photography will be dealt with here. They will be discussed from the standpoints of positioning and arranging, lighting, and setting up.

Positioning

At first glance the requirements of positioning would seen obvious—the subject is located at the camera with the area of interest toward the lens. Patients, when possible, and specimens should be placed in the "anatomical position," with the top at the upper part of the photograph. Such is the essence. Yet a simple clarity test should be made before the shutter is opened. The photographer, or the physician ordering the picture, should study the viewfinder or groundglass and imagine himself to be a typical member of the group for whom the photograph is intended. The physician, particularly, has a clear mental image of the subject. He should make sure the groundglass image coincides.

Allied to positioning is selection. It is good practice to standardize on three photographic views—full-length, half-length and close-up. Of course, there will be times when ultraclose-ups and other extra views will be needed. Such standardization is a necessity for records, but it will also help to orient viewers when routine photographs are shown, particularly when a series of related cases are presented.

The same principle can be extended to all types of medical records. It is customary and helpful to include an object of known size, such as a ruler, with a gross specimen.

When a close-up is made of a patient, some easily recognized anatomic landmark or contour should be included. However, this rule should not be forced to the point of losing detail through the inclusion of too much in the field. Sometimes another photograph can provide orientation. On others a phrase in the caption or title like "lesion on the shoulder" or an adjective like "axillary," will suffice. The best criterion is the purpose of the photograph. Is it a record of a shoulder with a lesion, or a lesion on a shoulder?

For certain subjects, several views of the same area are needed. Another useful feature is the inclusion of a normal subject for comparison with the abnormal (Figure 3).

While considering orientation, it should be pointed out that plain backgrounds are necessary. Cluttered or uneven surroundings for the subject are distracting and confuse the outline of the patient or specimen. The physician often attaches a roller windowshade to the ceiling of his office or examining room to provide a background.

A string grid provides a fiducial background for the somatotype. There are occasions when a grid would be useful in certain presentations of routine subjects made for other purposes. The grid is scratched into a clean sheet of acetate plastic. It is placed in contact with the paper during printing (obviously it must be kept free of dust).

Clothes are sometimes part of the surroundings. They should be removed from a region somewhat larger than the area of interest. Otherwise distracting, untidy, or even obscuring details mar the clar-

Figure 3. *The most graphic way to describe an anomaly with a photograph is to include a normal subject in the field for comparison.*

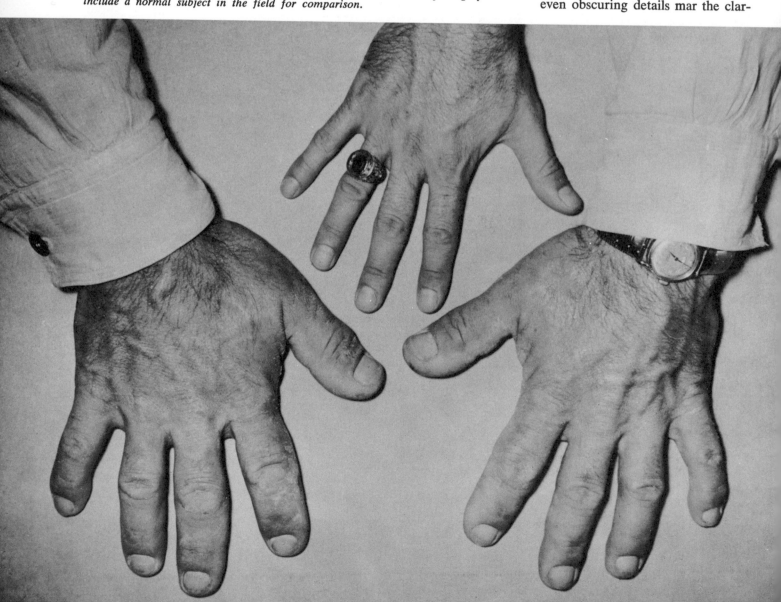

ity of the photograph. Of course, unnecessary nudity is purposeless. Therefore, the field should be confined to a pertinent area; the rest of the body, clothed or unclothed, should be omitted whenever possible.

Color laboratories are permitted to return processed slides depicting pudendal regions when the films are sent in with a note on a physician's or hospital's stationery or with an official form. The medical purposes of the photographs should be indicated.

A final point of positioning relates to perspective. Foreshortening occurs when the lens is relatively close to any subject. This is of no consequence for the majority of medical subjects. In certain fields fixed subject-to-lens distances must be adopted to minimize distortion and hold the residual amount constant. About 12 feet is suitable in orthopedic projects. Plastic and orthodontic surgeons have arrived at 5 feet as a good camera distance for records of the face.

Lighting

Equally important as positioning is lighting. Lighting can be considered to be of three types: optimum, standardized, and simple.

Optimum Lighting

Good medical photographic lighting is not hard to learn. There are two basic factors to understand: 1) don't overlight; and 2) gauge the visual effect.

First, a single main light is directed onto the subject and moved up and down, sideways, and around until the desired features of the condition appear strongly delineated to the eye in approximately the camera location. Almost always the main light should be higher than the camera.

When lighting a subject of full-figure size, the light will tend to fall off toward the bottom of the picture. A light at about camera height and at the same angle as the first light should be directed toward the knees. Its intensity should be studied and the distance varied until the general skin tones appear to be uniform from top to bottom. This can be checked with an exposure meter. When arranging this auxiliary main

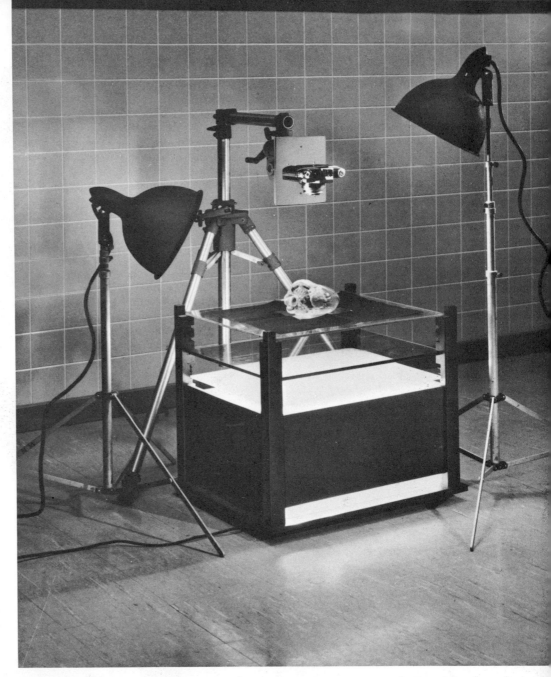

A standardized set-up for the photography of gross specimens. The "reflectors" are blackened so that they do not enlarge the source, though they protect the eyes of the photographer from glare.

light, particular attention should be paid to the highlights and shadows produced by the first light—they should not be destroyed by the second.

Once the main lighting has been established, it is merely necessary to reduce the shadow contrast a little with fill lighting, so that the film can accommodate the tone range. The shadows, though, should remain clearly evident. An exposure meter can be used to measure the skin brightness produced by main and fill lights separately. The ratio should be approximately 3:1 for

black-and-white photography and 2:1 for color. These values should be increased somewhat when there are no pronounced shadows or dark tones involved, because the body can be considered a light-toned subject with a short brightness range.

The fill light should be as close to the camera axis as possible, about two thirds the distance of the main light. Obviously, it should not be as intense as the main light, or the shadows would be "killed." Here too, it may be necessary, in photographing the full figure, to utilize two fill lights. They should both be

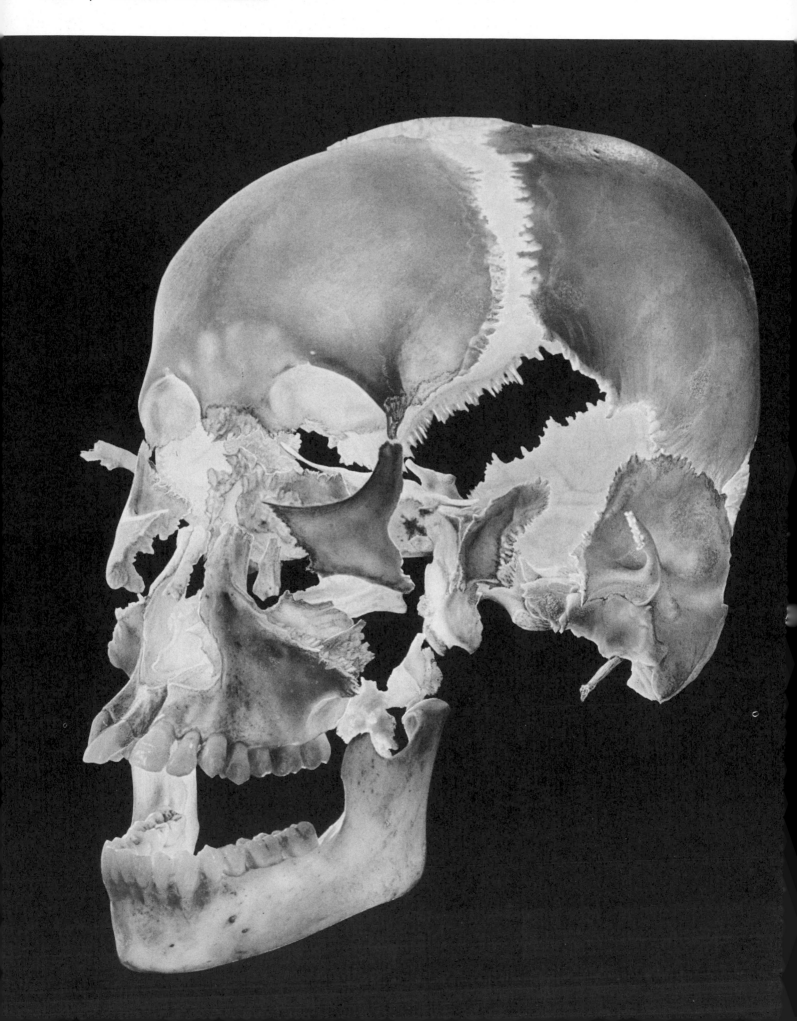

Figure 4. *This Beauchene skull is disarticulated and the pieces separated on wires. The wires have been removed on a master print with spotting colors, and the result copied for a forceful effect. The dramatic lighting was obtained by methods outlined in the text. The main light here was a small hidden flashlight bulb.*

at camera height, one with its center beam directed to the shoulders the other aimed at the knees.

The fill lighting should come from the main-light side of the camera when the subject is fairly flat, such as a shoulder or male chest, or when moderate roundness is to be slightly emphasized, or texture plus shape

recorded. It should be on the opposite side when prominent roundness produces a wide shadow, or when asymmetry is to be shown with a fairly even lateral intensity.

Lighting for infrared photography is a special "mapping" technique. The negative contrast is quite high; hence the lighting contrast has to be very low, or veins and other detail will be lost in the edge shadows. Four lights are usually required. These should be placed equidistantly on both sides of the camera. The lighting angle between the subject-lens axis and the lighting axes should be 55 degrees

horizontally and about 45 degrees vertically. Electronic-flash units provide sufficient infrared to make them very useful for infrared photography.

Since optimum lighting has to be observed as it is arranged, a point about electronic-flash units should be noted. They are available in studio types with modeling lights. Such an advantageous feature adds to the practicality they afford in offering heat-free illumination and

Diagram indicating how to construct a light box for the photography of gross specimens. This enables the background to be transilluminated to eliminate shadows.

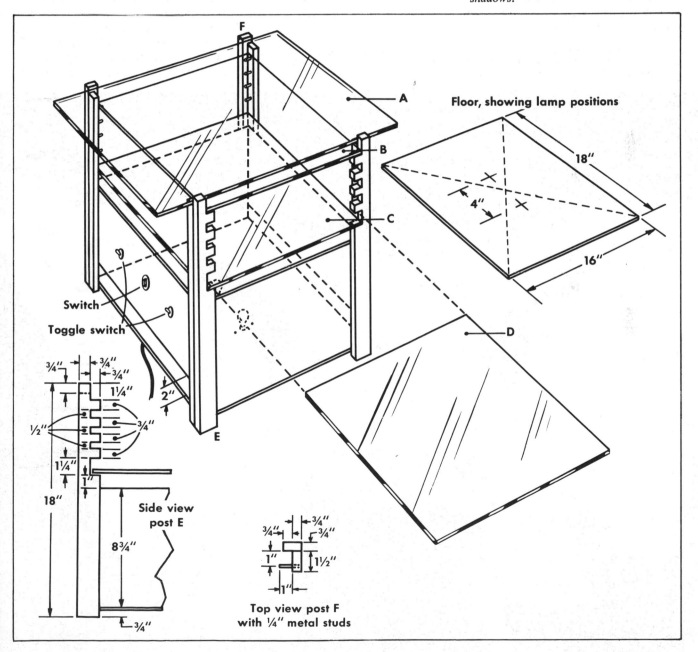

motion-free images of fidgety adults and active children.

Background lights complete an optimum set-up. In order to use them, about six feet of space behind the patient is required. A light-toned background provides good tone control; a pastel aquamarine is fine for color photography. For most work skin tones look normal when the background is half as bright as the average flesh tones. A light-toned background requires twice the meter reading than the patient yields. It tends to produce or emphasize swarthiness. A very dark background emphasizes body outlines, and makes the skin appear pale. A dark background is the easiest on which to control shadows.

The above principles apply equally to the lighting of apparatus and gross specimens. For the latter, the main-light angle sometimes has to be quite great in order to supply sufficient crosslighting for revealing texture. Also, only one main light is needed, though sometimes two fill lights can be employed when visual appraisal so indicates. The anatomical top of the specimen should be located toward the main lamp.

There is a special problem in lighting gross specimens: catchlight control. Some workers try to eliminate them with polarizing screens or by immersing the specimen in saline solution. However, specimens are almost always glistening wet and need tiny catchlights to create this

effect. A catchlight is a specular reflection of the light source and its reflector; the bigger the source, the bigger the catchlight.

To provide a small source, 500-watt, medium-screw base, clear-bulb projection lamps are utilized. The reflectors are blackened inside so that they do not contribute to the effective size of the source. They protect the eyes of the photographer from the discomfort of glare and reduce illumination to the camera and lens.

A light box that transilluminates the background for gross specimens has come into widespread use. This provides the shadowless background that is so desirable for the clear delineation of specimens.

Sometimes accent lighting is needed in photographing specimens, and this is particularly true in delin-

Figure 5. *Laboratory specimens, especially bones, present challenging lighting assignments. Here, small mirrors were employed to shine a little extra illumination onto the higher ridges to yield an optimum three-dimensional effect.*

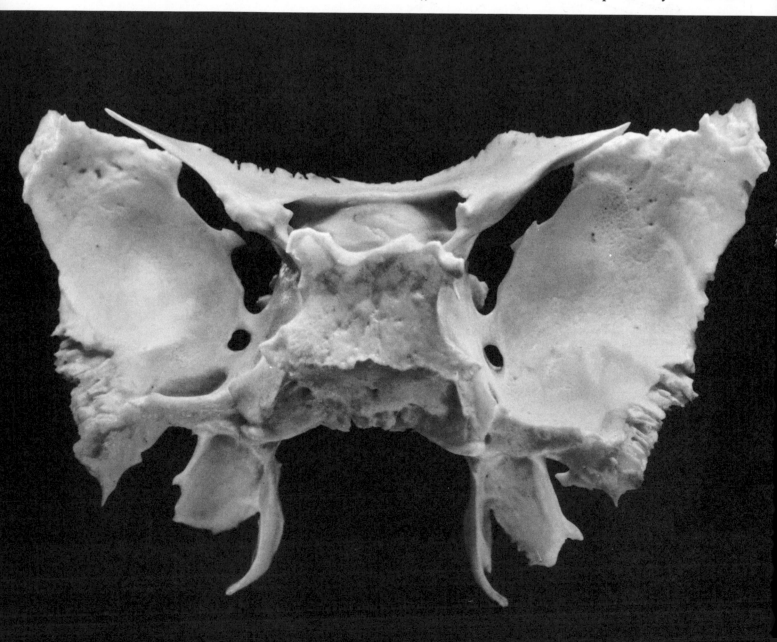

eating the intricacies of bones. Because the latter do not have tone contrasts, the delineation has to be done with light. Small mirrors may be used to accent the highest ridges of the specimen. This gives a true appearance of depth to the concave portions and "raises" the prominences. It is well to remember that the rim of a depression is light in tone. (See Figure 5.)

Even a bare bulb is proportionately like a diffuse floodlight for an average photomacrographic gross specimen. In order to produce a sufficiently "raw" light for a tiny specimen, a small microscope spotlight can be employed. The author obtains even more sharply defined lighting with the minute bare filament of the clear-glass bulbs intended for such spotlights. Fill-in light can be obtained for either means with mirrors, bits of foil, or blotters. Optimum lighting is nearly always required in photomacrography. Care should be taken to keep photomacrographic tissues and gross specimens moist with normal saline solution when making experiments.

Standardized Lighting

Patients, and gross specimens to some extent, lend themselves to standardized lighting set-ups. The lighting is fixed to provide a median between flat and contrasty effects. It has the advantages of being free from bad lighting errors and having a standard exposure. The method is the first one for beginners to adopt when learning medical photography, especially if the patient's condition is such that he would be wearied by the extended period needed in experimenting with optimum lighting. And even when the subject is in a condition to spend some time in the photographic department, a preliminary standardized record provides "insurance." The lights are arranged for a 3:1 or a 1:1 ratio (Figure 5).

Simple Lighting

Because it uses photoflash or electronic-flash illumination, the simple system is practically confined to patient photography. The term "simple" refers to the basic arrangement of hand-held portable camera and light. The complexity of the camera has no bearing on the basic

A sheet of heavy plate glass holds a book page flat for copying. The opposite page can be retained with a rubberband. It should be covered with black paper to prevent reflections on the page from being copied.

method. A range of cameras can be employed, from an elementary close-up camera with the absolute minimum of adjustments, to the advanced reflex with its precise and versatile components. (See Figure 5.)

The term "simple" also refers to the speed and convenience of operation. There will be many occasions when the expert will find the system valuable. For those with no photographic background at all, the system ensures successful efforts. This is especially true for close-up work, which requires considerable skill when other methods are

employed. Experienced photographers can be of service in arranging some cameras and viewfinding components for the beginner, and can calibrate the exposures required. The user can then make the few adjustments needed by rote. The three-view procedure is particularly compatible with the simple system.

The simple system is particularly useful in making a series of photographs depicting steps in a manual operation or large-scale procedures such as exercises following polio. It is also practical in working with children, whose attention

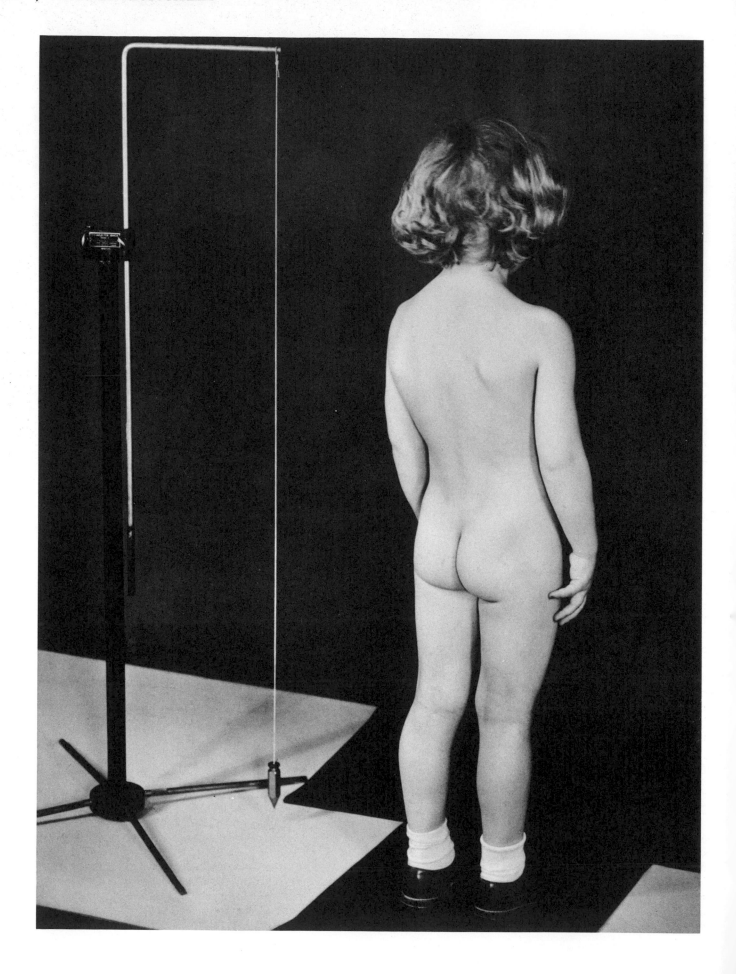

span is often not long enough for more formal photography.

Background shadows can be controlled; they cannot be eliminated. When a light-toned background is needed, the subject should be placed as close to it as possible. The shadow then becomes an unobstrusive thin line. If dark backgrounds are permissible, the subject can be brought out from the surface about four feet. The flash then does not carry to the background, so that both it and the shadow are recorded dark. For close-ups, the simple system provides "architectural" lighting. Skin texture is well shown.

After some experience has been gained with a simple set-up, versatility can be increased with easy variations. Sometimes the flash holder can be temporarily detached and held by hand on the side of the camera opposite its bracket.

Even though the lamp is close to the subject-lens axis in the simple system, the method has limitations in lighting body cavities, such as the mouth. Axial lighting is needed to illuminate the entire oral cavity, for example. This is obtained with a ring light, which is a circular electronic-flash tube designed for fitting around the lens.

Axial lighting is not suited to flat or shiny surfaces, nor for the rendition of texture. Reflector-type sidelights to accommodate such subjects, and also an ophthalmic light for photographing eyes, are available to augment ring lights.

Set-ups

Basic arrangements for patient and gross-specimen photography have already been presented in connection with lighting. There are some other items useful in photographing various subjects.

For patients. One helpful device in photographing patients is the plumb bob. It is important to ensure that the subject be depicted in an upright position in the photograph, so one

Figure 6. A plumb bob is necessary in posture studies. It can be on a portable stand, or when such work is routine, hung from the ceiling at the edge of the studio background. One edge of the print is made parallel to the vertical string. When grids are superimposed over the body, one of the upright lines is aligned with the string.

of the vertical edges can be printed parallel to the image of the plumb line, which need not appear in the picture (Figure 6).

Another indispensable unit is a posing chair. Many patients cannot stand for long; in fact some have to be photographed in a wheelchair. But if they can get up, a posing chair that obstructs the body as little as possible should be employed.

For those patients who cannot sit in a wheelchair, or for those who have to be photographed prone or supine, a high tripod and a low stepladder become the best expedient.

When much orthopedic photography is to be done, a large mirror can be suspended over an examination table at a 45-degree angle. The camera is fixed to a high tripod or stepladder, because the bottom edge of the mirror should not be much lower than six and a half feet, and because the camera has to be at a height that allows it to be directed horizontally toward the center of the mirror. A front-surface mirror is desirable but not absolutely necessary.

One further suggestion will be helpful here in connection with making still photographs in the operating room. Telephoto or long-focus lenses are generally necessary so that small fields can be recorded at safe and uncrowded working distances. With a view-type camera focal lengths of 12 or 14 inches are desirable. When a 35 mm camera is employed, a 135mm or 200mm lens is preferable. However, a set-up should be selected that can be focused for close range, so that fields of about 6×9 inches can be accommodated.

For copying. As in all photography, the type of camera used in copying will depend on the kind of photograph wanted. Quite often a camera with a groundglass back is employed for copying because of the ease in scaling. Horizontal or vertical copying stands can be utilized.

A point of lighting is worth considering, especially when glossy photographs form part of a composite original. The usual copying angle is given as 45 degrees, and this does theoretically preclude lamp glare along the lens axis. However, such a

rule fails to take the reflector into account. Sometimes the sector of the reflector nearer the lens axis produces a partially specular reflection at the edges of a shiny original. Therefore a safer procedure is to arrange the lamps so that an angle of 45 degrees exists between the camera-side rims of the reflectors and the lens axis.

The basic requirements for copying radiographs are an X-ray illuminator or a light box in addition to the copying stand. An intermediate transparency is first made. This is treated like a negative and printed to a facsimile slide or a paper print. A film with a long scale has to be used for the intermediate. Sometimes dodging or masking methods help to hold significant detail in light and dark areas.

It is also practical and convenient to copy radiographs with Kodachrome II film. In order to record the long density radiographic scale, exposure should be gauged to just yield density in the lightest areas. Then, to prevent the darkest areas from blocking up, a flashing exposure is made by double-exposure methods of the illuminator alone; it should be about $1/90$ of the basic exposure for the light areas.

For cinematography. Fundamentally, the procedures for making medical and research films are the same as those for other, nonmedical fields, depending on the application, of course. In the operating room the camera usually has to be mounted on a high stand. A platform step is required for the photographer.

Measures must be taken to fill the vital need for maintaining aseptic conditions. The photographer has to be masked and gowned and the stand draped with sterile sheets. Nothing loose on camera or lights can be tolerated, because of the danger of contaminating the surgical field with dropped equipment.

It is imperative, when inflammable anesthetic atmospheres are present, to use explosion-proof equipment for lighting. There is much work being done with the operating-room lights themselves because of their safety. However, they have a blue-green heat-absorbing glass in them. In some of the older models of operating-room light fixtures this adds a color tinge to color photographs. In many later types a heat-absorbing glass suitable for color photography has been incorporated.

The main operating light is designed to cover only the surgical field. When it is utilized alone in photographing some of the preparatory steps of an operation, the larger field required is not adequately lighted. This results in dark bluish corners in the motion-picture frame. The relatively large areas of such preliminary scenes are better lighted with portable operating stand lights.

The main light provides a logical lighting because it represents the lighting under which the procedures are actually viewed. The results are somewhat flat on the screen, however, because the three-dimensional effect of actually viewing the operation is missing. It can be satisfactorily introduced during filming by means of an operating stand light. This is placed opposite the camera on the other side of the table at about the same lighting angle as the camera angle. It is less intense than the main light, yet it furnishes some backlighted relief and highlights for adequate modeling. When making exposure-meter readings in such a set-up, the meter should be held on the side of the extra light in order to avoid picking up a misleading specular glare.

For surgical 16 mm filming at least two lenses should be available —of 25mm and 63mm focal length. It is also helpful to have on hand a 150mm objective, so that extreme close-ups can be recorded at a practical distance.

PHOTOGRAPHIC MATERIALS

Films, papers, and processing are covered elsewhere in this encyclopedia, but some considerations of their selection which apply specifically to medical photography should be made here. Medical subjects can be classified into three main categories according to the type of black-and-white rendition required.

Panchromatic renditions. These can be made with or without correction filters as the occasion demands. Contrast filters may be useful with contrasty films in copying some colored originals. The following clinical and gross-specimen subjects usually call for panchromatic photography: posture studies; marked morphologic anomalies and those complicated with colored or pigmented areas; isolated dark red areas with lighter reds or other light tones also in the field; surgical fields.

Orthochromatic renditions. These can be obtained with orthochromatic emulsions or with panchromatic films used in conjunction with a Kodak Wratten No. 66 filter (factor 2). One of the chief purposes of such a rendition is to provide slight emphasis for faint red rashes. Subjects can be summarized as follows: light red areas within normal tones; dark red areas which constitute the major part of the field (treated as "dark subjects" in calculating exposures); slight morphologic anomalies not complicated with colored areas.

Infrared renditions. Some of the subjects that record darker in infrared photography than they appear to the eye or which can be recorded in the absence of a visual manifestation are: venous blood showing through thin, normal, or moderately thickened superficial veins; details under a thickened cornea; hemangiomas; ulcer beds with marked venous stasis; tissue patterns under some superficial dermatological lesions; tattoo marks; certain pigmentations. Some that do not yield an enhanced infrared rendition should be noted: venous blood in thickened and tortuous varicose veins; veins under a layer of superficial fat; certain pigmentations.

Contrary to what is sometimes assumed, infrared photography cannot record details more than about one quarter inch below the skin. And it certainly cannot photograph internal organs through the several inches of external tissues.

The general set-up for surgical photography is illustrated here. Not all arrangements need be as elaborate, and they are discussed in the text. (Photo: Billy Burke Productions)

There is one more aspect of film selection that does not fall into the above categories. It is the copying of continuous-tone photographs alone or as parts of composite illustrations. Here Kodak Gravure Copy film is extremely valuable because it retains good gradations in the light tones that are often present in medical photographs.

COLOR PHOTOGRAPHY

The 35 mm color slide is in widespread use because of its light weight and compact size. The advanced op-

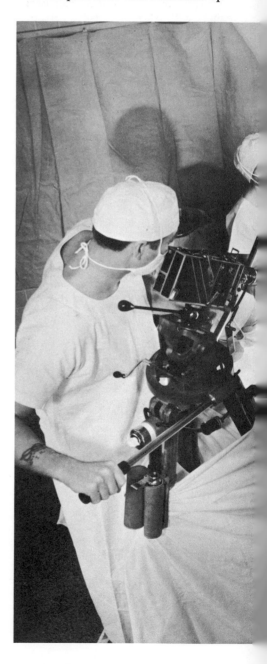

tical design of 35 mm projectors provides superior screen images. This, coupled with the quality and versatility of 35 mm cameras, makes the slide program a practical one. It is particularly convenient for the small clinic or the physician's office because a darkroom for loading and processing photographs is not needed. The slides are invaluable for those who travel to lecture.

Projectors with magazines allow lectures to be organized and filed readily as well as projected correctly. The slides can be programmed in synchronization with a sound track in a tape recorder for applications already discussed.

Large color transparencies are often used for $3^1/_4 \times 4$-inch slides for teaching lectures when they match older slides and when the lecture does not have to be given outside the institution. Display transparencies serve a number of uses. These large photographs can be duplicated to provide 2×2-inch slides.

Color photography is particularly valuable in teaching because those unfamiliar with the subject do not have to pause and try to make a mental translation from a black-and-white image. In fact, until they have had experience, this cannot be done. Of couse, when morphology alone is involved, color is not needed.

One point about color photography should not be overlooked— though requiring somewhat more care in exposure, it is much easier than black-and-white photography. It takes considerable lighting experience and other skills to make a good black-and-white rendition of colors. Yet color photography records them in a satisfactory fashion without the prerequisite of an extensive photographic background.

Furthermore, since color is so useful in presenting the subject quickly and unequivocally, it has major advantages in the teaching field. For example, a subject such as the characteristic "golden glow" of the skin seen in children who have accidentally swallowed ant poison could not be demonstrated in black-and-white at all. On the other hand, most common lesions have a characteristic red color, so that quite often a black-and-white rendition that delineates their distribution does present most of the information needed—it is, of course, necessary to visualize the darker areas as a pinkish red. Nevertheless, purplish lesions photograph to about the same black-and-white tones as red ones, and some confusion could arise here that could be avoided by color photography.

While it is practical to make all slides in color, it is not always economically feasible to plan the use of color engravings for publication, or large color prints or transparencies for display. Hence it is worthwhile to consider the purposes for which color is most valuable and make every effort to use it effectively. Efficiency demands that the unnecessary use of color be avoided. Color in medical publications should be employed only to impart vital information, and never just to serve as decoration.

As a general recommendation subjects should be photographed in color when color is the main feature of the condition, or when no darkroom is available, or when the subject material is not going to be used

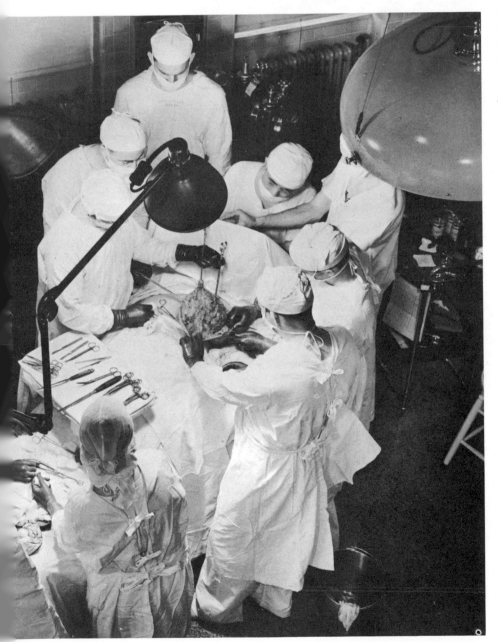

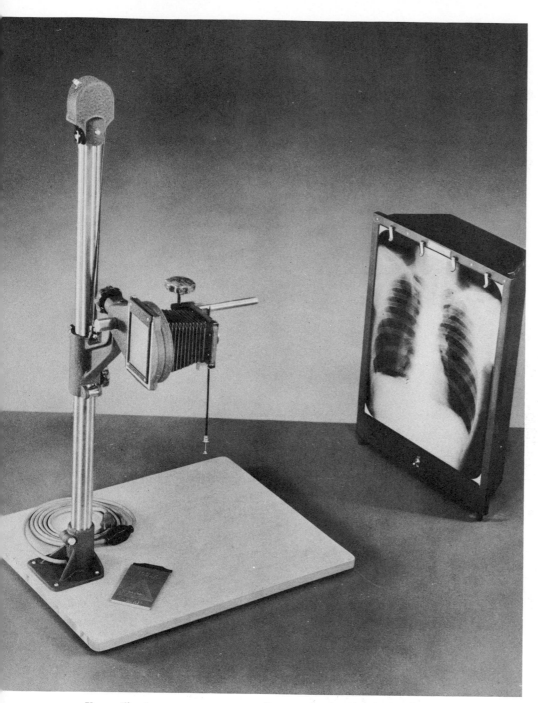

X-ray illuminators serve to transilluminate radiographs for copying. When much of this work is done a special light box can be constructed. It should allow for the introduction of paddles or masks behind the opal glass for dodging.

changes in color, but not absolute color values. No color photographic process can yet be expected to reproduce colors with photometric accuracy because of well-known practical tolerances in emulsion balance, exposure, and processing. Accordingly, when a research project involves color comparisons, color photographs can be employed only as useful guides. To gain the maximum benefits from them, a reproducible photographic set-up must be arranged so that the appearance of the subjects can be recorded consistently. The same care should be taken in positioning, framing, and lighting of the patients, animals, or tissues.

For studying changes in subjects and for checking the associated photographic records, standard conditions of illumination must be employed. Prints should be appraised under the same lighting used to examine the subjects. Color transparencies, on the other hand, should be viewed on a suitable transparency illuminator and checked against the subjects placed under the standard lighting established for making comparisons.

As new photographs of a subject are made, they should be evaluated as soon as possible. If the results do not show quite the right color balance, adjustments can be made during reprinting. The renditions of direct transparencies can be adjusted, when necessary, by binding color-compensating filters with them.

When the color differences are too slight to be accommodated by any color photographic process, it is often useful to make colored plastic, latex, or wax standards as guides. This is also necessary when the subject changes appearance during the period required for processing color photographs.

When a project spans several months, a year, or more, special procedures might be helpful. Enough film of the same emulsion number should be obtained at the beginning to serve for the entire program. It should be stored in a deep freezer and returned there after exposure. A roll should be taken out for defrosting at least 24 hours before it is placed in the

for black-and-white publication. If subjects available only in color form are needed for black-and-white publication, black-and-white prints can be made.

There are projects in which the routine records are required in color and it is impossible to foresee those which will be needed in black-and-white. This gives practicality to color-negative programs. Such

records can be used for miniature or larger slides, display transparencies and black-and-white prints— all from the master file negative.

For investigations involving long-term changes in patients, a consideration often arises as to whether color photographs can provide color standards for comparison. Color photography can be effective in demonstrating subtle variations or camera. When the records have all been made, the entire run should be sent to a reliable laboratory for processing at once. A letter requesting this service should be sent to the laboratory, and a carbon copy enclosed with the film.

Sometimes, for a particularly exacting project involving much time and expense, an additional safeguard may be deemed advisable. Two cameras can be utilized to provide two sets of records. The two batches of film can then be sent in at separate times to guard against loss in the mails or processing contingencies. The duplicate slides could be used in lectures or as extra records for study.

The author expresses appreciation to Charles C. Thomas, Publisher, for courtesy in the use of several illustrations from Gibson, H. Lou, 1960, *The Photography of Patients.*

□

MERCURY

Mercury is a silver-colored metal which has a number of peculiar characteristics. Probably the most outstanding of these is its low melting point—in the vicinity of 38F below zero (or −37C). Thus mercury is molten at all normal temperatures and is usually found in the liquid state. When cooled below -38 F by immersion in liquid air or dry ice, it becomes a hard, solid metal like any other; it is heavier than lead for an equal cubic content.

In its liquid form, mercury has a very high surface tension. Spilt mercury, instead of spreading out and wetting other surfaces, forms a convex surface—the familiar spheres which are practically impossible to pick up since any attempt to grasp them breaks them up into smaller spheres which scatter in all directions. It was this elusive property that gave mercury its early name, "quicksilver."

EFFECTS OF MERCURY

Mercury has a strong fogging effect on photographic emulsions. Even a small quantity scattered in a darkroom, possibly from a broken thermometer, can do considerable damage. Since it is nearly impossible to gather up, one can only wait for it to evaporate, which it does very slowly.

In photography, mercury was first used as a developer in the daguerreotype process. Here, the exposed plate was placed in a dark box over a heated plate of mercury, whose vapors were deposited preferentially on the exposed silver bromide, forming an image in silver-mercury amalgam. This image was usually treated with a gold toner to render it more permanent.

Mercuric chloride, sometimes known as bichloride of mercury, is used in photography as a silver-image bleach, especially in intensification processes. The silver image is bleached in a combination of mercuric chloride and potassium bromide, or sometimes mercuric chloride alone with some acid as activator. The bleached image is redeveloped in an ordinary developer. The final image consists of the original silver, plus a certain amount of mercury which accounts for its intensification. These images are not very permanent.

Another unusual use of mercury is to be found in the photography of odors. A dish of mercury is used, either alone or with a thin surface layer of a very fine white powder such as lycopodium. A drop of the perfume is floated on the pool of mercury, and the whole left undisturbed until such time as a pattern forms on the surface which appears to correspond with the type of odorous fragrant vapors emitted from the perfume. This pattern can be photographed in a strong crosslight.

Mercury has a number of other uses. Special electrical switches are made with a small glass tube of mercury and contacts sealed inside. When the tube is tilted, the mercury pool runs down to the contacts and makes the circuit; tilting in the opposite direction breaks it. Any possible spark is contained within the sealed tube. This is especially valuable for heavy inductive load, which would cause enough sparking to seriously damage other types of contact; it is also valuable for sparkless switches, as in the photographic equipment used in operating rooms or coal mines.

MERCURY-VAPOR LIGHTING

While scientists had known for years that an electrical discharge through vapor of mercury produced an eerie blue-green light, it was only in 1901 that Peter Cooper-Hewitt devised a practical light source based on this principle. For some years photographers made extensive use of the Cooper-Hewitt light. While not excessively bright to the eye, its output was entirely in the range to which color-blind and ortho films were sensitive, and it produced an effect on these films far out of proportion to the visual appearance of the light.

The early Cooper-Hewitt lights were simply long tubes with a small bulb at one end filled with a small pool of liquid mercury. An extra contact was built in the side of the bulb to start it. To start the tube, it was necessary to tilt it until the pool of mercury made contact with the starting electrode, forming an arc which vaporized some of the mercury and filled the long straight part of the tube with vapor.

When this was accomplished, the current was transferred from the starting contact to the electrode at the far end of the tube, and a long glow discharge was maintained through the length of the tube, while the heat of the discharge maintained enough mercury in the vapor state to keep the lamp lit. Mercury vapor which condensed to liquid on the upper part of the tube merely ran back into the pool and replenished it.

Crude as this method was, it was undeniably efficient, and movie studios covered whole ceilings with such lamps. Neighborhood photographers gave up their skylights and installed mercury-vapor lights. Only with the coming of panchromatic film did their use finally begin to diminish.

Advanced types of mercury-vapor lamps are still used for copying, producing photostats, and similar purposes in which color rendition is unimportant. The newer lamps can run on either a-c or d-c and are started electronically. Essentially they are still the long straight tubes emitting the same weird blue light. They can, of course, be made in other shapes—the M-shaped tube is used in enlargers as a highly actinic and well-diffused source of light, especially for large negatives.

HIGH-PRESSURE MERCURY LAMPS

All of the Cooper-Hewitt lamps are of the low-pressure type. The tube is pumped out to a vacuum before the mercury is poured in; the glow discharge will not take place if there is any air in the tube. The major disadvantage of the low-pressure mercury lamp is that its light consists of a few narrow bands of ultraviolet, blue, and green— a discontinuous spectrum containing no red.

As the pressure in a mercury lamp increases, however, a continuous spectrum begins to appear over the individual mercury lines. If the pressure is raised sufficiently, a snow-white light is emitted, still strong in blue and ultraviolet, but having an essentially continuous spectrum.

Such high-pressure mercury lamps obtain their pressures by small size and high-power loading; no air is present. When first turned on, the pressure is low and the light dim. As the lamp heats up, the pressure increases and the light gets brighter and brighter until the lamp reaches operating temperature.

Such lamps have a number of uses. If made in a quartz housing, (Hanovia lamps), the ultraviolet output is very large, and they are used for small sunlamps and, in larger sizes, for industrial sources of ultraviolet. The GE H-4 lamp is somewhat similar, but its quartz-mercury tube is enclosed in a larger glass housing which absorbs the far ultraviolet; it transmits enough near ultraviolet to be used for a sunlamp which will tan but not burn.

These lamps require special transformers for operation; they cannot simply be plugged into a socket. For home use, there is one mercury-vapor lamp in which the high-pressure tube is enclosed in a mushroom-shaped glass housing, like a reflector floodlamp. The housing also contains special resistors, and the whole thing can be screwed into any 115-volt light socket. They are sold mainly for use as suntan bulbs, but could be used for photographic purposes, such as contact printing on P.O.P. proofing stock, blueprinting, or illuminating a copy stand.

These lamps have exceedingly high light outputs in proportion to their size and current drain. The most remarkable of all the high-pressure mercury lamps is the special capillary lamp designed for high-speed microfilm printers and similar uses. This lamp is hardly bigger than a cigarette, yet it consumes 1000 watts and emits many times more light than any other 1000-watt source. The tiny tube must be enclosed within a larger glass tube; water is kept flowing through the space between the two tubes for cooling purposes, otherwise the lamp would rapidly overheat and destroy itself.

FLUORESCENT LAMPS

Fluorescent lamps are actually mercury-vapor lamps which contain a very small amount of mercury. The mercury collects in droplets on the walls when the lamp is cold. To start the common type of fluorescent lamp, a small filament is provided at each end of the tube which, when heated, vaporizes the mercury. When the mercury is properly vaporized, a small switch called a "starter" transfers the current to the ends of the tube. A glow discharge will then extend through the tube, just as in the other forms of vapor lamp.

The small amount of mercury in the tube results in a predominantly ultraviolet emission, with very little visible light. The inside of the tube itself is lined with a phosphor, a chemical that glows visibly when irradiated with ultraviolet. All the useful light in the fluorescent lamp comes from the glowing phosphor.

By proper choice of chemicals for the phosphors, the tube can be made to emit a cold blue-white light, a warmer white, or various colors, including blue, green, and red. Some colors are produced by making the lamp itself of colored glass, or by combining colored glass with a color-emitting phosphor.

For ultraviolet experiments, the so-called "black-light" bulb consists merely of the fluorescent tube without its phosphor. It is lined or coated instead with a filter dye which blocks off all visible light but passes the ultraviolet freely. These "black-light" lamps are used for ultraviolet photography, fluorescence experiments, advertising displays, reading fluorescent ink marks in laundries, and many other purposes. *Also see: Fluorography; Lighting Sources for Color.*

METALPHOTO

Metalphoto is a sensitized aluminum sheet used for imprinting instrument panels, nameplates, and similar items by photography. Unlike an ordinary photographic material, the sensitive silver halides do not lie on the surface, but within the pores of an anodized layer on the aluminum sheet. After processing, this layer is sealed by a simple heating process, making it almost completely scratchproof and impervious to damage.

The emulsion on Metalphoto is of contact speed and gives very high contrast. It is intended principally for line work, and high contrast negatives produce the best results. Continuous tone reproduction is also possible. Negatives can be made for engraving or offset by using a litho-type film and developing a litho-negative developer. The negative should look almost like a stencil with clear, transparent lines and completely opaque background or vice versa.

Because of the material's low speed and inherent blue-sensitivity, any paper safelight may be used. Exposure, developing, and fixing must be done under the safelight; subsequent washing and heat-sealing, in normal room light.

EXPOSING THE PLATE

Metalphoto is exposed by contact in the usual form of contact printer. Since the plate is considerably stiffer than printing paper, take particular care to secure good contact with the negative. The light should be strong enough to secure full exposure in 30 seconds or less. Due to the material's reciprocity characteristic, longer exposures under weaker light may not produce a full black.

For the sharpest image, contact printing should be done in a vacuum frame. With an arc light, this frame will produce positives of over-all uniform sharpness.

Plates can be made by enlargement if the lamphouse illumination is increased enough to give sufficient exposure. Use a photoflood lamp in the enlarger, or step up the brightness of the existing lamp with a Colortran or similar converter. In either case, the exposure must be kept within a maximum range of 30 to 45 seconds.

Double-coated Metalphoto is available for use where double-sided plates are needed. While exposing one side, protect the back of the plate with a sheet of the interleaving paper in which the plates were originally packed. This prevents abrasion marks caused by contact with the pressure back of the printing frame.

PROCESSING THE PLATE

Develop, just like a paper print. In addition to the developer supplied by the manufacturer (Metalphoto Developer DM-44), the plates will process well in Kodak D-19.

Developing time in the DM-44, developer is three to eight minutes. Allow an extra minute or two leeway if the image does not appear dark enough. However, over-development may cause a fogged background. Develop one plate at a time to avoid scratching.

After development, the plate should be rinsed under a faucet or placed in a conventional acetic acid shortstop. The plates should then be fixed in the usual acid hardening fixing bath, followed by washing in running water for about two minutes.

At this stage, the image is brown-black or dark sepia. To secure the full black image, tone the image in a gold-thiocyanate toner, which can be bought as Metalphoto Image Toner or be made up to the following formula:

Hot water (125 F or 52 C)
     24 ounces   750.0 cc
Ammonium thiocyanate
     3½ ounces   105.0 grams
Gold chloride 1% solution*
     2 ounces   60.0 cc
Add distilled water to make
     32 ounces   1.0 liter
* A one gram (15-grain) tube of gold chloride dissolved in 100 cc (3¼ ounces) of water.

Toning takes from one to five minutes, depending on the age of the toner solution. A fresh solution may bleach the image slightly so as a precaution let the toner stand overnight before use. The bleaching action can also be stopped by adding approximately 100 cc of exhausted toner to the fresh solution.

Toning must be done in glass or porcelain trays, not in any form of metal or porcelain-on-steel. Do not use stainless steel hangers for handling plates in the toner.

Be careful not to overtone, since the image may turn blue or bleach out. After toning, rinse plates in running water.

SEALING THE PLATES

At this stage, the image is permanent but still somewhat easy to damage. The image must now be sealed within the pores of the anodized coating of the plate. There are a number of ways of doing this, depending on just how hard a coating is desired. Immersing the plate in boiling water for 30 minutes is the simplest method. The water must be pure, either distilled or deionized, since impurities will cause the image to bleach or mottle. After sealing, the image is permanent and the plates may by dried. If necessary they can be polished without damage to the image.

There are various techniques of treating the anodized surface of the plates to color them, to make them fluorescent, or to produce multicolored effects. Instruction in all these variations, as well as in other methods of sealing plates are available from the manufacturer, Metalphoto Corp., 18531 S. Miles Rd., Cleveland 28, Ohio.

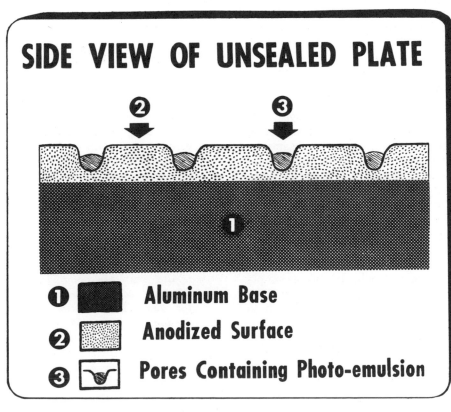

Printed from a Metalphoto plate that itself has been photographically printed and developed, then made permanent.

METRIC SYSTEM

The metric system is used universally as a system of weights and measures for scientific purposes. The basic unit in the system is the meter, which, when the metric system was first introduced in France was originally defined as $^1/_{10,000,000}$ of the distance from the earth's pole to the equator. Since this is not a very convenient standard for reference, a "standard meter" was made in the form of a metal bar and is now kept in Paris. Duplicates of this bar exist elsewhere, and each carries with it a record stating by what amount the succeeding bars differ from the length of the first meter bar.

What confuses some people is the relation between the inch and the meter, that is, 1 meter = 39.37 inches, and this latter figure looks formidable to handle. But when working with the metric system, no such conversion is ever necessary. All units in the metric system relate to each other by multiples of 10, making the system easier to use than one in which, for instance, 12 inches make 1 foot, or 5280 feet equal 1 mile. In the metric system, large distances are measured in kilometers, (1 km = 1000 meters) which offers no difficulty in calculation.

MULTIPLICATION AND DIVISION

The meter is multiplied and divided by 10, thus:

1000 meters = 1 kilometer (km)
100 meters = 1 hektometer
10 meters = 1 dekameter
$^1/_{10}$ meter = 1 decimeter
$^1/_{100}$ meter = 1 centimeter (cm)
$^1/_{1000}$ meter = 1 millimeter (mm)

There is an even smaller unit, used in scientific work, which is $^1/_{1,000,000}$ of a meter and is called a micron; its abbreviation is the Greek letter μ (mu).

This relationship is followed throughout the system, and the forenames are always the same. For example, the unit of liquid measure is the liter, and the unit of weight is the gram. Each can be multiplied and subdivided:

1000 liters = 1 kiloliter
100 liters = 1 hectoliter
10 liters = 1 dekaliter
$^1/_{10}$ liter = 1 deciliter
$^1/_{100}$ liter = 1 centiliter
$^1/_{1000}$ liter = 1 milliliter

The liter is a very convenient unit (it is slightly larger than a quart) and the various multiples and sub-multiples are seldom used. Large volumes are generally measured in liters and small ones in milliliters (sometimes, but not accurately, called "cubic centimeters").

The same relationship applies to grams:

1000 grams = 1 kilogram
100 grams = 1 hectogram
10 grams = 1 dekagram
$^1/_{10}$ gram = 1 decigram
$^1/_{100}$ gram = 1 centigram
$^1/_{1000}$ gram = 1 milligram

The gram is a very small unit (about $^1/_{30}$ of an ounce), so most of its subdivisions are seldom used. The kilogram is generally used in commerce; it is approximately 2.2 pounds. The metric ton (1000 kg) about equals the avoirdupois long ton (2240 pounds) and is used for measuring large quantities. For scientific work, the gram and the milligram are the only units employed to any extent.

Since the system is decimal, it is often just as convenient to use decimal notation rather than the intermediate multiples and submultiples, which may be confusing. Thus, rather than 1 decigram, it is usual to find the same amount written as 0.1 gram.

The same applies to lengths. On engineering drawings, measurements are not usually given in decimeters or centimeters, but simply in millimeters. Thus a length of 55 centimeters is usually written as 550.0 and understood to mean millimeters. The decimal point and zero following it are omitted unless the drawing requires high precision. On an ordinary drawing, then, the above dimension would be given simply as 550, and the mechanic making the part would understand it to mean millimeters.

Photographers should use the metric system whenever possible. It will, for one thing, eliminate all questions, when using formulas from abroad, as to what amount is actually meant. For instance, an American quart is 32 ounces, a British quart is 40 ounces; other similar discrepancies run through the two systems. But a gram is always a gram, a meter is always a meter, and a liter is always a liter.

If you are fitting out a darkroom for the first time, buy a metric balance and a set of gram weights; they are easier to use since they are calculated in multiples of 10. Avoirdupois ounces contain 437½ grains, and it is difficult to handle $^1/_8$ of an ounce that way, for example.

Use metric liquid measure. It is as easy to make a liter of developer as a quart, and much simpler to subdivide, especially into small parts. How many minims in a fluid dram, and how many fluid drams in an ounce? It is easier to use milliliters (or cubic centimeters), which run 1000 to the liter.

Use the Centigrade thermometer, You will normally develop at 20 C, which is about 68 F. The scale on the Centigrade thermometer is better spaced and easier to read. On a Centigrade thermometer, 0 is freezing (water), room temperature is about 20, and water boils at 100 degrees.

MICRO- AND MACROCINEMATOGRAPHY

HENRY ROGER
Rolab Photo-Science Laboratories, Sandy Hook, Conn.
[The author of this article is a pioneer in the field of micro- and macrocinematography. Both techniques are discussed here in detail. Subjects covered include applications, necessary equipment and accessories, illumination, focusing, heat absorption, exposure, and time-lapse work.]
• Also see: Microphotography Glossary; Microcinematography for Time Lapse; Microreproduction.

MICROMOTION PICTURES ARE MOTION pictures of relatively small objects which are enlarged on the negative film strip and further enlarged by projection upon a screen. The degree of enlargement on the negative ranges from actual size or a few diameters (two to three times the original size) to about one thousand diameters which is considered to be the limit of optical magnification.

In this country the technique is also known as motion photomicrography, cinemicroscopy, or microcinematography. Microphotography and microfilming refer to the reverse process, the reduction on negative film of relatively large objects (engineers' drawings, books, documents, checks) so that they can be filed in limited space.

The purpose of micromotion pictures is to record on motion-picture film the appearance and action of small objects as seen through a magnifying lens or a microscope. Micromotion pictures may thus become interesting and valuable parts of documentary or educational films. In this connection the system of microdemonstration on closed circuit TV has recently been devised —the television camera is mounted over a microscope and shows the microscopic field on the television screen.

Micromotion pictures are a valuable research aid in the study of microscopic phenomena in various branches of the natural sciences (biology, medicine, chemistry, physics, technology). Here the camera is an automatic recorder of phenomena taking place under the microscope.

Since the microscopic action is often too fast (or too slow) for the eye to follow, slow-motion and time-lapse techniques are employed in photographing these events.

Another important research function of micromotion pictures is to increase the visibility of the photographed micro-organisms by increasing contrast values. For example, a living-tissue cell has such delicate structure that its parts are often difficult to distinguish, especially at high magnification. (Unfortunately, stains used in histology to bring out differentiations and details cannot be employed.) But correctly chosen contrast filters and film emulsions will raise the contrast values to such a degree that the delicate structures become clearly visible on the screen.

Rolab microscopy laboratory with microcinema apparatus.

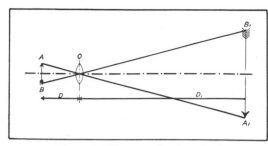

Figure 1. *Diagram showing the formation of an enlarged image.*

MACRO- AND MICROMOTION PICTURES

Often a distinction is made between macro- and micromotion pictures, or macro- and microphotography. (Editor's Note: Some confusion of terms may arise from the similarity of these names. Macrocinematography and microcinematography are the motion-picture versions of photomacrography and photomicrography. Microphotography, on the other hand, refers to a process of making small-copy negatives of large objects.)

Macro refers to the photography of small, solid, opaque objects relatively low (under 20 ×) magnifications. Macrophotography like ordinary photography uses incident illumination, light thrown upon the surface of the object at suitable angles.

Micro refers to photography which requires the use of microscopes, to the photography of microscopic objects at medium and high magnifications. Because most objects in this group are transparent, they must be illuminated by transmitted light. The photographer usually uses a single light source in combination with either single condensing lenses or compound condensing systems (substage condensers) depending upon the rate of magnification. Darkfield microscopy and metallography fit into this definition, as does similar work which uses vertical illuminators (opaque illuminators).

Micromotion pictures are based on the same optical principles as microprojection or photomicrography. The photographer must have a thorough knowledge of microscopic optics, experience in preparing the material to be photographed, and experience in ordinary motion-picture technique.

Any positive lens will magnify the object. In Figure 1, *O* represents a lens, *AB* the object, and *A'B'* the reversed image of the object *AB* as it would appear on a screen or the groundglass of a camera.

Note that the object is closer than the image to the lens. In order to take a magnified photograph, the distance from object to objective must be shorter than the distance from objective to image. Size of object equals size of image when the distance from object to objective is twice the focal length. The closer the object to the objective, the higher is the magnification until a point is reached at which an image is no longer formed. The location of this point depends upon the focal length of the objective used.

LOW-POWER MOTION PICTURES

Practically any of the objectives available for motion-picture photography could be used for low-power (macro) motion pictures, provided the camera is equipped with an extension device to move the objective forward. Depending upon the magnification desired, the extension may range from a fraction of an inch to several feet.

The objective for a given subject is facilitated by the following rules prevailing in ordinary close-up portrait photography. In photographing the head of a person, an objective with a relatively long focal length would be chosen in order to avoid distortions of perspective. For example, if a portrait were taken with too short a focal length, the eyes would be in focus while the nose would be too large; the ear, being further away from the objective, would appear too small in proportion. At the same time, both nose and ear might be out of focus because of the limited depth of field. Therefore, as a general rule a relatively long focal length is used for close-up photography.

The higher the magnification desired, the shorter the focal length of the objective. As the focal length decreases, the distance between object and objective also decreases until we reach a limit beyond which we cannot use ordinary objectives. This limit is about ten diameters on the negative. Further magnification requires a more complicated technique, to be discussed later.

As mentioned before, most objectives regularly supplied with motion-picture cameras—those of 25, 35, 50, 63, 75, and 100 mm focal length—may be used for low-power macromotion pictures. Symmetrical objectives serve a double purpose; they can be screwed apart and the front lens, which has a longer focal length than the combination, used separately. The unsymmetrical objectives such as Tessars must be reversed so that the rear lens faces the object. This is quite logical when one considers that the objective's normal use, the formation of a reduced image of a large object,

A high magnification photograph of a human ovum, left, and a single human spermatozoa, right.

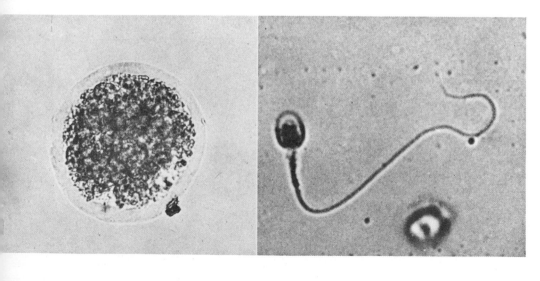

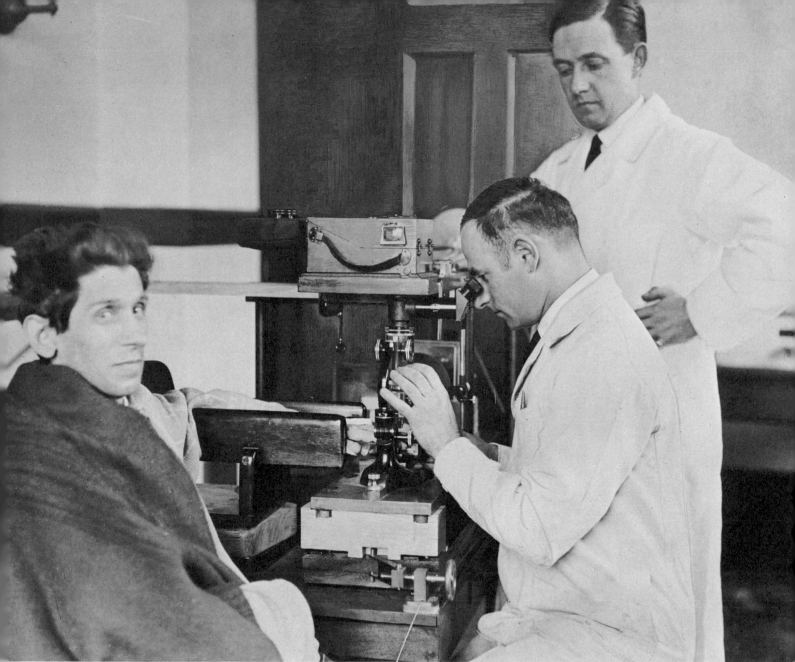

Figure 2. *Taking motion pictures of the blood circulation of a man. Special apparatus designed by the author.*

is also reversed.

Some camera manufacturers mount their objectives in oversize barrels. Part of the barrel acts as or is part of a sunshade. If this sunshade cannot be removed and prevents the object from being moved as close to the objective as is often necessary for macro work, the objective must either be used in the reversed position, or dismounted from its barrel and used in a special adapter with extension piece.

APPLICATIONS OF MICRO WORK

Medicine. Several years ago the author gave a micromotion-picture demonstration before a large group of scientists. The chairman of the meeting in his introduction said that he has never seen a more dramatic film than that which the audience was about to witness. The film showed what goes on inside the body, how tissue cells and blood cells actually behave. The growth of normal and malignant tissue could actually be seen, and it was also possible to study the behavior of single cells, mitotic cell division, phagocytosis, and the action of various agents upon cells.

An undulating membrane, surrounding white blood corpuscles and used by them to detect foreign bodies in the blood stream, was discovered by means of this motion picture. This phenomenon falsified the theory that white blood cells "sense" foreign bodies some distance away.

A great deal of work has been done on blood circulation, first in animals and later in man (Figure 2). The latter required the development of a new technique, since only reflected light could be used. The fold of the finger nail was selected as the best place to study the blood flow through capillaries. The surface of the skin was rendered optically homogeneous by an application of cedar wood oil, thus disturbing reflections were eliminated using polarized light. By using a specially constructed d-c arc lamp, the photographer obtained ten to twenty

16 mm TIME-LAPSE MOTION PICTURE CORRELATION TABLE

RATE OF EXPOSURE	SINGLE PICTURE TAKEN EVERY — Minute	Second	ACCELERATION AT PROJECTION SPEEDS — 16 f/sec	24 f/sec	10 / 400 Hrs	Min	Sec	20 / 800 Hrs	Min	Sec	50 / 2000 Hrs	Min	Sec	60 / 2400 Hrs	Min	Sec	80 / 3200 Hrs	Min	Sec	100 / 4000 Hrs	Min	Sec	FEET OF FILM / NUMBER OF IMAGES
1 PER HOUR	60		57600	86400	400			800			2000			2400			3200			4000			1 PER HOUR
2 " "	30		28800	43200	200			400			1000			1200			1600			2000			2 " "
3 " "	20		19200	28800	133	20		266	40		666	40		800			1066	40		1333	20		3 " "
4 " "	15		14400	21600	100			200			500			600			800			1000			4 " "
6 " "	10		9600	14400	66	40		133	20		333	20		400			533	20		666	40		6 " "
8 " "	7.5		7200	10800	50			100			250			300			400			500			8 " "
12 " "	5		4800	7200	33	20		66	40		166	40		200			266	40		333	20		12 " "
24 " "	2.5		2400	3600	16	40		33	20		83	20		100			133	20		166	40		24 " "
1 PER MINUTE		60	960	1440	6	40		13	20		33	20		40			53	20		66	40		1 PER MINUTE
2 " "		30	480	720	3	20		6	40		16	40		20			26	40		33	20		2 " "
3 " "		20	320	480	2	13	20	4	26	40	11	6	40	13	20		17	46	40	22	13	20	3 " "
4 " "		15	240	360	1	40		3	20		8	20		10			13	20		16	40		4 " "
6 " "		10	160	240	1	6	40	2	13	20	5	33	20	6	40		8	53	20	11	6	40	6 " "
8 " "		7.5	120	180		50		1	40		4	10		5			6	40		8	20		8 " "
12 " "		5	80	120		33	20	1	6	40	2	46	40	3	20		4	26	40	5	33	20	12 " "
24 " "		2.5	40	60		16	40		33	20	1	23	20	1	40		2	13	20	2	46	40	24 " "
30 " "		2	32	48		13	20		26	40	1	6	40	1	20		1	46	40	2	13	20	30 " "
60 " "		1	16	24		6	40		13	20		33	20		40			53	20	1	6	40	60 " "
2 PER SECOND		0.5	8	12		3	20		6	40		16	40		20			26	40		33	20	2 PER SECOND
4 " "		1/4	4	6		1	40		3	20		8	20		10			13	20		16	40	4 " "
6 " "		1/6	2.66	4		1	7.5		2	15		5	37		6	45		9			11	15	6 " "
8 " "		1/8	2	3			50		1	40		4	10		5			6	40		8	20	8 " "
10 " "		1/10	1.6	2.4			40		1	20		3	20		4			5	20		6	40	10 " "
16 " "		1/16	NORMAL SPEED	1.5			25			50		2	5		2	30		3	20		4	10	16 " "
24 " "		1/24	SLOWED DOWN	NORMAL SPEED			16 2/3			33		1	20		1	36		2	10		2	43	24 " "

"ROLAB" PHOTO-SCIENCE LABORATORIES

A 16 mm time-lapse motion-picture correlation table. Calculations are similar to the 35 mm chart.

exposures per second.

Bacteriology. Films have been made showing the growth of bacterial cultures, starting from a single cell and multiplying within a few hours to astronomical figures. Bacteriophage, a bacteria destroying agent, has also been recorded on film.

Not all germs move about rapidly. In fact a great many do not seem to move at all. However, typhoid bacteria are very active and have been used for interesting experiments. In one, for example, the destructive action of ultraviolet radiation on bacteria has been demonstrated. Many records have been made of spirochetes, such as the ones causing syphilis.

Interesting films, especially to brewers and bakers, have been made of budding yeast cells, starting with a single cell which gave rise to large cell colonies. The five-hour process is telescoped into forty seconds on the screen.

Chemistry. One micromotion picture, *Colloids,* shows the Brownian Motion of ultramicroscopic particles (caused by molecular bombardment), liquid and gaseous suspensions, the cataphoresis, magnetic phenomena on particles of iron oxide such as those contained in magnetic recording tape, and the production of colloids by the electric arc.

A micromotion picture, *The Magic of Oil,* shows lubricating oils exposed to freezing temperatures. In a tiny droplet of ordinary oil, large wax crystals form and gradually create a network which renders the oil viscous. Special winter oils remain fluid because their smaller singular wax crystals begin to form at lower temperatures.

Industry. A large carbon-black manufacturing concern has produced a micromotion picture, *Inside the Flame,* which tells the entire story of carbon black and its role as a fortifier of rubber goods such as automobile tires. Another motion picture, *Facts about Fabrics,* has several very interesting microscopic scenes which show the great variety of fabrics and their weave constructions.

Law. One of the most significant applications of micromotion pictures is as legal evidence, especially important in patent litigations. The evidence of micromotion pictures has been officially accepted by the courts. In one patent-infringement suit, brought by one of the leading ice-cream manufacturers of the country, one of the litigants had to prove adhesion between ice crystals and wood. He did so be showing a micromotion picture of relevant experiments carried on under the microscope.

MICROSCOPE AND ACCESSORIES

For medium and high magnifications (20× and over), the compound microscope may be used. A monocular wide tube is preferable because it prevents internal reflections (flare spots) from interfering with the image. For low magnifications, MicroTessars or Summars are used without eyepieces. The upper collar of the microscope tube should be removed before using.

A light trap, consisting of two sleeves made from either black cardboard or thin sheet metal, is used between microscope tube and camera to prevent stray light from reaching the film. A similar light trap is used between eyepiece and camera for the higher magnifications. (Figure 3.)

Although practically all the achromatic objectives and eyepieces regularly supplied with microscopes may be used for still photomicrography, a more careful selection of micro-optics must be made for motion-picture work. Since most subjects are alive and active, they require relatively short exposures. For this reason, dense monochrome and color-compensating filters to correct chromatic aberrations cannot be used. Apochromatic objectives in combination with compensating eyepieces are recommended, especially for high-power work.

For the lower powers, some achromatic objectives produce acceptable results. To be certain of their photographic performance, it is advisable to test them with diatoms or other test objects. It might be mentioned here that some achromats have excellent photographic qualities.

Eyepieces also must be carefully selected as to their optical performance. Some eyepieces which seem excellent for visual microscopy can produce disturbing flare spots on the film.

The higher the eyepiece magnification, the larger the circle of illumination produced on the plane of the image (focusing plane). However, since we want to utilize the maximum of light projected by the eyepiece into the film gate, the lower-power eyepieces are preferable.

Furthermore, although only the "initial" magnification of the objective determines resolution of detail (the eyepiece is only used for further "empty" magnification), the higher-power eyepieces can diminish the better definition of detail provided by the best objectives. Here, as in all microscopic work, resolution is more important than magnification.

ADJUSTMENTS FOR GOOD RESULTS

A few precautions have to be taken with the microscope to insure maximum resolution of detail. Precise alignment of the optical system of your microscope is a prerequisite for maximum sharpness and good photography in general. The following alignment procedure is suggested:

Instead of the usual microscope with a narrow tube and a revolving nosepiece for changing objectives, use a microscope with a wide photomicrographic tube and with individual slide holders for the objectives. These slide holders should have two-way adjustments for centering the objectives. Use a low-power 5× to 10× objective, together with a low-power eyepiece, to align the substage condenser with the upper part of the microscope.

Using a low-intensity light source, bring the iris diaphragm of the condenser into focus by closing the iris to the smallest opening, then racking the tube down until this opening appears in focus in the center of the visible area. If the opening is not centered, use the two adjustments on the slide holding the objective. Now open the iris slightly so that its contour is concentric with the round field of view. This procedure may be repeated, and corrected if necessary, using higher-power eyepieces.

Now rack the tube up again. Place a slide with cross line on the mechanical stage, then move this "centering slide" into the accurate center of the field. If your microscope has a rotating stage, adjust it so that the center (cross line) remains stationary while the stage is rotated. If mechanically possible, this position should be fixed so that the center does not accidentally get out of place.

Adjust the medium-high objectives on their individual slide holders in like manner. When you change low for high eyepieces you may still find slight inaccuracies which should be corrected at this time.

With a microscope thus accurately centered, it is easy to change from low to high power without losing the area on the slide under

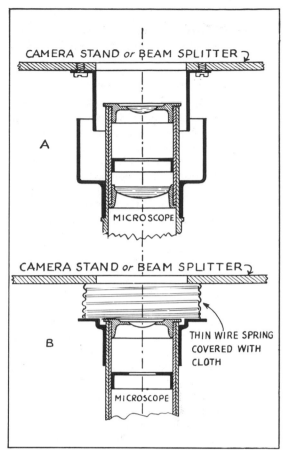

Above: Figure 3. *Pair of light-proof sleeves, A, and cloth bellows, B, used between the microscope and camera or between the microscope and beam-splitter observation tube.*

Below: Figure 4. *Roger S-F camera drive for single frame action.*

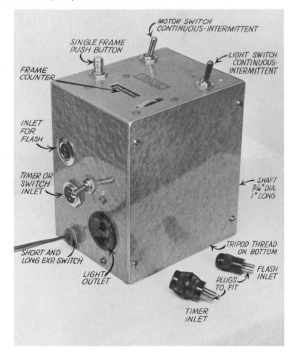

observation, besides having the best possible condition for excellent photography.

CAMERAS

Any good motion-picture camera will take micromotion pictures but a well-balanced precision mechanism is essential to sharp and steady pictures. Remember that not only the object is magnified but also any motion, even the slightest vibration of the equipment, can cause the photograph to be out of focus.

Professional 35 mm movie cameras (Bell & Howell, Mitchell) although of excellent construction, are too heavy to handle easily. The many attachments and devices on these cameras are useless in microwork. Also, these cameras have to be shifted from the taking position to the focusing position, which may disturb the delicate adjustments in microwork.

The ideal camera would have the following characteristics: 1) small size but sturdy construction; 2) simple, well-balanced, vibrationless mechanism; 3) direct focusing device on film gate with a very fine groundglass screen with cross line

or small circle indicating center; 4) the film gate as near as possible to the front of the camera to shorten the distance from the eyepiece to the image, often a decided advantage in critical illumination; 5) silent motor with adjustable speeds directly attached to camera or, better, a motor drive with flexible shaft, such as the Roger Single-Frame Camera Drive (Figure 4).

For stop-motion work the camera must have a single-frame shaft. It should be possible to open the camera and take out its film magazines without changing the taking position. This is a great help when short strips of film with test exposures are taken out for immediate development.

FILM

Black-and-white film is used predominantly with live biological material because of its higher sensitivity, the availability of different contrast characteristics and speeds, lower film and processing costs, and the advantage of being able to check results immediately with exposure and developing tests in the home darkroom.

Specimens which show good coloring at low magnifications lose their coloring in proportion to magnification. For example, red blood corpuscles are pink at low magnifications, brownish-yellow at medium magnifications, and clear as glass at high powers.

For time-lapse pictures of living tissue cells at low and high magnifications, fine-grain positive film produces more highly contrasted negatives which brings out the delicate structure of the cells often invisible to the naked eye.

Color film is used for micromotion pictures, mainly with colored specimens. However, it is difficult to determine correct exposure and there is not much exposure latitude in color emulsions. Exposure determination by photoelectric means is not satisfactory since only over-all intensity values can be measured without consideration of contrast.

The image area of a 35 mm negative is approximately 4.5 times larger than the area of a 16 mm film. Obviously it is much easier to focus on the larger area. In micromotion pictures, critical focusing presents a number of problems especially at higher magnifications. Even the finest groundglass screen is often much too coarse for the extremely delicate details of some objects and a clear glass with cross line is used instead. As is, the 35 mm image area is too small for critical focusing of these delicate structures; in fact many fine details may not register at all on the comparatively coarse negative emulsion. This problem is much greater in the 16 mm field.

However, the smaller image area in the 16 mm field gives better critical illumination than the 35 mm area. If the camera is located at the proper minimum distance above the microscope and within the pencil of light, the smaller area of the 16 mm film may receive 4.5 times more light intensity than the 35 mm film area. The advantage is obvious when working with biological material that is sensitive to light or heat or with darkfield illumination where the light comes from the specimen itself.

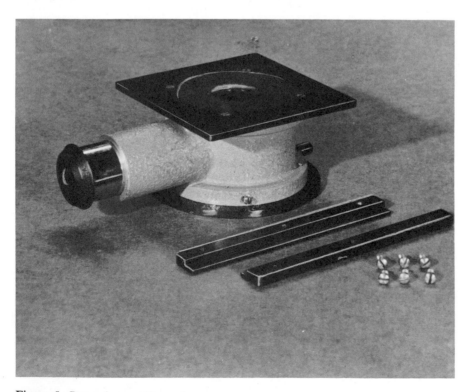

Figure 5. *Roger beam-splitter observation eyepiece.*

Figure 6. *The standard microcinema apparatus designed by the author. The apparatus is of heavy construction with a number of precision adjustments for correct optical alignment. The entire apparatus is built into a niche with folding doors for protection. The incubator at the center below the camera keeps the microscope and specimen at the required temperature. Doors on three sides make the specimens and adjustments accessible (some adjustments may be made from outside by extension screws). The optical bench is on leveling screws with vibration absorbers. The track carries a number of riders for lights, cooling or color filters, condensing lenses, and other equipment. The camera is screwed against a hinged plate and may be tipped into a horizontal position for change of film. It is also mounted on a sideways slide, making alignment with the microscope possible for the focusing device. At left are driving motors and at the right is the electric control panel.*

OPTICAL SET-UP

No single set-up, no matter how versatile and elaborate, can be used for all microcinematography. Depending upon the nature, size, and motion of the object to be photographed, the optical line-up of object, camera, motor, light source, may be vertical, horizontal, or a combination of both.

For low-power work not requiring the use of a microscope, the most widely used arrangement is a horizontal one whereby the centers of object, objective, and camera (film gate) are in line, permitting easy individual positioning of each part for focusing.

Since the camera is the heaviest part of the equipment, it should be kept stationary and the object moved for coarse focusing. The author uses an optical bench with three adjustable riders for object, objective with sleeve and focusing adjustment, background, as well as several stands holding various light sources. The objective is part of the optical bench and has no mechanical connection with the camera.

For this reason vibrations originating in the camera mechanism or motor are not transmitted to the objective.

The floor upon which the entire apparatus is placed should be absolutely rigid to eliminate even the slightest vibrations. Vibrations may be caused by nearby traffic, slamming of doors, noises of all kinds, even by the operator walking

The Rolab Microcinema Apparatus for taking motion pictures through a microscope. Platform with alignment stops for microscope, adjustable column, camera support with fixed and swivel plate with beam-centering device. Beam-splitter observation eyepiece with one inch adjustable double prism for simultaneous observation and photography of slide. Roger S-F camera drive and camera timer, lower left.

around the apparatus or the hum of transformers for low-voltage light sources.

Manufacturers of photomicrographic equipment suspend the base (optical bench), which supports the entire apparatus on coiled springs or upon rubber or felt cushions. In micromotion pictures, however, most disturbing vibrations are caused by the equipment itself. The equipment should be placed upon a very thick stone or concrete floor

which is isolated from building vibrations by layers of cork or other insulating material, or the base of the equipment should stand on pads of cork or sponge rubber.

A vertical set-up is best for most medium- and high-power micromotion pictures. Most objects are suspended in liquids and must therefore be kept in a horizontal position upon the stage of the microscope. At high power requiring the use of oil-immersion objec-

tives, the cedarwood oil used between the slide and objective and slide and condenser will run off if the microscope is used horizontally.

The vertical set-up is the most convenient for focusing and makes it possible to center the beam of light for critical illumination by adjusting the microscope mirror. The latter also permits easy switching from one light source to another.

The microscope can be used in a vertical position while the camera axis remains horizontal. A prism or first surface mirror above the eyepiece of the microscope throws the beam into the camera. The reflecting surface of the prism can also be made partially transparent. This will permit a fraction of the light beam coming directly from the microscope to continue in a straight line to a focusing plane at the equivalent distance of the film gate in the camera, which may be observed with a magnifier. The main drawback to this right-angle set-up is the fact that every height adjustment of the microscope tube requires a corresponding height adjustment of the camera.

STANDARD APPARATUS

With the Standard Microcinematographic Apparatus (Figure 6), adjustments over a wide range of speeds and magnifications can be made within a few seconds.

The equipment consists of four main units which are separate from one another in order to eliminate the transmission of vibrations. Unit 1, the optical bench, carries the microscope and the light source or sources with condensers, cooling cells, filters. Unit 2 is the camera, an observation tube (beam splitter), a focusing and light-centering device, motor for raising or lowering camera platform, electric relay for intermittent operation, and rotating shutter. Unit 3 consists of the two motor drives, one for high- and the other for low-frequency operation, the latter coupled with the intermittent-timing relay. Unit 4 is the electric-control panel which may be considered a central operating system for the light, the motors, the timing device, and for any additional apparatus such as incubators. The electrical equipment, including timing mechanism and motor drive, can be built into separate compact, portable units which can be mounted on a suitable stand. The entire apparatus may be closed in by a folding door which protects everything within the compartment.

OPERATING PROCEDURE

Let us say for example we wish to take a motion picture of some living yeast cells. The specimen, properly prepared on a slide, is placed on the stage of the microscope. The light source in this case

Figure 7. *Table to determine rate of exposure per hour, per minute, or per second for 35 mm film. Example: an action taking 3½ hours is to be photographed on 50 feet of 35 mm film. Select the time from the 50-feet column which is closest to 3½ hours. In this case, it is 3 hours, 20 minutes. Follow this to the left or right and find the rate of exposures—4 per minute. The rate of acceleration may also be found by consulting the acceleration columns on the same horizontal line.*

Rate of Exposures	Single Pictures taken every		Acceleration at Projection Speeds of		Length of Time to Take:																											
					10			20			40			50			62 ½			100			200			300			400			← Feet of Film
					160			320			640			800			1000			1600			3200			4800			6400			← Numb. of Images
	Min.	Sec.	16 F.S.	24 F.S.	Hours	Min.	Sec.	Hours	Min.	Sec	Hours	Min	Sec.	Hours	Min.	Sec.	Hours	Min.	Sec	Hours	Min.	Sec	Hours	Min	Sec	Hours	Min.	Sec	Hours	Min.	Sec	
1 per Hour	60		57600	86400	160			320			640			800			1000			1600			3200			4800			6400			1 per Hour
2 " "	30		28800	43200	80			160			320			400			500			800			1600			2400			3200			2 " "
3 " "	20		19200	28800	53	20		106	40		213	20		266	40		333	20		533	20		1066	40		1600			2133	20		3 " "
4 " "	15		14400	21600	40			80			160			200			250			400			800			1200			1600			4 " "
6 " "	10		9600	14400	26	40		53	20		106	40		133	20		166	40		266	40		533	20		800			1066	40		6 " "
8 " "	7½		7200	10800	20			40			80			100			125			200			400			600			800			8 " "
12 " "	5		4800	7200	13	20		26	40		53	20		66	40		83	20		133	20		266	40		400			533	20		12 " "
24 " "	2½		2400	3600	6	40		13	20		26	40		33	20		41	40		66	40		133	20		200			266	40		24 " "
1 per Min.		60	960	1440	2	40		5	20		10	40		13	20		16	40		26	40		53	20		80			106	40		1 per Min.
2 " "		30	480	720	1	20		2	40		5	20		6	40		8	20		13	20		26	40		40			53	20		2 " "
3 " "		20	320	480		53	20	1	46	40	3	33	20	4	26	40	5	33	20	8	53	20	17	46	40	26	40		35	33	20	3 " "
4 " "		15	240	360		40		1	20		2	40		3	20		4	10		6	40		13	20		20			26	40		4 " "
6 " "		10	160	240		26	60		53	20	1	46	40	2	13	20	2	46	40	4	26	40	8	53	20	13	20		17	46	40	6 " "
8 " "		7½	120	180		20			40		1	20		1	40		2	5		3	20		6	40		10			13	20		8 " "
12 " "		5	80	120		13	20		26	40		53	20	1	6	50	1	23	20	2	13	40	4	27	20	6	40		8	54	40	12 " "
24 " "		2½	40	60		6	40		13	20		26	40		33	25		41	40	1	6	50	2	13	40	3	20		2	27	20	24 " "
30 " "		2	32	48		5	20		10	40		21	20		26	40		33	20		53	20	1	46	40	2	40		3	33	20	30 " "
60 " "		1	16	24		2	40		5	20		10	40		13	20		16	40		26	40		53	20	1	20		1	46	40	60 " "
2 per Sec.		½	8	12		1	20		2	40		5	20		6	40		8	20		13	20		26	40		40			53	20	2 per Sec.
4 " "		¼	4	6			40		1	20		2	40		3	20		4	10		6	40		13	20		20			26	40	4 " "
6 " "		⅙	2.66	4			27⅓			53⅓		1	36⅔		2	13⅓		2	46⅔		4	26⅔		8	53⅓		13	20		17	46⅔	6 " "
8 " "		⅛	2	3			20			40		1	20		1	40		2	5		3	20		6	40		10			13	20	8 " "
10 " "		1/10	1.6	2.4			16			32		1	4		1	20		1	40		2	40		5	20		8			10	40	10 " "
16 " "		1/16	normal speed	1.5			10			20			40			50		1	2½		1	40		3	20		5			6	40	16 " "
24 " "		1/24	slowed down 0.66	normal speed			6⅔			13⅓			26⅔			33⅓			41⅔		1	6⅔		2	13⅓		3	20		4	26⅔	24 " "
32 " "		1/32	slowed down 0.50	slowed down 0.75			5			10			20			25			31¼			50		1	40		2	30		3	20	32 " "

would probably be an incandescent lamp in combination with a light green filter to protect the specimen from heat and give maximum contrast. We focus first with a low-power objective in order to locate a field. After finding a suitable area, we raise the magnification by changing the objective. In both adjusting the microscope and selecting a proper field, we should consider the photographic effect.

Next we calculate the rate of growth (in this case upon the basis of experience) in terms of time and magnification. Then we have to consider the length of time at which the action should be reproduced on the screen. This calculation for time-lapse work is facilitated by the use of the time-lapse correlation table (Figure 7) which enables us to find within a few seconds the time interval (frames per minute or hour) and length of film (or number of frames). Now we set our dial on the correct figure on the control panel (Figure 6).

Assuming that the focusing device (on the same level with the film gate in the camera) is in position, we check our focus with that of the observation tube. We then switch over to the groundglass for adjusting even distribution of light which may be properly corrected and centered by slightly adjusting the microscope mirror.

To move the camera into shooting position, we move the drop handle over to the stop position. This automatically engages the driving mechanism with the camera. The apparatus is now ready, for exposure tests or actual pictures.

The above procedure refers to pictures taken in brightfield illumination. Much more light intensity is required for darkfield work where only the comparatively small amount of light reflected from the specimen itself is utilized for exposure. In time-lapse work a stronger incandescent light will suffice. Normal speed or slow motion which we use for faster moving objects, such as typhoid bacteria, requires a powerful arc lamp.

In the latter case, we would use the revolving shutter, making sure that it is synchronized with the camera shutter. This can easily be checked by looking through the camera telescope finder and watching the shutter opening. The revolving shutter makes it possible to regulate the exposure within limits by adjusting the blades to a wider or narrower opening.

ILLUMINATION

The most frequently used light source is the incandescent lamp because of its convenience, variety, and availability. The diameter of the area to be illuminated should determine the size of the lamp. Since most lamps are used with condensing systems which project the image of the light source, in this case the filament, upon the object, one would use a larger light source for larger areas and low power, and a smaller light source with relatively greater field intensity for smaller areas and high power. Ordinary projection lamps, as used in commercial projectors, fall into the first group, the small low-voltage lamps with "concentrated" filaments belong to the latter group.

When the incandescent lamp fails to produce sufficient intensity for exposure, the arc lamp, which is a much more powerful and actinic light source, is used. Although a-c current may be used in series with the necessary step-down transformers or rheostats, d-c is preferable because of its relatively higher field intensity emitted from the flame of the positive carbon. Other light sources include Point-O-Light, zirconium arc, and mercury arc.

For low-power micromotion pictures of solid (opaque) objects, the rules of illumination for ordinary photography may be adhered to; conditions are the same except that the objects are in miniature.

In high-power work with the microscope, the image of the light source is produced in the plane of the object slide. A practical way of adjusting the light is the following: move the light source and condenser back and forth along the optical track until a circle of light covers three-quarters of the microscope mirror, plane side up. Then adjust the mirror until the circle of light which it reflects covers the lower

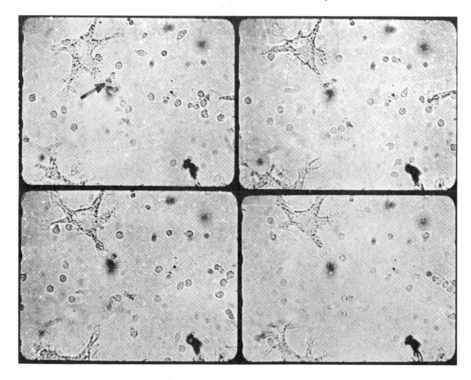

How a large cell takes up a small cell and "digests" it is shown in this strip of the phagocytosis of a lymphocyte by a large leucocyte of guinea pig. Small cell, A, indicated by arrow, will be taken up; large cell, B, stretches out pseudopod towards small cell; small cell, C, inside of pseudopod; small cell, D, still visible, is drawn further into the large cell.

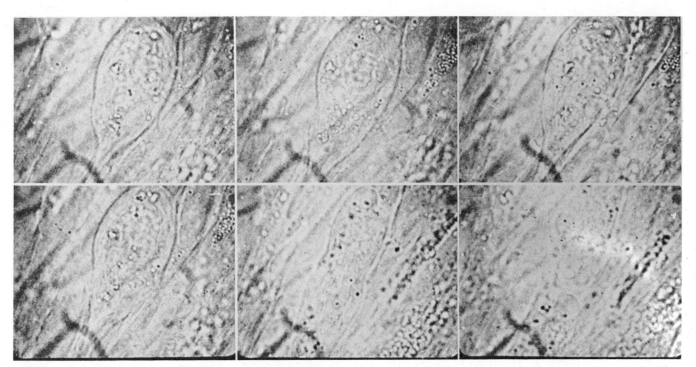

Cell division (mitosis) of a tissue cell (fibroblast). The cell, normally of elongated shape, begins to become round, A, and the nucleus, now visible in the upper part, begins to travel further down, B. The nucleus then shows signs of agitation, C, and begins to divide, D. As the nucleus divides, chromosomes are seen, E, and the fibroblast begins to indent on both sides. Both cells finally separate, F, with vigorous agitation. This is live material, no stains are used as they are toxic to cells.

surface of the substage condenser. It may be necessary to make slight adjustments of light source, condenser, mirror, or substage in order to obtain maximum illumination, image definition, and contrast.

MICROCINEMA EQUIPMENT (16 mm)

In addition to microscope and camera, 16 mm microcinema equipment has three separate parts: camera timer or intervallometer, single-frame motor drive, stand or apparatus upon which the microscope is placed together with the camera and its motor drive. These are the same three basic units contained in the standard microcinema apparatus for 35 mm film.

The Rolab Microcinema Apparatus for a 16 mm camera consists of: base plate with stops for the microscope, column with shaft and keyway for height adjustment, fixed and swivel plates with camera bracket, beam-centering tube, beam-splitter observation eyepiece on slide, single-frame camera drive mounted on a separate bracket and connected to the camera by a flexible connector. All the upper parts may be moved out of the way to clear the microscope for visual work, or the microscope may also be removed. When microscope and camera are recombined, they are automatically aligned by the align-

ment stops on the base plate.

The rotation of the upper part with camera has other advantages. A second microscope can be mounted opposite the first at 180 degrees for macrocine work and, if properly aligned, for microcinematography. The sliding arrangement which usually holds the beam-splitter observation tube may in this case hold a Micro-Tessar or Summar with focusing bellows. The magazines can be removed and returned without dismounting the camera body.

The S-F Camera Drive may be pulled back or removed by loosening a tripod screw on the bottom of the unit and a slot on the bracket. This disengages it from the camera so that the spring motor can be operated at higher speeds.

This equipment permits the use of two light sources with only the substage mirror on the microscope needing adjustment when changed from one light source to the other. A push button operates the S-F Camera Drive single-frame (for testing). For time-lapse work the

Roger Camera Timer model "I" will operate the camera by remote control automatically at various time intervals.

For practical reasons, a set of time intervals has been established. These intervals, adjustable by turning three dials, are: 1, 2, 3, 6, 12 and 24 frames per hour; 1, 2, 3, 4, 6, and 8 frames per minute. Changing from one to another will not affect the exposure once found correct for a particular emulsion. Faster speeds are of course possible, either by operating the camera drive at "continuous" instead of "intermittent" or by using the spring motor of the camera.

Although any 16 mm camera may be used with this equipment, the Cine-Special has a reflex finder, located parallel with and above the Beam-splitter observation eyepiece, which permits comparison and accurate adjustment of the field.

HEAT ABSORPTION

All light sources produce heat. This is objectionable because heat may injure or destroy the specimen or even parts of the microscope. Some biological objects, such as tissue cells, blood, or bacteria, are so sensitive to temperature that special precautions must be taken to cut down heat and light must be kept to the minimum necessary for exposure. Heat absorbers (glass cells filled with liquid or filters made of heat-absorbing glass) are placed between the light source condenser and the microscope, or between condenser lenses when the condensing system consists of more than one lens. The liquid in the cell may be distilled water or a weak solution of copper sulfate combined with a few drops of sulfuric acid. Recipes for other heat-absorbing liquids may be found in books on microscopy.

When continuous light is employed, a great amount of heat can be prevented from reaching the microscope by using a revolving shutter. This shutter, however, must be synchronized with the shutter in the camera.

FOCUSING DEVICES

The usefulness of micromotion pictures depends upon the photographic quality of the original negative. The operator's primary concern must be to obtain a sharp image.

In microscopy, the depth of field can be measured only in microns (1 micron $= \frac{1}{1000}$ mm). At medium and high magnifications, the slightest touch of the micrometer screw may throw the image completely out of focus.

Even the finest groundglass screen is much too coarse to focus critically on these extremely delicate structures. We therefore focus on the virtual image appearing in the exact plane of the film emulsion, using a well-corrected magnifying eyepiece. A clear plane glass with a cross line, circle, or rectangular frame etched on the focusing surface indicates the center or the limits of field respectively. The etched lines are also used to check or correct the

focusing eyepiece.

The focusing device is mounted on a movable slide together with the camera. The focusing plane of this device takes exactly the same level as the film emulsion above the microscope.

By means of a swivel, either the eyepiece with cross line or a fine groundglass screen with light shade may be moved into position. The groundglass screen is used here to center the beam of light and, if necessary, to correct its distribution. Some microscope oculars cause flare spots which register on the film as light areas; these may be detected on the groundglass.

For time-lapse work with intervals of a few seconds or more, this focusing device is easy to use between exposures. It is also used to check focus before taking pic-

Figure 8. *Rolab microcinema apparatus set-up for low temperature motion pictures. A 35 mm motion-picture camera is in position. The freezing device is in left foreground, between the camera timer and microscope. Note the ice on the tubing.*

tures when no particular action has to be followed. The advantage lies in the fact that all light reaches the film without loss by reflection as would be the case with beam-splitting devices.

When action has to be observed while the camera is operating, a special observation eyepiece with beam splitter is used (Figure 5). Two rectangular prisms are cemented together into a glass cube. One of the prisms is coated with semi-transparent silver or aluminum and forms a single-plane 45-degree mirror, diagonally positioned within the cube, which reflects part of the beam sideways into the eyepiece. The beam splitter eyepiece of the standard apparatus slides into position underneath the camera platform and automatically aligns with microscope and camera. No mechanical connection exists between these two except light sleeves or flexible bellows (Figure 3) as generally used in still photomicrography.

A few manufacturers of microscopes have placed on the market micromotion-picture apparatus with beam-splitting eyepieces attached directly to the tube of a vertically-mounted microscope. The camera is screwed on an adjustable stand in the horizontal position and receives its image-forming beam from the beam splitter.

Unlike the beam-splitting eyepiece on the Standard apparatus, the reflected beam is thrown into the camera. An adjustment of the microscope tube along its track requires a corresponding height-adjustment of the camera. This may be avoided by attaching the beam-splitter eyepiece directly to the camera. Such an arrangement, however, offers no guarantee of sharp pictures because the reflecting surface becomes an integral part of the camera, the vibrations of which may even be magnified.

EXPOSURE

In still photomicrography, a number of factors determine correct exposure, such as the structure of the specimen, its color and contrast, magnification employed, type of light source, its opacity, adjustment of substage condenser, emulsion speed, development, cooling, and color filters. To all these we must add the motion-picture speed which ranges from one exposure per hour to 64 or more per second. The best and shortest way to success is to make tests and record every possible factor of each exposure.

Attempts have been made to measure and calculate the exposure with photoelectric cells. In order to be useful under all conditions, a photoelectric meter must have an extremely wide range; the faintest trace of light should produce a noticeable indication on the meter's dial.

There are two types of meters. In one, a system of shunt resistors connects a self-generating photocell with a sensitive galvanometer, thus possessing several ranges of sensitivity. Another, more sensitive, type uses a photoelectric cell in combination with an amplifier system and a microammeter. The most logical place for the photocell is on the "receiving end" of the optical system, namely near the film gate where the image is formed.

PREPARATION OF MATERIAL

Two factors must be considered. First, the specimen must be prepared in such a way that it acts normally or gives a desired effect. Secondly, the preparation must suit whatever optical requirements are necessary to assure optimum photographic results. The difficulty of fulfilling these requirements increases proportionately with increasing rates of magnification.

Medical and biological material, living micro-organisms, for example, will not behave naturally unless they are kept under conditions as close to normal as possible. For living cells certain special culture techniques must be followed closely, or the cells will die from contamination by bacteria or molds, toxic effects of certain types of glass or other substances, lack of oxygen or carbon dioxide, change of temperature, or too much light. Deviation in the chemical composition or pH balance of the culture may cause the cells to deteriorate. Special culture flasks or chambers have been developed for still and motion-picture photography, which make it possible to use high-power oil-immersion objectives with very short working distances.

Bacteria and protozoa must be prepared in their particular media and transferred to slides before they are photographed. To prevent evaporation, the cover slip must be sealed to the slide by a ring of vaseline or paraffin.

For taking pictures of the blood circulation small animals, such as frogs, are used. After they are anaesthetized, they are mounted on a stiff board in which a small hole is drilled for transmitting light. The board with the animal in place is then either fastened or held down with weights to the microscope stage.

Embryos or other small animals require special mounting techniques; much is left to the ingenuity of the operator. This is also true in chemistry and physics where practically every new problem requires a new technique.

For the study of materials at high temperature, small heating units are used. These are made from sheet asbestos, mica, and a small coil of nichron or platinum wire, whose ends are connected with electric current in series with a rheostat. Care must be taken that all optical parts on the microscope are protected from excessive heat.

For low temperature work a refrigerant, cooled down to the desired temperature by a miniature freezing device (Figure 8) is circulated through a hollow cooling cell on the microscope stage. Here special care must be taken to prevent condensation of moisture on optical surfaces which would blur the picture.

There is practically no limit to what can be demonstrated with the aid of motion pictures. It is up to the operator to work out the details particular to his problems. The entomologist who wishes to study and demonstrate the behavior of small insects under varying degrees of atmospheric pressure will have to develop a small pressure or vacuum chamber for his specimens. The chemist who wishes to make a study of electrochemical phenomena under the microscope will devise an apparatus with the necessary electrodes. The physicist who wishes to demonstrate the Brownian Movement of small particles suspended in gas will construct a small metal chamber with windows for illumination and an inlet and outlet for the gas. The industrial laboratory worker studying the effects of corrosion will build a device in which the specimen can be exposed to the corrosive action of various agents.

SUMMARY

Micromotion pictures have unlimited application in research and demonstration. Many a detail may easily be overlooked unless we see it in motion; often we are only able to detect a bird in the foliage of a tree in the act of flying away.

Since our medium is motion pictures, there should be some motion in the object to make it effective. Lifeless objects may be rotated by means of a synchronous clock motor, or a small moving pointer may be used to point out one or several features.

Today, microscopic scenes constitute the backbone of many documentary or industrial motion pictures. They have replaced animated drawings to a certain extent since animation is never quite so convincing as the real thing. More important, through the medium of micromotion pictures, people who never have a chance to look through a microscope are able to see what is going on in a new and strange world.

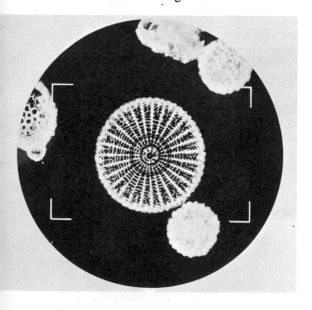

MICROCINEMATOGRAPHY FOR TIME LAPSE

H. W. ZIELER
Zieler Instrument Company, Inc., Boston, Mass.

[As the field of medical and biological research expands, there is a growing demand for specific information on the assembly and operation of microcinematography equipment. The author has designed and made available special equipment for this exacting and interesting work. Now the cinematographer with average experience who is interested in specialized research can use the equipment and get good time-lapse microcinematography films.]

• *Also see: Photomicrography; Time-Lapse Photography.*

LIVING CELLS AND OTHER SMALL objects that can be seen only through the microscope undergo morphological changes which are of interest to the microscopist. Some of these changes occur so slowly that the continuity of their progress cannot be detected by visual observation. These changes may be reproduced in accelerated form by taking series of photomicrographs of the objects on motion-picture film at suitably selected equal time intervals, and by projecting the films thus obtained as motion pictures at normal speeds of 16 or 24 frames per second.

If, for example, growing cells of animal tissues in cultures are photographed through the microscope at the rate of one picture per minute for a period of 24 hours, and the film is then projected at the rate of 24 frames per second, the morphological changes are visually accelerated so that they seem to occur within one minute. This method of photomicrography is called "time-lapse microcinematography." Interest in this relatively old

Since the microscope produces a circular image, a frame establishing the camera's point of view is tremendously helpful in framing the specimen.

field of photomicrography has recently revived with the development of new techniques for studying cells growing in tissue cultures on various media. In cancer research, for instance, it is the aim of the scientist to find substances which inhibit the growth of cancer cells but do not affect the growth of normal cells. This inhibited, or unaffected, growth of cells can be studied in time-lapse micromotion pictures.

Since the availability of commercially produced complete assemblies for time-lapse microcinematography is somewhat limited, many microscopists have assembled their own equipment from commercially available components, mechanically modified to suit special requirements. An assembly which is offered commercially as a unit (Figure 1) consists of:

1. The microscope with illumination system.
2. The optical focusing and viewing device (beam splitter).
3. The motion-picture camera.
4. The shutter-actuating device.
5. The intervallometer.
6. The stand holding microscope and camera in alignment.
7. The incubator (optional).

THE MICROSCOPE

Any microscope with monocular tube, or combination monocular-binocular phototube, is suitable for microcinematography. Preferably, it should have a built-in illumination system, including a light source of adequate intensity. The illumination system should include aperture and field iris diaphragms and a centering device for the condenser. Since the microscope in Figure 1 is in an incubator, it is also equipped with extension gears attached by horizontal axes to adjustment knobs on a mechanical stage. Additional extension gears have been provided for coarse and fine focusing of the image from outside the incubator.

OPTICAL FOCUSING AND VIEWING DEVICE

When the microscope is used for visual observation, the objective forms the intermediate image in the focal plane of the eyepiece. The rays then pass through the eye lens of the eyepiece to form a virtual

Figure 1. *The Zieler assembly for time-lapse microcinematography. The various component parts operation are described in the text.*

image at infinity. Finally, the rays emerging from the eyepiece are intercepted by the observer's eye, the lens of which forms the final image on the retina.

For microcinematography, however, the final image must be formed in the plane of the film. Since the dimensions of the frame (8 × 11 mm for 16 mm film) are relatively small, the film must be placed close to the eyepiece. Although it is possible to refocus the microscope for image formation at this close distance, the quality of the resulting image is inferior because spherical and chromatical aberrations arise when: 1) the intermediate image is formed at a

distance which is less than the optical tube length for which the objective is corrected; and 2) the final image is formed at a finite distance for which the eyepiece is not chromatically corrected.

These aberrations are eliminated by interposing an auxiliary lens between eyepiece and film plane. A lens of short focal length (about 1½ inch) is attached to the motion-picture camera and focused independently to infinity so that its rear focal plane coincides with the film plane. It is in a metal mount which does not protrude much beyond the surface of the front lens

so that the entire divergent bundle of rays emerging from the eyepiece is collected and transmitted by the lens. An aplanatic magnifier of 6 to 8× magnification can be used for this purpose (Figure 2).

A beam-splitting prism is mounted between the eyepiece and the auxiliary lens. It transmits about two thirds of the image-forming rays that pass through the auxiliary lens and forms an image on the film. It reflects about one third the rays that pass through a lateral viewing telescope. Its objective forms a real image in the rear focal plane. The rays continue through the eyepiece

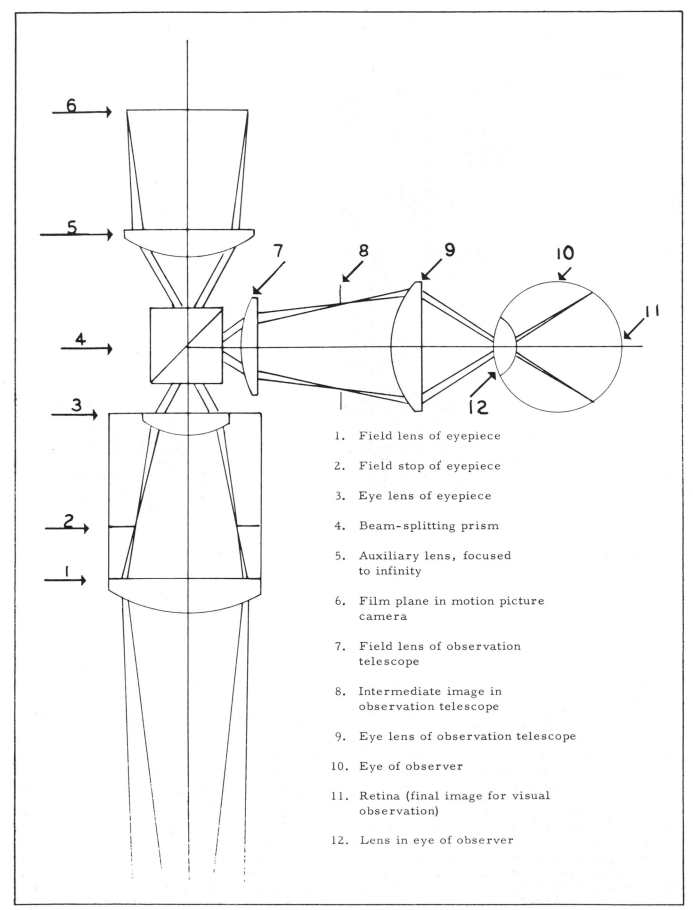

1. Field lens of eyepiece

2. Field stop of eyepiece

3. Eye lens of eyepiece

4. Beam-splitting prism

5. Auxiliary lens, focused to infinity

6. Film plane in motion picture camera

7. Field lens of observation telescope

8. Intermediate image in observation telescope

9. Eye lens of observation telescope

10. Eye of observer

11. Retina (final image for visual observation)

12. Lens in eye of observer

Figure 2. *A special beam-splitting eyepiece mounted between microscope and motion-picture camera lens permits the operator to see and focus the specimen.*

of the telescope and enter the observer's eye, where they form the final image on the retina. The observer sees this image "at infinity."

A rectangle of fine hair lines in the rear focal plane of the objective of the telescope indicates how much of the circular area of the field of view is reproduced on the rectangular film frame. The eye lens of the telescope is adjustable and can be focused on the hair lines. When hair lines and microimage are simultaneously in focus visually, the image is also in focus in the film plane. This method of focusing and viewing the image makes the objective and the eyepiece perform under optical conditions identical to those of visual observation, where their correction is at an optimum.

THE MOTION-PICTURE CAMERA

The Bolex camera (Figure 1) has a film capacity of 100 feet, which is adequate for most time-lapse photography. Cameras with a film capacity of as much as 400 feet are available. For time-lapse work, the spring motor of the Bolex can be disengaged, and a motor can be coupled to the outlet for the hand crank. The release button can be moved to a position for single exposures. There are other motion-picture cameras with similar features for time-lapse microcinematography, some equipped with daylight-loading film magazines. Although the film capacity of a daylight-loading magazine is only 50 feet, a new length of film can be loaded within a few seconds, practically without interruption of the continuity.

THE SHUTTER-ACTUATING DEVICE

In Figure 1, an electric motor is coupled to the hand-crank shaft of the Bolex camera. The motor, with a system of gears in a housing, receives electrical impulses from the intervallometer. For time exposures, it rotates $1/16$ of a revolution to open the shutter, and, after expiration of the selected length of time for the exposure, it rotates another $1/16$ of a revolution to close the shutter and to transport the film to the next frame.

For instantaneous exposures, an-other impulse from the intervallometer causes the motor to rotate $1/8$ of a revolution, the shutter now opens and closes for an instantaneous exposure of approximately $1/10$ of a second.

There is a push button and also an optional connection for a foot switch so that the motor can be operated continuously for taking motion pictures, at normal or reduced speeds. Since the motor is connected to the hand-crank shaft, rewinding of the spring motor is, of course, no longer necessary.

It is possible to operate the Bolex shutter with a solenoid, but pulsing action of the solenoid causes vibrations which require additional devices to be fully absorbed.

THE INTERVALLOMETER

The length of the time interval between pictures is varied by setting the pointer to the desired value on one of the two dials of the intervallometer. The pointer of the second dial is set to the desired time exposure.

It is desirable to have facilities on the intervallometer for a continuous or an intermittent operation of the light source. For short (less than five seconds) intervals between pictures, the light source is usually switched on continuously. For long intervals, the light source is turned on shortly before the exposure and off when the shutter closes. For objects which are sensitive to light, it is possible to provide minimum exposure by using an electronic-flash unit synchronized to the shutter.

In order to hold microscope and camera in correct alignment, the microscope is clamped to a metal base plate which rests on a sheet of rubber about one fourth of an inch thick. The whole unit rests on the baseboard of the stand. A carrying arm with platform can be moved up and down by a rack and pinion, clamped in any desired position, and swung in and out of the light path. The camera, with its gear box and other attachments, is mounted on a common plate and fastened to the platform of the carrying arm. This arrangement absorbs vibrations up to the highest magnifica-tions. There is no direct contact between motion-picture camera and beam splitter since the upper portion of the light-proof connecting sleeve does not touch the lower portion; therefore, the transmission of vibrations to the optical system is avoided.

In order for living animal cells to continue growing in cultures, the temperature of the culture must be maintained at approximately 37 C. Although it is possible to place a heating stage on the object stage of the microscope, it is better to place the entire microscope in an "incubator," preferably made of transparent plastic. It is also desirable to have extension focusing gears and operating gears as shown in Figure 1.

TIME-LAPSE MICROMOTION PICTURES

After having made the electrical connections and loaded the motion-picture camera, the preliminary adjustments of the microscope are made while the master switch of the intervallometer is in the OFF position. A special switch makes it possible to by-pass the intervallometer to turn on the light source of the microscope.

The preliminary adjustments of the microscope, including selection of the illumination method and the objective, are routine procedures with which the microscopist is familiar. They need not be described here. Upon completion of these adjustments, the length of the interval between exposures and the length of the exposure itself must be determined.

Interval between exposures. The interval between exposures can be determined with the following formula:

$$I = \frac{a \times 3600}{b \times c}$$

$I =$ Interval between exposures *in seconds.*

$a =$ Number of *hours* of the event to be photographed.

$b =$ Number of *seconds* into which this event is to be condensed by projection.

$c =$ Number of frames per second projected by the motion-picture projector.

There is a fury of activity taking place in this garden, but it is invisible to the naked eye. With the aid of a microscope and time-lapse photography, these slow changes can be observed and recorded.

Example: Morphological changes of the object occurring within 12 hours are to be photographed with time lapses so that when the film is projected at the rate of 24 pictures per second, the events are condensed into a period of 2 minutes (120 seconds).

$$a = 12 \qquad b = 120 \qquad c = 24$$

$$I = \frac{12 \times 3600}{120 \times 24} = 15 \text{ seconds}$$

The pointer of the interval dial is to be set to 15 seconds.

Length of the exposure. The length of exposure can be determined with a photoelectric exposure meter. The photoelectric cell in light-proof housing with extension tube is held against the eye lens of the observation telescope. The reciprocal value of the deflection of the needle on the indicating meter is then multiplied by a second value determined by the sensitivity rating of the film.

Example: A photovolt Photoelectric Exposure Meter Model 501-M is used. It has four sensitivity ranges, each adjacent rating 10 times more sensitive. On range No. 1 (lowest sensitivity), the factor for a film of ASA rating 10 is 5. Therefore, on range No. 2 it is 50, on range No. 3 it is 500, and on range No. 4 it is 5000. A film with an ASA rating of 60 is used. The needle deflects to 50 on range No. 3. The exposure time is:

$$E = \frac{1 \times 500}{50 \times 6} = \frac{5}{3} \text{ seconds}$$

The pointer of the exposure dial is to be set to $\frac{5}{3} = 1.6$ seconds.

Length of film. The length of film to be used during the period within which time-lapse pictures are taken is determined by dividing the total number of seconds in the period by the number of seconds in the interval.

Example: When pictures are taken at intervals of 15 seconds for 12 hours (12×3600 seconds), the total number of frames exposed is:

$$\frac{12 \times 3600}{15} = 2880 \text{ frames}$$

Each foot of film contains 40 exposures. The total length of film exposed is:

$$\frac{2880}{40} = 72 \text{ feet}$$

After the pointers of the two dials are set, the light switch is set, either to RUN (microscope light source turned on about one-fourth second before the shutter opens and off when the shutter closes) or to SET (microscope light source lit continuously). The time-lapse switch is set to TIME, the master switch is turned on, and the equipment starts to take time-lapse micromotion pictures. A frame counter can be attached to the intervallometer. When this device is set to 2880 frames, for example, the equipment will be turned off automatically when 2880 frames have been exposed.

MICROPHOTOGRAPHY GLOSSARY

[Here is a glossary of the terms most frequently encountered in the field of microphotography.]
• *Also see: Chemical Glossary; Color Photography Glossary; Glossary (page 197).*

Actifilm: a trademark of the Ozalid Corp., for a sheet of diazo film.

ammonia process: two-component diazo process in which both the diazo and the coupler are on the base, and development is achieved by neutralizing the acidic stabilizers by evaporating aqueous ammonia.

aperture card: a card with a rectangular hole specifically designed to hold a frame of microfilm.

archival quality (archival standards): standards of permanence for photographic films established by the ASA. There are separate standards for raw film and for processed film.

azo dye: dye formed by the reaction or coupling of a diazo and coupler, as in the diazo process.

background: the area of a drawing, microfilm or print, exclusive of line work, lettering, or other information.

background density: the density of the noninformation area of an image on microfilm.

bleed through: undesired appearance of back-printed information in the photograph of the front of a document.

block indexing: a system of indexing microfilm on which documents are photographed in groups or "blocks" identified by readily distinguishable numbers.

blow-back: an enlarged print made from microfilm.

book carriage: a device which permits the rapid photographing of large bound books. The carriage has balanced or spring-loaded platens to support the covers of the book. With spring-loaded platens, two pages may be photographed at a time.

book holder: a device which permits the photographing of bound books under glass. It consists of balanced or spring-loaded platens mounted in a box with a hinged glass cover. It is used to hold bound books which cannot otherwise be held flat enough to permit full coverage while photographing.

camera, rotary: a type of microfilm camera that photographs documents while they are being moved by some form of transport mechanism. The document transport mechanism is connected to a film transport mechanism which moved by some form of transport so that there is no relative movement between the film and the image of the document.

conditioning: 1) a process of restoring microfilm for active use after a period of storage, generally including rehumidifying and cleaning; 2) a preliminary treatment given to material such as aperture cards before specific tests are made (generally the material is kept for a definite length of time at a specific temperature and humidity).

Copyflo: a trademark of Xerox, Inc., for electrostatic printers.

Copytron: a trademark of Charles Bruning Company, Inc., for an electrofax-type printer.

coupler: in diazo printing the coupler is a compound which combines with the unexposed diazonium salt to form the dye image.

cutting lines (chopping lines): lines added at the time of microfilming to permit automatic cutting of prints reproduced on roll paper.

diameters - reduction, enlargement, magnification: a measure of the number of times a given linear dimension of an object is reduced or enlarged by an optical system.

diazo material: a slow-print film or paper sensitized by azo dyes which, after exposure to light strong in the blue through ultraviolet spectrum and development by ammonia vapor or alkaline solution, forms an image. Diazo material generally produces non-reversible images—a positive image will produce a positive image and a negative image will produce a negative image.

dimensional stability: a term applied to the relative ability of photographic materials to maintain their size and shape during and after processing, and also under various conditions of temperature and humidity.

Electrofax: a trademark of Radio Corporation of America for a zinc-oxide coated paper used in an electrostatic reproduction process capable of creating and maintaining an image on paper.

electrostatic: this term is used to identify certain dry photographic processes wherein photosensitive materials are electrically charged and a latent image produced by projection and developed with ionized carbon toner.

enlargement ratio: the ratio of the linear measurement of a micro-image of a document to the linear measurement of the enlarged image, expressed as $5\times$, $20\times$, and so on.

Filmac: a trademark of the Minnesota Mining and Manufacturing Company for a microfilm reader-printer and related supplies.

Film-A-Record: a trademark of Remington Rand Co. for a line of microfilm products.

film, unitized: a roll of microfilm separated into individual frames or strips and inserted in a carrier.

flash card: any target, generally printed with distinctive markings, which is photographed to facilitate indexing of film.

flats: a term used to describe two pieces of glass, polished to a high degree of smoothness and flatness and used to hold film in readers and enlargers.

generation: a measure of the remoteness of the copy from the original document; the picture taken of the document is termed "first generation"; microfilm copies made from this "first generation" are termed "second generation"; copies from the "second generation" are termed "third generation"; and so on.

image position: the arrangement of objects or images with respect to the axis of the film.

indexing film: any method of annotating, by flash cards for example, a division of material being photographed; used so a given document may be easily located.

insert film: microfilm strip cut in a length to fit a film holder.

intermediate: a reproducible copy (which may be microfilm) made from the original document, which is used to make further copies.

interpreter: an EAM card machine which senses a punched card and prints the information on that card.

Kalfax: a trademark for the microfilm of the Kalvar Corp.

macroscopic: large enough to be seen by the unaided eye.

master film: any film, but generally a negative, which is carefully inspected and then used for producing further reproductions.

master microfilm card: an aperture card containing microfilm, generally a negative, which is used for producing further reproductions.

Microcard: a trademark for a micro-opaque card manufactured by the Microcard Corporation.

microfiche: microfilm produced by a camera in the form of multiple images in grid pattern on a card-size sheet of film, rather than as sequential images on a roll of film. Used primarily in Europe.

Micro-File: a trademark for a line of microfilm products of the Eastman Kodak Co.

microimage: a unit of information, such as a page of text or a drawing too small to be read by the unaided eye.

Microline: a trademark of the Ozalid Corp. for a line of microfilm products.

microphotography: the application of photographic processes to reproduce copy in sizes too small to be read by the unaided eye. Not to be confused with photomicrograph.

microproduction: copy rendered in sizes too small to be read by the unaided eye—they may be produced photographically or by other means on either transparent or opaque materials; also the process of making such images.

original: material from which copies are made, such as handwritten copy, printed matter, drawings, or photographs.

pagination: a term referring to the arrangement of pages or micro-images of pages on a microfilm or micro-opaque.

reader: a projection device for viewing an enlarged microimage.

reader-printer: a machine which combines the functions of a reader and an enlarger-printer.

reflex copying: a method of photocopying in which light passes through the sensitized paper and emulsion, strikes the material being copied, and reflects back to the emulsion.

simplex: an image-positioning technique in rotary-camera microfilming; images are photographed across the full width of the film.

Xerography: a dry electrostatic photographic process using a charged photoconductive plate to record the image.

(Reproduced by permission from the copyrighted book, *Glossary of Terms,* The National Microfilm Association.)

SEMINARY STUDENTS   **ESTHER BUBLEY**

This photograph is a tour de force of repetition, both in theme content and the physical placement of the figures. Rather than waiting for a visually complicated cluster of students, Miss Bubley caught them in this straight-lined progression, accented by the nearly parallel lines of the sidewalks. Academic rules of composition are broken, in that the figures appear bound to walk out of the picture at lower right. The roadway accentuates this momentum.

Although in motion, the figures have a static quality. Their placement in the photo could be called repetitious by academicians, but somehow they arrest the attention—so much so that we almost fail to notice a fourth cluster of students in the distant center at top.

Notice how the post at the exact corner of the building above center right helps to define the clear-cut, simple lines of the composition.

Dépêches officielles
2me Série 1646

Pour copie conforme
Le Directeur Gén.
L'Inspecteur
de Lafolly

Service des DÉPÊCHES PAR PIGEONS VOYAGEURS organisé par
M. STEENACKERS, DIRECTEUR GÉNÉRAL DES TÉLÉGRAPHES ET DES POSTES
M. MERCADIER, Rue de Grenelle-Saint-Germain, 103, PARIS.

Dépêches officielles 2me Série 1647

Pour copie conforme. Le Direct.r Gén.l J. ... P. Inspecteur de Lafolly

MICROREPRODUCTION

Vernon D. Tate

Executive Secretary, National Microfilm Association Librarian, U.S. Naval Academy

[The fantastic growth and vitality of the microreproduction industry is revealed in this informative and timely article. Discussed in detail is the theory of microreproduction and its many practical applications. In addition an extensive bibliography is provided.]

• *Also see: Copying and Close-up Photography; Films When and How to Use Them.*

Microphotography today is a large and important industry with a gross annual volume in excess of $250,000,000. Although basic approaches in the field remain in outline much as they were 20 years ago, greatly improved techniques, excellent instrumentation, breakthroughs in several important component fields and above all acceptance and wide application underlie a growth pattern which can only be described as phenomenal. The faith of the pioneers who devoted so much of their talent, ingenuity, and money to the field has certainly been well justified.

It is clear that all of the data relating to equipment, processes, possibilities, and applications cannot be compressed into the space that is presently available here. Even a reasonably concise full treatment would require one or more volumes. As an example, a glossary of the field now in a second edition requires 50 double column pages just to cover the essential vocabulary now in use. *(Glossary of Terms for Microphotography and Reproduction Made From Micro-Images* edited by D. M. Avedon, National Microfilm Association, 1962.) Even this study is obsolescent and is in process of revision.

The best method of procedure seems to be to present the subject

Official dispatches sent by carrier pigeons. Prints were made from the microscopic film that was placed in a quill and affixed to one of the major feathers of the pigeon's tail.

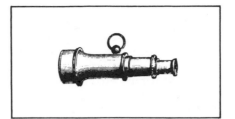

Miniature telescope containing a microscopic photograph and a lens to magnify the image. This viewer was in use around 1867.

as simply as possible, retaining enough of the historical background to afford perspective while supplying liberal reference to the literature so that the interested individual may follow the subject as far as his interest and available time will allow. A word about sources may be pertinent. In addition to books mentioned herein, there are numerous periodicals which carry frequent articles of interest. In addition there are monographs, reports, standards, and other documents dealing with special subjects. Companies in the field publish catalogs, data sheets, booklets, and reprints of articles relevant to their products.

The National Microfilm Association, whose publications will be frequently mentioned, holds an annual convention. The most recent, the 12th, held in 1963 in San Francisco was attended by about 5000 people. The exhibit section required 85 booths to show the equipment, supplies, and accessories now in use in the field. A full program of formal papers, discussions, and panel sessions occupied three days. All of the 32 papers and discussions will appear in the 12th annual volume of *Proceedings.* These annual volumes are a mine of information, and while the earlier ones are now out of print, sets can usually be found in large public, university, and research libraries.

DEFINITION

A microphotograph is a reduced-size documentary reproduction in photofacsimile which is too small to be read by the unaided eye. Usually, though not always, microphotographs are made of textual originals. They may be prepared on film, glass, paper, or other supports and may appear as single or consecutive, negative or positive images on rolls of film 16, 35, 70 or even 105 mm in width. They may also appear in strips, as single exposures mounted in aperture cards or other unitizing devices, as for example, coded "chips" in high-speed data handling devices, or in numerous other forms. A group of microreproductions arranged in rows on a sheet of film is termed a microfiche. A counterpart is an opaque card or sheet containing several rows of images. When this card is the same size as the standard library card, 7.5×12.5 cm it becomes a Microcard ${}_R$.

The basic technique by which these miniature facsimiles are produced is known as microfilming, microcopying, or microreproduction and the product as microfilm, microcopy, or a microphotograph. In recent years, a generic term microform has come into popular use to describe the processes, products, and their many variations.

EQUIPMENT

Microreproductions are made with cameras of various types. There are two basic types, the rotary and the flatbed (planetary) cameras. The rotary camera utilizes a rotating drum or a similar feed in conjunction with synchronized film movement and illumination. A document fed into a slot in the machine is illuminated and as it passes a narrow field, the camera feeds a proportional amount of film to make the exposure. Suitable only for bank checks, cards, loose sheets, and similar originals, equipment of this type is usually made for use with 16 mm film and is widely

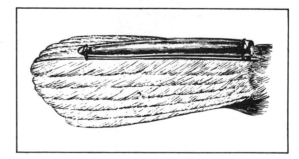

Quill containing microscopic dispatches showing method of attachment to carrier pigeon.

used in banking, business, and similar fields.

Flat-bed or planetary cameras, on the other hand, are made for 16, 35, 70 or 105 mm film and may accept one or more sizes. In simplest form, this type comprises a base with a vertical mast on which the camera bracket may be moved up and down to achieve different reduction ratios. Lighting and control devices, moving or static copyholders of many styles for flat sheets, bound books, engineering drawings, and the like are provided as required. The original is placed in position on the copyholder and the exposure is made.

Flatbed cameras are slower in operation than rotary types but compensate for their comparative lack of speed by versatility and precision in operation.

A variant type used for preparing microfiche and the matrices from which opaque microforms are printed is known as a "step-and-repeat" camera. The only significant difference is in the movement of the film holder. The film holder is made to accept a flat sheet of film which moves in precise relationship on a checkerboard pattern to produce the rows of images on a single sheet that the microfiche or sheet micropaque formats require.

PROCESSING

Processing methods are essentially similar to those used in any photographic process and may be carried out in small scale with hand equipment or by machine. Most microfilm is processed on large precision machines capable of operating at high speeds. They deliver the film dry and ready for inspection and further treatment. Roll positive is printed in continuous printers, usually in rolls of 1000 feet, but the completed-roll microfilm is supplied for use in a standard 100-foot roll. While the foregoing is written with silver-halide microfilm in mind, it should be noted that diazo, Kalvar, and other films are also extensively employed.

Since the small image cannot be read by the unaided eye, means must be employed to make it legible and useful. The spread of equipment and methods employed for this purpose is tremendous. Enlargements on paper, often called "blow-backs," can be made to original size, larger, or smaller as desired. Equipment for this purpose, some of it of high capacity, is widely used. Visual reading of the microform is provided by means ranging from the hand lens (for low reduction) or low-power microscope to highly sophisticated reading consoles equipped with various devices for locating and manipulating any desired image. The other main visual-reading method is projection.

A light source, a means for holding the microform in position, a projection lens, and a screen, all combined in an enclosure, result in a device anomalously known as a reading **machine**, which could be termed more properly, a machine for reading. The variations and elaborations of this essentially simple outline are endless but can be subdivided, by the type of screen used, into translucent- and opaque-screen readers. Each has particular advantages and both are useful. Other points of difference include the size and kind of microform for which the instrument is designed, the method of holding and transporting it, the range of magnification, and various

Recordak Microfile Copying Machine, Model MRD-2. Takes 16 mm and 35 mm film in 100-foot lengths. Reduction ratios from 5 to 21 diameters.

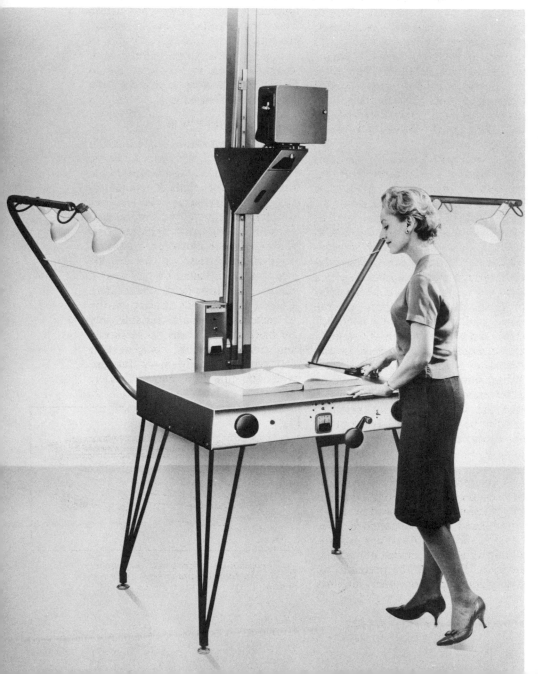

Projection and transcription of the enlarged microscopic dispatches brought by carrier pigeons.

other factors. Some reading machines are equipped to make enlarged paper copies and are known as reader-printers.

In addition to cameras and reading machines, there are many other types of equipment used in microreproduction: processing machines for film, printers, darkroom enlargers, inspection equipment, rewinds, splicing equipment, and many other items. The basic source for equipment information for the entire field is the *Guide to Microreproduction Equipment,* edited by Hubbard W. Ballou and published by the National Microfilm Association. The current (1962) edition contains 519 pages; an 87 page *Supplement A* to the *Guide* was issued in 1963. In addition to pictures of equipment, factual data including prices are supplied. It has been estimated that to acquire one of every item Listed would require an investment well into six figures.

TERMINOLOGY

Not infrequently, *microphotography* is confused with *photomicrography* or photography with a microscope, a technique that is used for quite different purposes. Moreover, the same terms have opposite meanings in the English and German systems of scientific no-

menclature. The former invariably applies the term microphotography to a greatly reduced photograph of a large original and photomicrography to a greatly enlarged photograph made with the aid of a microscope of a small object; the latter uses equivalent terms but reverses their meaning, microphotography being photography with a microscope while photomicrography refers to a minute photograph of a large original. Shortly before the outbreak of World War II, the International Standards Association drafted a preliminary agreement standardizing the terminology according to the English usage. The name and reference are now standard throughout the world.

In recent years, an additional term, *macrophotography* has come to be applied to larger than actual-size photographs of small (for example, insects) as distinguished from microscopic objects. Macrophotographs are made with combinations of photographic equipment not including a compound microscope.

FILMS

There are certain basic considerations in microreproduction, some of them quite elementary, which must always be borne in mind. The film in microfilm is photographic. At the present time the negative film in common use is a special slow-

speed panchromatic silver halide with a distinctive sensitometric curve. This film may be coated with an antihalation backing that is either removed in processing or subsequently. Alternatively, clear-base film can be used. The base is acetate prepared in accordance with specifications formulated for permanent record use by the National Bureau of Standards. The image on exposed and processed negative microfilm is negative, that is the values of the original are inverted. Black printing on a white background on a microfilm negative appears as white (transparent) letters on an opaque (black) background.

Positive microfilms, made usually by contact from negatives, restore the reversed values; in the illustration just cited a positive print would show the printing as black (opaque) on a white (transparent) background. Positive-silver film coated on acetate base is not color sensitive and is much slower than negative film. It is intended for machine printing and processing.

Two important duplicating films, diazotype (usually called diazo) and Kalvar should be mentioned at this point. Neither is a "silver" film and each has special characteristics that make it particularly useful in the broad range of microreproduction processes. Diazo film is made by incorporating photosensitive dye-

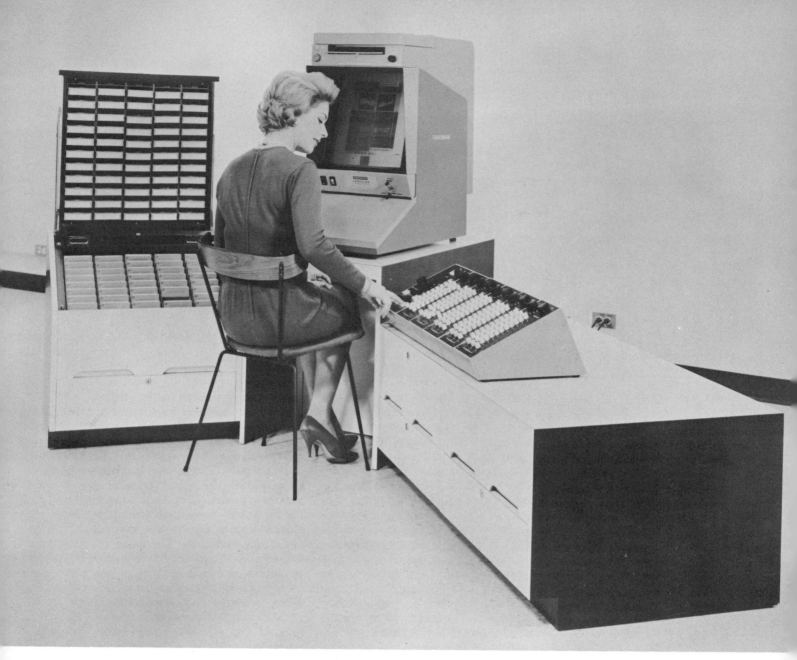

Recordak Microcode high-speed reference station for locating any document from a condensed file of up to a million pages on microfilm. A paper print of the abstract file can be made at the same time. The record file is automatically scanned for locating the microdocuments.

stuffs on a film base. After exposure by contact under strong illumination (the material is much slower than "silver" film) processing which involves dye coupling is achieved in a chamber into which ammonia vapor is introduced. Diazo films are virtually grainless and are direct-working, that is produce a negative from a negative and a positive from a positive.

The Kalvar process is relatively new and is based on a light-scattering effect of photosensitive chemicals sensitive to heat. Exposure is made by ultraviolet light and development is by heat (225 F). No chemical developers or other agents are required and the process is dry. A special heat fixation can be applied for copies from which prints are to be made; this process is negative-working.

It should be stressed that neither diazo nor Kalvar are presently suitable for camera use. Film size always refers to width for roll film which may be, as has been indicated, 16, 35, 70 or 105 mm; an 8-mm variant comprising two rows of images in a 16-mm film is sometimes used. Microfiche sizes are expressed in sheet dimensions, as for example 7.5 × 12.5 cm. The standard roll of microfilm is 100-feet in length. Perforations, essential for motion pictures, are not required or used in microfilming except in a few instances for coding.

Frame size refers to the amount of film area in the camera available to receive the microfilm image for a single exposure. Placement concerns the orientation of the image with respect to the frame size and the film dimensions. It can best be considered in terms of the reading line. A page of printed matter can be placed in microfilm so that the reading line is parallel to the length of the film, or alternatively parallel to the width of the film. Placement is an important consideration because it affects the type of utilization media to be employed, the ratio of reduction, and film economy.

Two additional terms, ratio of reduction and resolution or resolving power, are so important that they deserve somewhat fuller treatment.

RATIO OF REDUCTION

If an ordinary 6×9-inch book page were microfilmed at a ratio of reduction of 8 times (as low as is commonly used), the resulting microfilm negative would measure $1^1/_8 \times$ ¾-inches. This is linear reduction. An area reduction of the same page would reduce the 54 square inches of the original to .84375 sq. in., or ×64.

Leaving out of account certain tricks in manipulation used mainly for photomechanical work, the reduction is always proportional. If the length of the document is reduced, the width is reduced to the same degree. In microphotography, *ratio of reduction* refers to linear reduction. It may be expressed as a fraction of the original dimension or size, as $^1/_8$, or as in optics as 8× or ×8 (using the × before the figure to denote reduction and after it as 8× to denote

enlargement). It may also be expressed in diameters; a ratio of reduction of 10 diameters, for example, means the same thing as ×10.

Ratio of reduction is one of the most important and least systematically considered factors in microphotography. It is one of the cornerstones of the art, for the ability of the technique to reproduce originals at considerable degrees of reduction and to make effective use of the copies so produced is basic. The economies of the situation which allow copies to be produced inexpensively, or below the financial limitations of competitive processes are also basic.

Ratio of reduction is not a simple matter. It is a function of the original itself, camera, lighting, resolving power of lens, film and processing, methods of intended use and many other factors including cost. Commercial working applications presently range upward to about 40 diameters. Laboratory and experimental work have demonstrated the practicability of making reductions in excess of 100 diameters. Interestingly enough, some of the early 19th-century microfilms were made at much greater reductions than those now commonly employed.

During World War II the "microdot" process used in espionage reduced a full legal-size page of text to the dimensions of a single dot the size of a period made by a typewriter. Even today many of the processes used to make microdots remain classified. A good indication of these methods that can be used will be found in G. W. W. Stevens *"Microphotography: Photography at Extreme Resolution."*

Resolving Power

Resolving power, sometimes called resolution, is at the heart of the microfilm process. The ability of photographic materials and suitable equipment to reduce textual images by as much as 100 times their linear dimensions, and then to recreate them by enlargement for viewing or for the making of facsimiles is fundamental. Resolving power is as much a function of the original, the camera including adjustments, the lighting, and the proper exposure as it is of the film and lens employed.

The National Bureau of Standards has developed methods of testing resolution which are relatively simple and efficient. They are widely used. The basis is a resolution chart, and the sheet "Instructions for the use of the National Bureau of Standards Microcopy

Last messages from Custer, June 25 and 26, 1876. The pencil messages were on slips of paper and microfilmed. The National Archives photo.

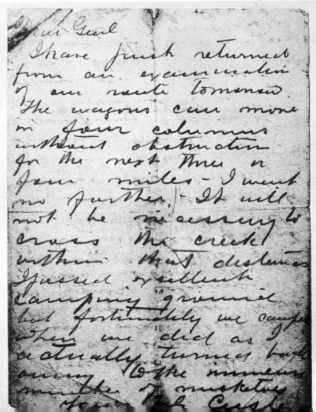

Resolution Test Chart" prepared by the Photographic Technology Section is so informative and important that it is reproduced in its entirety in the following paragraphs. (It should be noted that a new resolution chart is in process of preparation. It will be essentially similar to the one now in use although a few values have been altered to make some of the computations somewhat easier.)

"In general, the reduction in dimensions of documents obtainable by photographic methods, such as by the use of microcopying camera, is limited by the resolution of the lens and of the film (emulsion). The resolving power of the best photographic lenses of short focal length in the center of the field is higher than the resolving power of the best film. At 20 or 30 degrees off the axis of the lens the resolution usually falls off to about one-half of that at the center of the field, or less. The resolving power of films ranges from 40 lines per millimeter for ordinary negative films and 60 to 70 for positive motion-picture films to about 130-150 lines per millimeter for the best microcopying films.

"Equal in importance to the resolution of lens and film is the proper positioning (focusing) of the lens. Very often we find that the focusing scale of the camera lens is in error so that the full resolving power of the lens and film is not attained. Of course, cameras subject to vibration, either from faulty design or from heavy machinery in the building, will not give highly resolved negatives.

"In order to evaluate the performance of microcopying cameras the resolution test-chart was prepared. This chart consists of a series of line-patterns, the lines and spaces being of equal width. Each pattern contains two sets of lines, one set at right angles to the other. The patterns range from one to ten lines per millimeter. Not less than three of these charts are placed on the copy board of the camera so that in the picture area, one chart is in the center of the field, one at the center of the long side, and another at the corner. The last two charts are oriented so that one set of lines of the patterns is radial with respect to the center of the field and the other set of lines is tangential.

"The group of charts is then photographed in the usual manner. To test the focus of the lens a series of photographs is made with small changes in focusing-scale readings, care being taken to record each reading on the card for future reference. After the films have been developed, the negatives are examined with a microscope using a magnification of about 40 diameters. The number of lines per millimeter, in the smallest pattern in which the lines can be counted with certainty, multiplied by the reduction ratio, gives the resolution. For example, if the smallest pattern of the chart resolved contains 7.9 lines per millimeter and the reduction ratio is 10, the resolution will be 79 lines per millimeter.

"In the center of the field the resolution should be independent of the orientation of the patterns. Away from the center of the field, it will be found that the resolution for radial and tangential patterns is not the same and, futhermore, will change with the distance. This effect is caused by aberrations of the lens. If in the center of the field, the resolution of lines in one direction is less than that in another direction, it indicates that the camera was vibrating during exposure or that there was a relative motion

Thermo-Fax Filmac 100 Reader-Printer made by Minnesota Mining and Manufacturing Co. Microfilm records on 16 mm, 35 mm, or on aperture cards can be copied or reproduced in a few seconds on an 8½ × 11 sheet.

of the image with respect to the film. In order to check the camera for vibration, make several exposures with the chart in the center of the field in one orientation, then turn it through an angle of 45° and make several more exposures. If the lines in both directions at both orientations are equally resolved, the camera is free from vibration.

"In cameras of the type in which the document being copied and the film move during exposure, there is the possibility that the relative motions may be improperly matched so that the document is moved either too fast or too slow with respect to the motion of the film. This can be checked by photographing resolution charts at the center of the field. If the camera is properly adjusted, the lines parallel to the motion and perpendicular to it will be equally resolved. Otherwise the lines parallel to the motion will show a higher resolution than those perpendicular to the motion.

"The lowest resolution in any part of the picture area, the size and style of type, and the reduction ratio are factors determining the quality of reproduction on microcopying film. Three grades of reproduction, sufficient for the needs of practical microcopying, have been defined. They are:
1. Excellent copy—details of type clearly defined.
2. Legible copy—readable without difficulty although serifs and fine details of type not clearly defined.
3. Decipherable copy—readable with difficulty, letters, e, c, and o partly closed.

"A correlation of these factors for commonly used styles of type has been established for these three grades of reproduction as follows:
1. For excellent copy, the height of the lower case letter e, as recorded on the film, should not be less than the distance across eight lines of the smallest resolution pattern resolved by the particular camera and film combination employed.
2. For legible copy, the height of the e should be not less than the distance across five lines

Remington Rand Model F 440, designed for viewing 35 mm film images mounted in aperture cards. Screen is 10½ × 12 inches, magnification 15 times.

of the smallest pattern resolved.
3. For decipherable copy, the height of the e should be not less than the distance across three lines of the smallest pattern resolved.

"For example, if it is desired to copy a newspaper, on which the height of the smallest e is 1.5 millimeters, at a reduction ratio of 19×, the minimum resolution required for the three grades of reproduction are:
1. For excellent copy, 101 lines per millimeter.
2. For legible copy, 63 lines per millimeter.
3. For decipherable copy, 38 lines per millimeter.

"It is recommended that several photographs of the resolution charts be made on every roll of microcopy film used, at the beginning of the roll, or preferably at both ends of the roll. This practice will provide a convenient means of continually checking both the operation and performance of the microcopying equipment, which can be referred to at any time."

It may be useful at this juncture to survey briefly some of the forms of microreproductions in common use and to include a few remarks on format and purpose. The following list is by no means complete and the comments are not to be considered exhaustive.

MICROTRANSPARENCIES
(Translucent projection)

16 mm microfilm: usual form 100-foot roll; used for commercial, industrial, governmental and other documents and files, bank checks, catalog cards, and similar materials.

35 mm microfilm: 100-foot roll, shorter rolls, strips, unitized; used for library, archival, academic purposes; governmental records of many types; industrial and business documentation including plans and specifications; and for many other uses.

70 mm microfilm: roll form, often unitized; used principally for engineering drawings and plans and large originals.

105 mm microfilm: unitized; used for large engineering drawings and plans and for special graphic reproduction purposes.

Microfiche (sheet film): rows of images on film sheets 3×5 inches or other size; used principally for academic purposes, more commonly in Europe than in the United States. A recent commercial development employs a sheet $6 \times 4\frac{1}{2}$ inches with 98 images. It is used by Micro-Photo of Cleveland, Ohio as a publication medium.

MICROPAQUES
(Reflex or Epidiascopic projection)

Microcard: (Name copyright by Microcard Corporation) consists of card 7.5×12.5 cm (approximately 3×5 inches) containing rows of images. An edition process primarily used for academic purposes.

Microprint cards: similar format and use to microcards, produced by many firms.

Microprint: generic term for micro-images on paper.

Microlexs: proprietary format featuring multiple rows of images sometimes as many as 300 pages on a paper card approximately 9 square inches; principally used for reproducing and publishing law books; an edition process.

Readex Microprint: a proprietary process whereby 10 rows of 10 pages each are printed from a

Church Catalogue
English Literature

Nos. 316— 3869
Dibdin — Gray, Thomas

Readex Microprint   *   New York

Readex Microprint card contains 100 pages on one side of a 6×9 inch card.

micronegative on each side of a paper sheet 6×9 inches. An edition process, the final product is nonphotographic and produced by a printing press.

Microstrip, Microtape: contact paper prints from 16 or 35 mm roll- or strip-microfilm negatives; usually cut into individual pages or short lengths and mounted on cards or sheets; used for hospital, personnel, financial and other records.

All of the foregoing are listed in general terms. There are exceptions and other formats.

THE TECHNIQUE

The technique of microphotography is popularly regarded as new and as an offshoot of motion-picture practice. Actually it is neither, and may boast a distinguished lineage dating back to the early days of photography. The publication by Daguerre of his process in 1839 heralded the practical adoption of photography. Two years later, the distinguished English microscopist and photographic pioneer, Dancer, reported that he had succeeded in reproducing a printed handbill 14 inches long on a negative ¼-inch long. Some examples of Dancer's work still exist. Other microscopists and experimenters followed and were successful, although their achievements were regarded by photographers and the general public as interesting but wholly impractical laboratory feats.

In his *Dictionary of Photography* of 1858, Thomas Sutton included the following definition of microphotography. "*Microphotography:* Under this head may be included two different processes. One is of little or no practical utility and consists of copying objects on an exceedingly small scale. The photograph is intended to be viewed through a magnifier or microscope. The other, which is a branch of photography of the highest interest and importance consists in producing enlarged photographs of minute objects—that is, in fixing the images obtained in the microscope."

HISTORY

As frequently happens, the first practical application of the process was in the manufacture of novelties wherein microscopic photographs of individuals, groups, famous documents, and sometimes (it must be admitted) naughty ladies, were incorporated. These photographs, usually in the form of transparencies, were mounted in souvenir fans, miniature telescopes, and similar trinkets.

The eminent French photographer, Dagron, was the first to employ textual microphotography on a large scale. He had established a studio in Paris for the manufacture of miniature souvenir novelties and in 1870 found his business ruined by the Franco-Prussian War of 1870-71. The city of Paris itself was so closely besieged that no means of communication with the outside world remained, save for an occasional balloon built in the city and floated over the lines to unoccupied territory. Carrier pigeons sent from Paris in the balloons later returned to the city with dispatches, but their maximum load was a thin sheet of paper only two or three inches square.

Dagron developed a plan to reproduce dispatches on microfilm at great reductions, thereby increasing the amount of information that could be transmitted by pigeon post. Accordingly, he embarked with an assistant and his equipment in a balloon and, after numerous vicissitudes, escaped to Tours. Arrangements were there made to have all public and private letters or dispatches printed on large sheets of paper each of which could contain about 300,000 characters. These were reduced photographically to a size of approximately 50 × 70 mm. Twenty thin collodion films encased in a quill could be carried by a single pigeon.

Upon arrival in Paris the films were projected on a large screen and transcribed by a number of copyists. Later, photographic enlargements on paper were made. In all, more than 100,000 dispatches were sent to Paris in this manner. It was the practice to make up and send 40 sets of each, as the mortality of the carrier pigeons through cold, rifle fire, and the falcons employed by the Prussians as interceptors was very great. Some of these original microscopic

*Readex Microprint Reader Model-C for use with the Microprint cards. 20×
magnification ratio. Viewing screen size 9×11 3/8 inches, green tinted.*

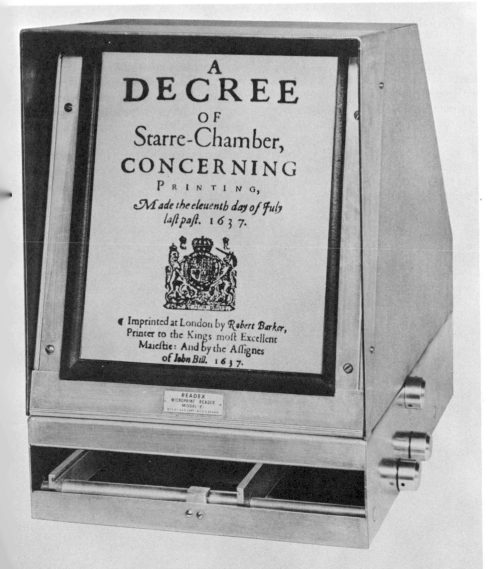

dispatches still exist and may be read without difficulty.

However desirable the process appeared in time of war, it proved too expensive to compete with normal peacetime methods of communication and microphotography again became, for almost half a century, an intellectual plaything and a challenge to experimenters. (A complete discussion of the achievements of Dancer and Dagron will be found in Frederic Luther's *Microflim: A History, 1839-1900.)*

Numerous attempts were made to apply microphotograpy on a practical basis, usually to library or scholarly work, but these were usually ended by the high cost of materials. However, with the development and popularization of motion pictures in the early years of the present century, quantities of excellent film became available at low prices and some research workers, using plate and cut film cameras for documentary reproduction, became intrigued with the possibilities of microfilm as an economical substitute.

One of the pioneers was Dr. Amandus Johnson, Director of the American Swedish Historical Museum. He built a camera using 35 mm nonperforated film for making reproductions of documents pertaining to America for Swedish archives. Dr. Johnson stated that he conceived the idea, which was original, after noting the clarity with which printed titles appeared on the projection screen in a moving-picture theater. With the special camera, of which several improved models were made, many thousands of pages were reproduced in ensuing years.

The introduction of the 35 mm camera provided photographers with a workable medium for making microfilm in a reasonable quantity at relatively slight expense. Accessories were promptly supplied by manufacturers, and word of mouth advertising and accounts in scientific, scholarly, and photographic journals widely publicized the technique. By 1930 it was in widespread use.

The problem was also approached with a view toward incorporating microphotography into business as a record-making and accounting medium. George P. McCarthy developed an instrument, which later became known as the Recordak, to reproduce bank checks on 16 mm film. A corporation known as the Recordak Corporation, a subsidiary of the Eastman Kodak Company, was organized in 1928 to develop, manufacture, and market the equipment. An early decision of the corporation not to sell the services of microphotographic reproduction to business organizations profoundly influenced later commercial development.

The decade 1930 to 1940 was marked by tremendous expansion. Microphotography became a multimillion dollar business. Specialized cameras, reading machines, processing and printing equipment, sensitive materials, and accessories became available; laboratories were established in many libraries, universities, and private business houses; commercial organizations and technicians entered the field; applications multiplied and pyramided.

Specialization in types of microphotographic activity appeared and, while amateurs continued to employ the technique with limited makeshift equipment, heavily capitalized laboratories and enterprises developed. Microphotography ceased to be a particular photographic technique and became a record-administration and control system in which photography plays a vital role.

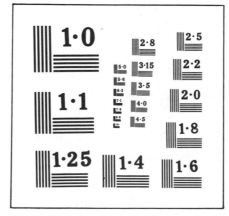

Microcopy resolution test chart from the National Bureau of Standards.

APPLICATIONS

It would be impossible to list in detail all or even most of the applications of microphotography or the fields wherein it has been used. There are, however, several broad general applications that may be noted. Summarized, these are as follows:

1. Protection and preservation of records.
2. Reduction of bulk files.
3. Making research and other materials available for use.
4. Collection of data.
5. Substitution for conventional photography.
6. Administrative accounting and business uses.

Protecting Records

Microphotography is one of the most convenient methods yet developed for protecting original records of all types. This phase of activity is sometimes known as insurance copying, for a microfilm of an original or a file deposited in a bank vault or other safe storage place remote from the location of the original is the cheapest type of insurance that can be obtained.

In wartime, ordinary hazards are immensely multiplied and sabotage, bombing, and other contingencies have already destroyed great quantities of records. In England microphotography is being used as an effective safeguard; many commercial institutions are microfilming their records and working papers on a day-to-day basis. As soon as the films are processed, they are immediately sent to storage locations in remote localities where danger from enemy activity is greatly reduced.

The great bombing raids or the so-called fire raids on London destroyed large and small businesses alike. Many of these were able to resume operation almost immediately through the utilization of microphotographic copies of correspondence files, bills, orders, minute books, ledgers, and other financial papers, catalogs, specifications, blueprints, plans, and the like. An equipment manufacturer holding important defense contracts in this

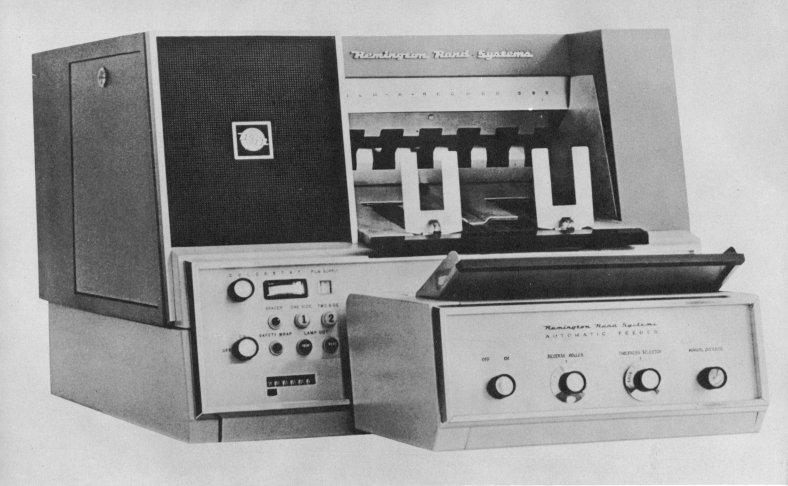

Film-A-Record 555 Microfilm camera that photographs both sides of a document simultaneously at the rate of 125 paper feet a minute. 16 mm film in lengths up to 200 feet. Automatic leader and trailer winding, spacing button for indexing, voltmeter to indicate voltage to lamps.

country recently stated that if his drafting room should be destroyed by any contingency, unique blueprints, working drawings, plans, and specifications could be reproduced from security microfilm copies and production would only be interrupted for a few days at most.

Even in peacetime the hazards of nuclear war are ever present. The destructive potential is so great as to overshadow any peril hitherto known. Since records are the life blood of so many industries and activities, vast microfilm projects have been undertaken to protect them. Mere preservation on safely stored microfilm is not enough. Facilities exist to provide disaster protection deep underground in so-called "head" installations. Similarly protected production laboratories are maintained in adjacent areas so that the stored records can be recreated in paper facsimile as needed.

Unexposed silver film may be fogged and ruined by radiation. This fact has spurred the search for suitable materials and processes that are immune to this hazard. Several have been developed and a number of immediate uses for them have been found.

It is unfortunately true that many records are being created without sufficient thought being given to their permanence. Poor quality paper and ink or impermanent methods of duplication are the principal offenders. It is quite possible and practicable to microfilm such records on receipt and preserve them permanently in microfilm form. Great quantities of records have been microfilmed for this purpose alone. As it is easy to make duplicate microfilms by automatic machines, a duplicate stored elsewhere is excellent insurance.

One of the grave problems faced by libraries everywhere is created by the fact that wood pulp paper is impermanent and carries within itself the seeds of its own destruction after a relatively short period of time. Since 1870 when it came into widespread use, thousands of titles in all fields have been printed on this impermanent stock. Einstein's first published scientific paper, for example, appeared in a periodical printed on wood pulp paper and was subject to chemical deterioration. Newspapers are notorious in this regard, and it is now standard practice to microfilm current issues an back files; over 500 newspapers are now preserved only on microfilm. Soon a large-scale program for microfilming books and periodicals will be launched. The initial studies are well advanced and it is clear that microreproduction is the only practicable method of insuring the perpetuation of these titles.

Saving Storage Space

Storage space in urban areas is expensive and executives continually deplore the expense of accumulating and housing files. It is possible

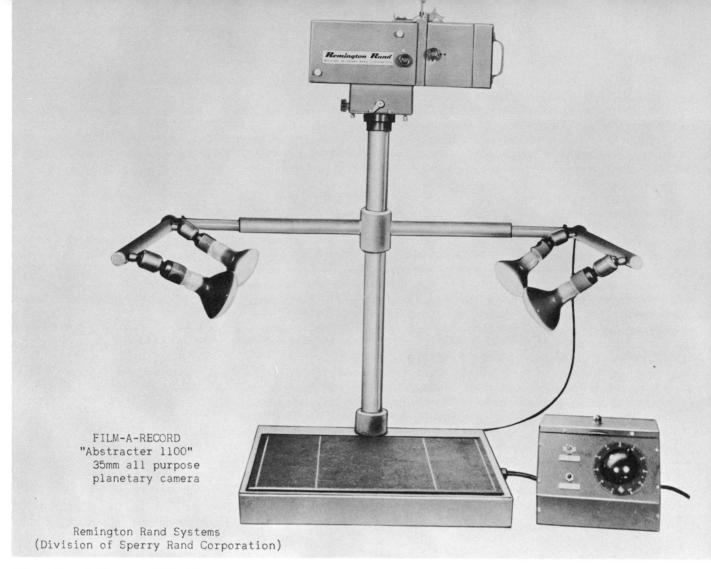

FILM-A-RECORD
"Abstracter 1100"
35mm all purpose
planetary camera

Remington Rand Systems
(Division of Sperry Rand Corporation)

Film-A-Record Abstractor 1100. 35 mm all-purpose planetary camera supplied by the Remington Rand Systems. A portable camera for copying records up to 20×24 inches.

through microphotography to reduce the required file space more than 95 percent. To cite a specific example, 30 million pages of a filled-in tabular statistical form exists in a government depository. It occupies approximately 9000 cubic feet of storage space. If placed on microfilm, the storage space could be reduced to less than 5 percent of the original bulk or roughly 450 cubic feet. The original file weighs roughly 300 tons; the microfilm would weigh 1½ tons. If the cost of housing this material is computed at 25 to 50 cents per cubic feet per year, the savings effected in a very few years in housing costs alone would more than defray the entire cost of microfilming.

It has been demonstrated that microfilm copies are actually easier to consult in many instances than the originals; a given record may be located from a microfilm file long before a clerk could walk from the office to the particular file drawer in a conventional file room. If at any time reproduction in paper facsimile to original size should become necessary, these can be produced on semi-automatic machines at low unit cost. In the Government, as well as in private industry, many perplexing space problems are being solved through microphotography.

Multiplication of Use

Microphotography is equally important in making materials available for use. Documents need never be out of file if copies are available and any item may be consulted at any time. Working tools, such as indexes, catalogs, reference works, and card files may be duplicated in several places. In library practice, it is not the custom in this country to loan rare books, manuscripts, or other valuable and fragile materials. As a consequence, research workers have been compelled, sometimes at considerable expense, to travel to the location of the originals or to obtain manual transcriptions which are never fully reliable, or to use photostat or conventional photographic copies which are reliable but expensive.

Now for the first time it is possible for copies of rare books, manuscripts, and other library and archival treasures to be procured in quantity at a reasonable price. New developments in electrostatic enlarging and other methods of making enlarged paper prints in quantity at low cost have further extended the range of possibilities in this area.

It is possible to utilize microphotography as a substitute for conventional photographic duplication, particularly with documentary or related materials. Photostats, for example, have been used in great quantities and while microphotography will not replace the photostat machine, it does supplement and extend its facilities particularly when long files of material are being reproduced. Full-tone photographic prints are being duplicated with considerable success through the use of microphotography.

It is no longer necessary to make copy negatives full size; microfilm cameras are used and the miniature reproductions are enlarged to the desired size. The photographic identification cards which are now almost universally employed in defense factories, government agencies, and related organizations, are in large part made with microphotographic equipment.

At the present time, microphotography is being used in virtually every field of endeavor. Its ramifications are a reflection of the complexity of modern life. Commercial microphotography began in banks and was intended to supply copies of checks passing through the bank. Formerly, as these were cleared they were returned to the depositor without a record other than the usual ledger entries being preserved. This procedure was generally unsatisfactory and frequently caused difficulty and financial loss.

Department stores, insurance companies, and business enterprises generally, use microphotography in billing and accounting operations. Some department stores prepare bills directly from microfilm reproductions of sales checks and tabulated ledger records. Transportation companies formerly had duplicate waybills prepared to send with shipments of goods after the goods were loaded for shipment; trains were often delayed in yards for several hours while the duplicate waybills were prepared. Now the originals are sent and microfilm copies are retained for the permanent record thus saving a great

Reproduction of 18th-century Spanish manuscript printed from a 24×36 mm microfilm negative.

deal of time and money.

Auditors and accountants, instead of traveling to branch plants and offices and remaining in the field for several months, now make their audits from microfilm copies of all required papers that are regularly forwarded to the central office. A small well-equiped staff can do more work faster, more accurately, and at considerable savings in cost.

Even in the apparently small item of postage, considerable savings can be effected. Before World War II, it was possible to send three letter-size sheets of ordinary bond paper, five letter-size sheets of manifold paper, or seven feet of 35 mm microfilm from Washington, D. C. to Hong Kong by air mail for 70 cents, the rate for ½ ounce. From 6 to 10 sheets of ordinary typewritten material, or the equivalent, could be sent at this rate. Seven feet of 35 mm microfilm could contain 56 maps, plans, blueprints, or tracings up to 30 or 40 inches or even larger, or 112 pages of typewritten manuscript or printed material (if the material were specially prepared for the purpose, 224 pages) at the same rate. The contrast is startling and if microphotography is used there are no errors in transcription.

Conversely, microfilms have been used to insure unique originals against loss in transit. Some publishers microfilm all manuscripts

before they are sent out to be read or sent to the printer. This practice has proved its worth in numerous instances. Statistical tabulations, nonalphabetic material, or oriental-language documents have been difficult to transfer rapidly from one place to another. Cable or telegraphic transmission is difficult. Microfilm and airmail offer a convenient and inexpensive solution. For example, the Shostakovich Seventh Symphony was first performed in this country from a score reproduced on microfilm and brought by air from Europe.

In academic and scientific work, archives, libraries, and museums use microphotography for a great variety of purposes, many of which parallel uses already discussed. Rare and unique documents or printed works may be filmed for preservation against loss or to protect them from the wear and tear of constant use.

Research and Records

For research purposes, a microfilm will serve as well as the original, and fragile documents may be thus safeguarded from further damage. Newspaper are a good example. They are notoriously fragile and impermanent, for the low-grade wood-pulp paper used is prone to chemical change, discoloration, and deterioration after a relatively short period of time. Through microphotography, newspapers may be

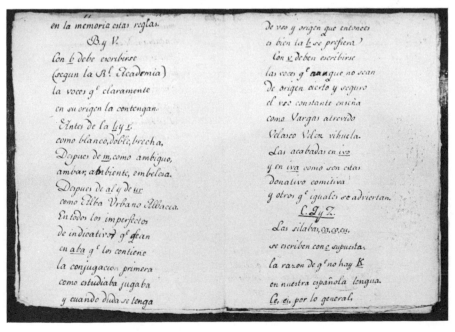

transferred to a stable, permanent medium and a microfilm copy on a suitable reading machine is much more usable than the large bound volumes formerly preserved in libraries. Several million pages of past and current newspaper have already been placed on microfilm, and many publishers film current files regularly and retain the microfilm as their permanent record.

Microphotography is being used to gather material that is no longer available for purchase. The newer libraries, for example, cannot hope to duplicate rare manuscript holdings of older institutions that have been collecting perhaps for a century or more; there are no originals to be had at any price. Microfilms, however, are readily procured and inexpensive. Personal or family papers, business or professional records, are frequently copied to be added to working collections. Gaps in collections or long series of rare materials required for particular purposes may be procured on microfilm.

Interlibrary loans which are expensive and generally unsatisfactory can be eliminated through the use of microphotography. Instead of securing the use of a volume for a short period of time, a borrowing library may secure a microfilm facsimile, often for the same price that would be paid for transportation if the original volume were loaned. When microcopies are supplied, the owning library will always have the book available on its own shelves and will run no risk of loss or damage in transit.

Rare or fragile volumes which have not customarily been loaned are equally available on microfilm. In the preparation of catalogs, calendars, indexes, and finding media of all types, microphotography serves many useful purposes. Museums may produce pictorial catalogs of the objects in their collections; regional-library catalogs may be built up through the filming of the card catalogs of many institutions and subsequent comparison and merging. Working lists, shelf lists, and bibliographies may be exchanged freely.

Bulky supplementary documents,

or pictorial or graphic appendices may accompany a printed book in the form of a volume on microfilm in order to supply a demand that is usually considerably smaller than that for the general discussion. In periodical publication, the same procedure and benefits are realized. *Mathematical Reviews,* an abstracting journal, publishes insofar as possible, abstracts of all articles appearing anywhere in the world dealing with mathematics. Many of these are published in obscure journals available in only a few libraries. Through a special arrangement, subscribers may secure a complete microfilm copy of any article abstracted at a nominal cost.

GOVERNMENTAL PARTICIPATION

No discussion of microphotography would be complete without mention of the participation of the Federal Government. Actually the microphotographic activities of the government represents a good cross section of current applications. The Government has archives, libraries, and museums. It operates businesses or business-like activities, manufactures certain items, conducts research, and for its own purposes utilizes every known technique of microcopying, sometimes on a vast scale. There is virtually no known activity that is not represented to some degree by a parallel in governmental operations.

A few examples may be of interest. Most human activities begin with vital statistics. The records of the Bureau of the Census are preserved on microfilm, and the decennial and other census projects are implemented in part by high-capacity, mechanized information-retrieval systems based on microfilm. One of these was designed at the National Bureau of Standards and bears the code name FOSDIC; it is, by the way, also used by the Weather Bureau.

Most Americans come under the provisions of the Social Security System; the entire operational base of the system is microfilm. A large building on the outskirts of Baltimore houses the vital components. The rapidity and perfection of ref-

Section of newspaper microfilm storage vault. Micro-Photo division, Bell & Howell, Cleveland. The vault contains 150 million newspaper pages on nearly 3000 miles of microfilm; storage in 1000-foot reels, controlled temperature 70 F, relative humidity 50% permanently maintained.

erence achieved is a source of constant amazement to the visitor. Again most Americans have some contact with the Treasury Department which uses many variations of microfilm. The records of Congress and of the Executive branch are, for the most part, safely filmed. The Department of Defense is responsible for wide-ranging developments and programs in fields as divergent as the reproduction of engineering drawings and documentation (a system which has revolutionized procurement and accounting systems and saved large sums of

In any technology the momentum generated by increased usage tends to expand capacity and improve speed and precision of operation. The tendency in electronics toward progressive miniaturization is evident in microreproduction. While the proved horizon of ×100 plus minification has not been commercially attempted, it is possible and, if the need arises, will be used. Although the larger microfilm sizes are used far more extensively now than formerly and seem to have established secure fields for their capabilities, the larger originals are being reproduced on the smaller film sizes with complete satisfaction. Better lenses, emulsions, cameras, improved processing, and "know how" are the reasons.

Coincident with improved facilities has come the need for fully accepted standards, for any industry is dependent on standards for sound progress. These have been provided and while coverage is not yet complete (the microfiche field is a noteworthy exception) it is broad enough for full-scale operation and is steadily improving.

New concepts and methods have been exceedingly important. So long as microfilm remained a preservation, security, and low-volume dissemination medium, except for special applications, it could not compete to advantage with many other well-established methods. The shifts from this more or less static concept to that of the dynamics of day-to-day-operations is probably the most significant attitude change of the period, and has already had far-reaching effects. Unitization, high-speed production of enlarged facsimiles at low cost, and mechanized data-handling systems using microforms are highly important developments. In fact the "total-systems concept" with microforms in a central or subsidiary role became the avenue through which the concept of active day-to-day applications was applied (See *The Active Uses of Microfilm,* ed. by J. F. Scanlan and Thomas G. Nanney, New York, Wolf Business Publications, 1962, 117 pp.)

money) to mechanized data-handling systems of breathtaking speed and encyclopedic coverage.

Microfilm has a part in the space program and related activities. The National Archives maintain extensive technical facilities to preserve and make its vast holdings available on microfilm. The Library of Congress operates the Photoduplication Service which is the largest and most complete scholarly laboratory for microreproduction in the world. The regulatory Commissions make extensive use of microtechnology. The National Bureau of Standards has set up basic standards and has in addition designed and constructed equipment of various types. The list could be extended infinitely.

If the myriad applications in the Federal Government were known and the gross output tabulated, if the similar applications by state and local governments were included and the total from nongovernmental sources were added, it would be easy to see why microreproduction has become a great industry. The remarkable fact seems to be that while a minor amount of displacement of earlier processes was inevitable, much of the growth represents penetration and exploitation of entirely new fields.

The solid foundation on which it was based has been earlier described in some detail. Similar extensive treatment for the present day situation is not feasible, and in a rapidly moving area may not be desirable, but some of the reasons for the forward surge do merit closer examination.

UNITIZATION

Unitization is certainly not new. The idea is simple—merely the use of a single microform reproduction in the same way that the original sheet of paper would be used, as a unit. Obviously the small dimensions and relative fragility of the microfilm page posed difficulties. Many solutions were brought forward.

The *aperture card* consisted of a card with a die-cut aperture into which a frame of microfilm, which could contain a single or several images, was mounted. There are numerous variants including one which provides a transparent pocket to receive the film.

The *"filmsort" card* combined a microfilm image with a punched card for high-speed sorting. With it came a gamut of accessory equipment: mounters, printers, readers, even reader-printers, copiers, and many others. A product of the Microfilm Division of the Minnesota Mining and Manufacturing Company, it has achieved wide acceptance and use.

Another unitization plan provided *acetate sleeves* for any desired film width and length. These sleeves are sometimes made up in combination with card stock in the form of cards or card-size receptacles that could be manipulated like index cards. They solved the problem of open-end files. Personnel and hospital records could be quickly brought up to date by adding single or multiple microfilm as required.

Reading machines and other equipment to use insert-card forms exist in ample quantity and variety. The larger microforms, notably 70 and 105 mm, offered lesser problems, for they could be utilized in simple acetate jackets which in some cases were supplied with card stock attachments for titles and filing identification. Micropaque formats could also be unitized with relative ease. By printing microfilm images on paper they could be affixed to a card and read in micropaque readers, precisely in the same manner as with the insert cards.

The introduction of pressure-compounds was a useful refinement. Of the many variations Microtape, seems to be most widely used. Interestingly enough the insert cards and the micropaque equivalents approximate in function, as they approach in format, the corresponding microfiche and opaque-sheet forms with the exception that in the former new material can be added from time to time.

PAPER FACSIMILES

Enlarged paper facsimiles of microforms has always been a convenient utilization method. As single-sheet enlarging techniques gave way to enlarging on roll paper, the processing of long rolls of paper was mechanized and many ingenious machines were developed for this purpose.

The cost curve for silver-photographic processes, however, rests on the square-inch cost of developed paper and regardless of mechanization, a limit is quickly reached. For small quantities of work the process is satisfactory and competitive but for larger quantities, the aggregate cost is formidable. New technology in the form of electrostatic reproduction developed rapidly and made possible many activities that had not hitherto been feasible. In addition to the production of prints in quantity, whole books could be reproduced in editions of a single copy.

ELECTROSTATIC PRINTING

Electrostatic printing from microfilm depends on principles quite different from those of conventional photography. A selenium plate, among other substances, can be photosensitized by exposure to a high-tension electrical field. A microfilm image can be projected on this field. A toner, essentially small particles of synthetic resin bearing colored matter, will adhere selectively, producing an image which can be transferred to paper and fixer as a permanent image by heat. Other variations of the process use treated paper, but the important fact is that the costs are very low as compared to other processes.

The input microfilm can be in roll or unitized form; in fact such microfilm is being made whose only function is to be used to make these enlarged prints, and after use it is discarded. The output, paper prints, may be delivered as cut sheets, or may be folded like a Chinese book and bound. Two-side reproduction is possible. The large Copyflo and Copytron machines of the Xerox Corporation and the Charles Bruning Company respectively, are illustrations of the automated application of this principle. There are many others.

STORAGE RETRIEVAL

Information is an elusive and valuable commodity. Scientific research, during World War II and the two uneasy decades following created such floods of data that traditional methods of handling, storing, and using documentation became overtaxed and inadequate. For statistical data computers were intensively developed. For textual and graphic data the microforms were an obvious selection. Storage is no problem but retrieval, especially at high speeds, is quite another matter. Coding to identify particular documents, or with more precision the complete contents of a single document, is far from simple. Even now, after the expenditure of much time and a great deal of money, this problem is far from ultimate solution.

Mechanization, or automation as the popular idiom now has it, was less troublesome but not without complications. Many useful and practical systems have resulted, and development work is going forward in this area rapidly. For some reason it is customary to refer to these systems by their code names. Mention has been made of FOSDIC and there are numerous others: CRIS, FILESEARCH, MEDIA MICROCITE, MINICARD, MIRACODE and WALNUT, are a few of them.

In general, the high-speed storage-retrieval systems work with microimages in the form of long rolls, sheets, strips, or as small discrete "chips." Coding and finding information may be supplied in the form of coding "bits" photographed on the film; magnetic tape, perforations, and other devices are also used. Operational characteristics include amount of material maintained in file, speed and precision of reference, and output. The output may be in the form of a visual image, an enlarged paper print, or a duplicate microform.

An aperture card which can be punched and manipulated by machines is an excellent data-storage and retrieval device. A reading machine using well-made and coded microfilm performs the same function, especially if a reader-printer is used and enlarged prints are added to the output. It is quite apparent that high-speed microdata storage and retrieval systems offer much promise for the future. (See: Bagg, T. C. and Stevens, M. E., *Information Selection Systems Retrieving Replica Copies,* National Bureau of Standards Technical Note 157, 1962, 172 pp.)

RECENT DEVELOPMENTS

It would be interesting to speculate about many other technological possibilities. Closed-circuit television with microfilm is in use. This reveals an entire gamut of related possibility. Microimages can be stored on tape or wire and recreated. Wide-band television transmission from 16 mm microfilm input, to 16 mm microfilm output, between New York and Washington D.C., was demonstrated some years ago. The electrostatic processes have been employed experimentally in microdimensions; the process called microxerography may one day become important.

There are new substances and materials under test. Even some of the older materials can assume new characteristics. Diazo which has been considered too slow to be anything but a contact medium may in the future become usable for projection printing. A recently demonstrated enlarger produces micro-images by projection on diazo paper.

One of the most important developments of the past two decades has been the demonstrated success of microforms in the large and important field of engineering documentation, specifically activities connected with the Department of Defense. Conventional methods of handling engineering documents and plans proved inadequate to the needs of the Department, its contractors, and subcontractors. Microfilm began to be employed, but in the absence of commonly accepted specifications, difficulties in application and interpretation were encountered.

In 1959 an ad hoc committee of government and industry personnel, convened to study this problem, produced after a long series of studies a series of mutually acceptable specifications (See: *NMA Informational Monograph No. 1,* "DoD Engineering-Data Microreproduction Standards and Specifications", 1963, pp. 151.) The coverage and clarity of these specifications make them practically an instruction book in microfilm operations, and their importance cannot be overestimated. Not only have they resulted in the saving of millions of dollars for the many government programs, but they are

Microfiche is a translucent sheet of 6×4 1/8 inch film. Each Microfiche contains multiple microimages o pages arranged in rows, and has the advantage of film plus the flexibility of the index card concept. Micro-Photo division, Bell & Howell Co.

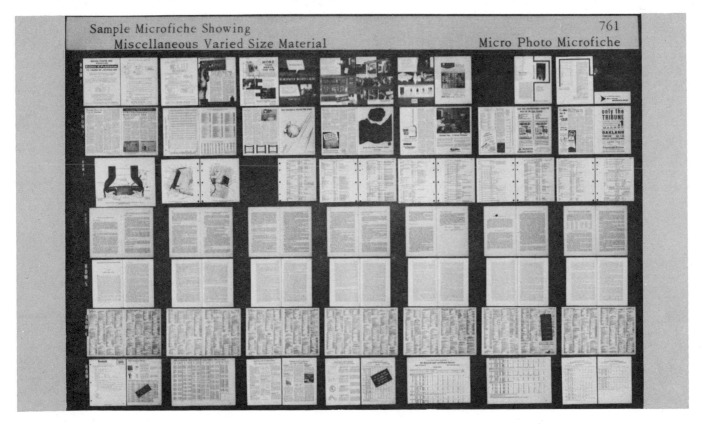

also now being adopted by private industry sometimes in modified form. They promise to bring about wholly new and more efficient operating methods in these fields.

THE MICROREPRODUCTION INDUSTRY

The microreproduction industry itself is an interesting study. There are many large, well-organized companies with branches and offices throughout the country. Individual service companies provide local and sometimes regional coverage. An association of individually-owned service companies offers national coverage. In addition many companies specialize in certain types of service, for example, land-title work, hospital records, library and documentary operations and the like. Many industries operate "in-house" microreproduction facilities supplementing these as required with contract services.

The same situation prevails in government where some of the largest and most important projects are undertaken. Experimental and development work is under way in many locations and connections. The community is small indeed that does not have contact in some way with the ramifications of this great industry, and a growing number of individuals are acquiring personal microform-reading equipment.

Microreproduction is a world-wide technique, and although it is probably not so widely used in most other countries as in the United States, its use is increasing rapidly. It has been predicted that the microforms will become a vital medium of world-wide communication, and rapid progress is being made toward this goal.

Finally, one measure of the stature and vitality of an industry is the extent and efficiency of its own internal communications. The National Microfilm Association, formed in 1942, was established to provide a common meeting ground for manufacturers, service companies, industry representatives, scientists, technicians, librarians, archivists, users, in a word anyone interested in the field. The annual meetings and conventions begun in 1952 have increased in size and importance in each succeeding year. The printed records of these meetings (*Proceedings* Vols. I to XII) now constitute basic documentation for the field. A bi-monthly journal, the *National MICRO-NEWS,* extends and supplements the annual volumes. Additional publications, the *Glossary,* the *Guide to Microreproduction Equipment* and others, are authoritative, essential books.

The following selected bibliography has been compiled to extend the necessarily limited coverage herein. Regretfully, the periodical literature which is extensive could not be covered but a list of selected periodicals whose pages contain frequent items of interest to the field has been added.

American Standards Association
10 East 40th Street, New York, New York
Publications
Note particularly publications of Committees PH5, Z38 and Z39.

Avedon, D. M., Editor
Glossary of Terms for Microphotography and Reproductions made from Micro-Images
Annapolis, Md.: National Microfilm Association, 1962, 50 pp.
Standard for terminology.

Bagg, Thomas C. and Stevens, Mary Elizabeth
Information Selection Systems Retrieving Replica Copies: A State-of-the-Art Report
Washington, D.C.: U.S. Government Printing Office, 172 pp.
A valuable and impartial survey of 15 systems includes an excellent bibliography.

Ballou, Hubbard W., editor
Guide to Microreproduction Equipment
Annapolis, Md.: National Microfilm Association, 1962, 519 pp.

Ballou, Hubbard W., editor
Supplement A to the 1962 Guide to Microreproduction Equipment
Annapolis, Md.: National Microfilm Association, 1963, 87 pp.
Affords impartial illustrated coverage including prices and specifications.
The basic book in the field on the subject.

Basic Standards and Specifications of the Department of Defense-Engineering Data
Microreproduction Systems
Annapolis, Md.: National Microfilm Association, 1963, 151 pp.
Excellent reference and informative source for field.

Current Research and Development in Scientific Documentation, No. 11
Washington, D. C.: National Science Foundation, 1962, 440 pp.
Valuable as a guide to research in progress throughout the world (as reported). Some microform projects included. See earlier

971.2 Northwest, Canadian - Description and travel. F 1060.8
McLean, John, 1799. [v.2–Card 1 (of 3)–p. i-viii, 10-111]
Notes of twenty-five years' service... [13,412 LCP]

Example of Microcard micropaque publication medium. This card 7.5×12.5 cm (same size as a standard library card) holds 112 pages of text, 56 pages each side of the card.

Recordak MPC-1 Microfilm Reader. Rotatable head, automatic focus, high-speed winding crank and scanning handle. Will accommodate 16 or 35 mm roll film and Filmsort aperture cards.

volumes for further information.

Davison, George H., editor
1962 Review of Equipment for Microtext
London: The Library Association, 1962, 146 pp.
British survey incomplete and elementary, contains some information not readily found elsewhere.

Diaz, Albert James, editor
Guide to Microforms in Print
Washington, D. C.: Microcard Editions, Inc., 1963, 90 pp.
Catalog of material published in microform.

Even, Arthur D.
Engineering Data Processing System Design
New York: Van Nostrand, 1960, 282 pp.
Excellent study of microreproduction and engineering documentation.

Frank, Otto
Die Mikrofilmtechnik
Stuttgart, Germany: Dorotheen-Verlag, 1961, 336 pp.
General survey valuable for information on foreign equipment, methods and concepts. German text.

Hawken, William R.
Photocopying from Bound Volumes
Chicago: American Library Association, 1963, 208 pp.
Does not deal with microform processes but contains details of corollary operations.

Hawken, William R.
Enlarged Prints from Library Microforms
Chicago: American Library Association, 1963, 131 pp.
Full discussion of several models of reader-printers and other equipment.

Hawkins, Reginald
Production of Micro-Forms
New Brunswick, N.J.: Rutgers, 1960, 208 pp.
Survey of literature to date emphasis on Library applications.

Korte, Thomas H., Meyers, Thomas C., Beery, John W.
Microfilm Aperture Card System
Ohio: Wright-Patterson AFB, 1960, 149 pp. charts.
Excellent discussion of aperture card systems and uses.

Lewis, Chester M. and Offenhauser, William H., Jr.
Microrecording: Industrial and Library Applications
New York: Interscience Publishers, Inc., 1956, 456 pp.
While not up-to-date, is still valuable.

Luther, Frederic
Microfilm: A History, 1839-1900
Annapolis, Md.: National Microfilm Association, 1959, 195 pp.
Good historical account for period covered.

Micro-Mechanized Engineering Data for Automated Logistics
Ohio: Wright-Patterson AFB, 1959, 61 pp.
Project MEDAL - aperture card data.

Readex Microprint Publications, 1963
New York: Readex Microprint Corporation, 1963, 191 pp.
Catalog of material available in form of Readex microprint.

Reproductions Reference Guide
New York: Wolf Business Publications, 1963, 250 pp.
Third edition of working reference guide of reproduction processes market by the editors of ODR Reproductions Review. Technical and management sections; buyer's guide.

Ridenour Louis N., Shaw, Ralph

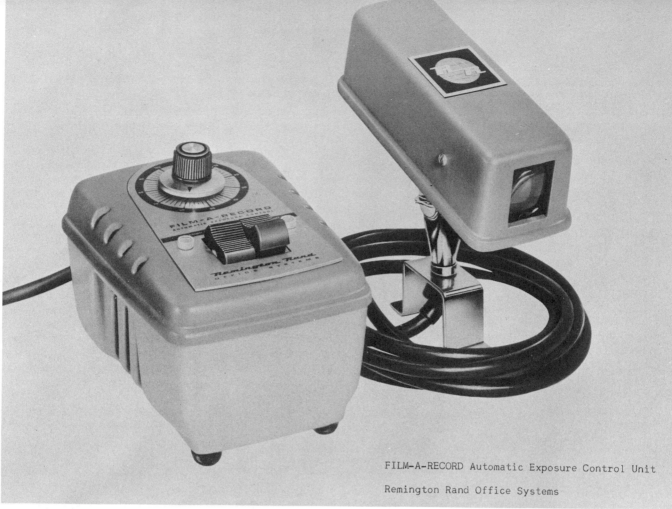

FILM-A-RECORD Automatic Exposure Control Unit

Remington Rand Office Systems

Film-A-Record Automatic exposure control unit for rotary microfilm cameras. Completely eliminates the need for any manual adjustments for light values or intensities. Remington Rand Systems.

R. and Hill, Albert G.
Bibliography in an Age of Science
Urbana, Ill.: University of Illinois Press, 1951, 90 pp.
Three early papers worth reading for background information on possibilities of mechanized documentation.

Scanlan, James F. and Nanney, Thomas G., editors
The Active Uses of Microfilm
New York: Wolf Business Publications, Inc., 1962, 117 pp.
Useful wel-illustrated guide to the uses of microfilm. Informative for beginners.

Stevens, G.W.W.
Microphotography: Photography at Extreme Resolution
New York: John Wiley & Sons Inc., 1957, 326 pp.
Excellent study of high degrees of minification.

Steward, Jean and Hickey, Doralyn and others
Reading Devices for Micro-Images

New Brunswick, N.J.: Rutgers, 1960, 205 pp.
Survey with excerpts of earlier literature. Intended for library field.

Tate, Vernon D., editor
Proceedings of the National Microfilm Association
Annapolis, Maryland
Vol. I, 1952, 61 pp.
Vol. II, 1953, 88 pp.
Vol. III, 1954, 97 pp.
Vol. IV, 1955, 110 pp.
Vol. V, 1956, 118 pp.
Vol. VI, never published
Vol. VII, 1958, 209 pp.
Vol. VIII, 1959, 298 pp.
Vol. IX, 1960, 244 pp.
Vol. X, 1961, 305 pp.
Vol. XI, 1962, 360 pp.
Vol. XII, 1963, in process
The papers presented in these volumes constitute the largest collection of diversified information about microreproduction available.

Tilton, Eva Maude, editor

Union List of Publications in Opaque Microforms
New York: The Scarecrow Press, Inc., 1959, 346 pp.
Lists of materials published in these formats.

Verry, H. R.
Document Copying and Reproduction Processes
London: Fountain Press, 1958, 328 pp.
British survey of processes.

List of Selected Journals:
Abstracts of Photographic Science & Engineering Literature
American Documentation
Industrial Photography
Journal of the Optical Society of America
Library Resources and Technical Services
National Bureau of Standards Technical News Bulletin
National MICRO-NEWS
ODR Reproductions Review
Photo Methods for Industry (PMI)
Reproduction Engineer
Special Libraries
The Office